AF226168

ABRAHAM LINCOLN.

From a photograph taken by Hesler in June, 1860

ABRAHAM LINCOLN

THE MAN OF THE PEOPLE

BY

NORMAN HAPGOOD

AUTHOR OF "LITERARY STATESMEN," "A LIFE OF
DANIEL WEBSTER," ETC.

WITH FRONTISPIECE

THE CHRISTIAN HERALD BIBLE HOUSE
NEW YORK CITY

PREFACE

To an American in sympathy with his country, loving her as she is, not wishing her essentially different, there can be few historical figures as attractive as Abraham Lincoln. Unequalled, since Washington, in service to the nation, he is unrivalled among our statesmen in the closeness with which he represents our land.

> "He was the North, the South, the East, the West,
> The thrall, the master, all of us in one."

The biography of such a man can afford honesty. Some have omitted what was not pretty. Others have apologized for it. Many would like to improve the rugged and homely face with a touch of rouge or magnesia. Surely this is trivial. Let us not try to make our great man like other great men. Let us allow him to reach as high as the saints in one direction, and as high as Rabelais in another. Let him be the prairie male as well as the sage and martyr, the deft politician as well as the generous statesman. Paint him as he is. He will still be great, nobler than ever, because more real. Better the truth and strength and beauty that are, than any fiction less human and less profound. Following the real Lincoln from the hovel to the White House, from the village girls and the tavern stories to Gettysburg and the second inaugural, we live grandly, up and down, to the right and to the left, breathing the air of the plains, the mountains, the closet, the hospital, of poetic superstition and of the sanest wisdom, and we see that life is good, that our nation is good, and that it is well to know the truth.

Lincoln himself refused to read a life of Burke because he believed that biographies were indiscriminate eulogies. Praise and blame have small place, and suppression, none, in the story of a large soul. It is not when justice is done that the heavens fall.

Thirty-four years have passed since Lincoln's death. A generation, unborn when he was shot, is now thinking and writing. It starts without the passions of the strife. We no longer see the problems as black and white. One of us has said recently that the negro was freed in the South that he might be lynched in Ohio. We now see the threads of right and wrong distinct yet tangled, as Lincoln saw them, even when he stood in the centre of the storm. Those who weathered the gale have left their memories of the pilot. The material is in. The opportunity is here for any who can use it.

The present biography is not a history of the Civil War. It is not an argument about emancipation or reconstruction. It is solely the personal history of Abraham Lincoln as it appears to one of his countrymen. To that particular reader an anecdote or a picturesque phrase often seems more important than a bill or a message to Congress. He has tried to select those incidents which are doubly true, because they are at once actual and significant, and this truth is as likely to inhere in the amusing as in the solemn.

To give credit for the sources of an impression, which is often breathed from the air of daily thought and conversation, is not easy, but a few words are due to the principal books on the subject. Nothing compares in value with Lincoln's own words, and the two volumes of his papers and correspondence are worth all that has been written about him. The official biography by Nicolay and Hay contains much valuable material not to be found elsewhere. Herndon has told the President's early life with refreshing honesty, and with more information than any one else. Lamon has shown vividly the side of Lincoln which naturally came out when he was in the company of his exuberant marshal. Whitney's " Life on the Circuit with Lincoln " is full of good stories of the western bar, and the President's relation to it. Nobody has made the politician's adroitness so real as Colonel McClure. Miss Tarbell has gathered some facts to supplement and correct Herndon and others. Morse's biography, in the American Statesmen Series, is an orderly and serious account of Lincoln's relation to the principal public questions. The other works are legion, but these have seemed, to the present writer, most fertile among the books dealing mainly with Lincoln. It is true, however, that a short impression, incidental to some other object, may be worth a volume. Thus flashes of the greatest value have been given by Emerson, Lowell, Greeley, Grant, Blaine, McClellan, and Sherman. Singularly enough, perhaps, almost nothing of worth has been written about Lincoln in foreign countries. It is probable, also, that in his own country, while flashes have been given by great compatriots, and indispensable records left by other contemporaries, most of the permanent lives, large and small, picturesque and technical, remain to be written.

N. H.

New York, July, 1899.

NOTE

The frontispiece to this volume, which is generally acknowledged to be the best portrait of Lincoln, is reproduced from a negative made at Springfield, Illinois, June, 1860, by Alexander Hesler of Chicago. The negative is now owned by Mr. George B. Ayres of Philadelphia, who has very kindly placed his copyrighted enlargement at the disposal of the publishers.

I take pleasure in acknowledging my indebtedness to Messrs. Houghton, Mifflin, & Co. for permission to print the quotation from Lowell's "Commemoration Ode," and to Messrs. Small, Maynard, & Co. for their kindness in allowing me to use Whitman's poem, "Oh Captain, my Captain!"

N. H.

CONTENTS

ABRAHAM LINCOLN

CHAPTER I

ORIGIN AND CHILDHOOD

WHEN Lowell calls Lincoln the first American, and when Emerson rejoices that a middle-class nation was wise enough to select a middle-class president, the importance of that ruler's social origin is suggested. He sprang from the great base of the national life, with few traditions, no knowledge of other lands and times, confronting a wilderness and its pioneers, longing for light, but having to work for every ray. Thrown intellectually naked into the world, his education had to be directly from the nature of the men and women who passed before him, so that when he came to his great trial, he had to pilot a people whose peculiarities he intimately knew. The fathers of the Revolution were cultivated Englishmen confronting Englishmen. Lincoln's whole nature grew in our soil, and when he was asked to rule a distracted country, native strength, honesty, and shrewdness had as their foundation an intimacy with the kinds of human nature which formed the conflicting masses.

His family emigrated from Norfolk, England, in 1637. His grandfather, Abraham, left Virginia, where he was a fairly prosperous farmer, to follow in the wake of the aspiring pioneer, Daniel Boone. In 1780, he sold 240 acres of land for "five thousand pounds current money of Virginia," and moved to Kentucky, where, in the custom of the time, he "entered" a large amount of land, settling near one tract on Long Run, in Jefferson County, to clear a farm. As the Indians were dangerous, there were but eighteen houses in the territory, practically all of the population, which in 1784 was thirty thousand, living, the Linkhorns among them, in the fifty-two stockades. In 1788, while he and his three sons were at work in the clearing, a stray shot from an Indian killed him. An inventory of his personal estate was made, according to Miss Tarbell, as follows : —

"At a meeting of the Nelson County Court, October 10, 1788, present Benjamin Pope, James Rogers, Gabriel Cox, and James Baird, on the motion of John Coldwell, he was appointed administrator of the goods and chattels of Abraham Lincoln, and gave bond in one thousand pounds, with Richard Parker security.

"At the same time John Alvary, Peter Syburt, Christopher Boston, and William (John (?)) Stuck, or any three of them, were appointed appraisers.

"March 10, 1789, the appraisers made the following return :

	£	s.	d.
1 Sorrel horse	8		
1 Black horse	9	10	
1 Red cow and calf	4	10	
1 Brindle cow and calf	4	10	
1 Red cow and calf	5		
1 Brindle bull yearling	1		
1 Brindle heifer yearling	1		
Bar Spear-plough and tackling	2	5	
3 Weeding hoes	7	6	
Flax wheel		6	
Pair smoothing irons		15	
1 Dozen pewter plates	1	10	
2 Pewter dishes		17	6
Dutch oven and cule, weighing 15 pounds		15	
Small iron kettle and cule, weighing 12 pounds		12	
Tool adds		10	
Hand saw		5	
One inch auger		6	
Three-quarter auger		4	6
Half-inch auger		3	
Drawing-knife		3	
Currying-knife		10	
Currier's knife and barking-iron		6	
Old smooth-bar gun		10	
Rifle gun		55	
Rifle gun	3	10	
2 Pott trammels		14	
1 Feather bed and furniture	5	10	
Ditto	8	5	
1 Bed and turkey feathers and furniture	1	10	

						£	s.	d.
Steeking-iron	.	.	.	.	.		1	6
Candle-stick	.	.	.	.	.		1	6
One axe . . . , . . .								9

> Peter Syburt,
> Christopher Boston,
> John Stuck."

Of the sons, the eldest, Mordecai, who inherited most of the land, seems to have been prosperous and esteemed, besides being a good teller of stories, a fighter, and a fierce hater of Indians. According to his famous nephew, he had "run off with all the talents of the family." Certainly few fell to Thomas, the youngest, who later became father to Abraham. He was taken by his widowed mother to Washington County, where he became a carpenter and cabinet maker, knowing his trade, but too lazy to make much use of it. He was entirely illiterate, but he also had social qualities, among them the ability to tell the stories picked up in a vagrant life, and to make himself respected in a fight when his pacific soul was stirred. He was a Jackson Democrat who couldn't write his name, until his first wife taught him to scrawl it, the farthest reach of education he ever acquired. His name was under the circumstances unstable, but in Indiana it showed a general drift toward Lickern, away from the favorite Kentucky form of Linckorn, settling in its present spelling many years later in Illinois. Tom was taken with spasms of religion, belonging part of the time to no denomination and again to several in succession, none of which affected the truth of the statement made by his relative John Hanks: "Happiness was the end of life with him."

On June 12, 1806, near Beachland in Washington County, Kentucky, Thomas married Nancy Hanks, the daughter of Joseph Hanks of Elizabethtown, in whose shop he had learned his trade. She is said to have been sensitive, melancholy, brooding, frail, with native refinement, the rudiments of education, and delicate instincts, qualities which failed to make her marriage an ideal one. Tom, settling in Elizabethtown, continued his uneventful pursuit of ease, combining it with sufficient effort to keep the family alive. After one daughter had been born, he moved to his farm, about fourteen miles from Elizabethtown, where his wife bore a son named Abraham. To an artist who was painting his portrait Lincoln once furnished this memorandum: "I was born February 12, 1809, in the then Hardin County, Kentucky, at a point within the new county of La Rue, a mile or a mile and a half from where Hodgens Mill now is. My parents being dead, and my own memory not serving, I

know of no means of identifying the precise locality.   It was on Nolin Creek."

This infant began life in what was called a
camp, because it was made of poles. Had it been
made of logs, it would have been called a cabin.
It was about fourteen feet square and had no
floor.   Life on the frontier was not luxurious, and
little Abraham's father was not the most enter-
prising of the settlers.   However, Abraham did
not care much just then, and he was but four
when his father, who spent his life in moving,
went onto another farm, fifteen miles to the north-
east, on Knob Creek.   In 1816, when Abraham
was seven, Tom took another change, this time
sampling Indiana.   Gathering together everything he owned in the way of goods and family,
he proceeded on horseback, aided by one wagon,
to a new farm near Little Pigeon Creek, about
fifteen miles north of the Ohio River, and a mile
and a half east of Gentryville, in Spencer County,
a village in which Abe, as he was always called,
soon found company and the ideas which cluster
about a country store increased by contributions
from the craft which passed down the Ohio.   So
primitive was the country that on the journey
Tom was in places compelled to cut his way
through the forest.   When he reached his destination he put into the hand of the seven-year-old
Abe an axe, with which the boy helped make a

clearing and build a camp. This camp was one of the proudest achievements of Tom's history. It was half-faced, which signifies that it was a shed of poles, entirely open on one side, roughly protecting the wife and two small children from the weather in the other three directions. In this shed, winter and summer, the family lived a whole year, while Tom and Abe cleared a little patch for corn and Tom built a permanent dwelling. Into this mansion he moved before it was half completed, and found it so attractive that he left it for a year or two without doors, windows, or floor. For chairs there were three-legged stools; the bedstead was made of poles stuck between the logs in the angle of the cabin, the outside corner supported by a crotched stick driven into the ground; the bedclothes were skins. When Abe went to bed, however, it was not in this, the only room in the cabin, but in the loft, on a bunch of leaves, which he reached by climbing a ladder made of wooden pegs driven into the logs. There was a dining-room table, consisting of a large, hewed log standing on four legs, and the nourishment was prepared and served by Mrs. Lincoln with the aid of a pot, a kettle, a skillet, and a few tin and pewter dishes. Abe did not always fully enjoy what this table offered him; for when his father, in one of his pious moods, asked a blessing on a meal consisting wholly of roasted potatoes, the boy is related to have ventured the comment that they were mighty poor blessings. Sometimes raw potatoes were peeled for dessert, and as wheat was rare, corn dodger served as bread. Cooking in that region was worthy of the material on which it worked.

The woods, full of malaria, breathed out frequent epidemics, one of which, the milk-sick, raging in Pigeon Creek in 1818, in October took the life of Nancy Hanks Lincoln. Tom made a coffin of green lumber, cut with a whip-saw, and taking his children and a handful of Gentryville friends, buried her. The little son felt mournful over the sad and hasty spectacle, and several months later, the story goes, when a wandering clergyman happened by, the boy induced him to go along with him to the grave and give to the dead mother more solemn rites.

It is probable, however, that when Abraham Lincoln in after years spoke of his angel of a mother, or his sainted mother, it was not of this frail woman that he thought, but of the stronger and more decisive person with whom his father filled her place. Tom had wished to marry Sarah Busch when he was a bachelor, but Sarah was not impressed by his talents and chose a man named Johnson. A very few months after Nancy died Tom started for Kentucky, where his old friend was the widowed mother of three children.

To her he offered himself again, alleging reformed habits and an improved worldly condition. On these representations she took him, and soon after Abraham and his sister saw their cabin approached by the most prosperous woman who had ever entered their lives. In the wagon which carried her goods were furniture, cooking utensils, and bedding of a magnificence and luxury beyond their experience. Not too much cast down by the contrast between her husband's story and his cabin, she took both him and it in hand. She forced him to put in doors and floors, and perhaps windows, which consisted of greased paper over a hole, and she taught the children some of the order and habits of civilization.

Abraham, now aged ten, was a queer, homely boy, with irregular face, coarse features, protruding ears, strong limbs, and an ambitious mind. If he had been to school in Kentucky, it was nothing to count; and although he was now eager to learn, and had the opportunity occasionally, when work was slack, to take advantage of some institution which kept open when there happened to be a floating schoolmaster, he later estimated that his entire schooling put together would add up to about one year. The wandering gentlemen who furnished the instruction needed to know something about the three R's and a good deal about the physical domination of rough boys.

The first Indiana school attended by the little Lincoln was kept by Hazel Dorsey, and stood a mile and a half from his father's cabin.   It was made of logs, high enough for a man to stand erect under the loft.   The floor was of split logs, the chimney of poles and clay, the windows of the usual greased paper pasted on pieces of split board which covered an aperture made by cutting out parts of two logs. Abraham is supposed not to have been quick, but to have stood high through his industry and keen interest.   Although the boy was so useful with his axe that he was often taken from school, even when it existed, to work at home, or be hired out to others, he got partly even by studying on Sundays or on the way to and from work, perhaps even when he was driving the team or doing other industrial chores and learning the rudiments of his father's trade.

At fourteen he received another taste of instruction under the guidance of one Andrew Crawford, and the progress in his nature and knowledge is shown by the fact that at this period he sat with a schoolmate, Amy Roby, on the bank of the river, and, while both dangled their feet in the water, explained to his girl companion that the motion of the moon, which seemed to be rising above the neighboring hills, was only illusion.   By this time he probably knew a good deal, for he was going weekly to Gentryville to

read the Louisville newspaper, and the few books
which existed in the neighborhood he learned
thoroughly. The Bible was at hand, and he read
it, but, his stepmother says, " he sought more congenial books." These more congenial volumes included Æsop's "Fables," which probably confirmed
his inherited tendency to speak in parables;
" Robinson Crusoe "; " The Pilgrim's Progress,"
which was no more successful than the Bible in
bringing out religion; a history of the United
States; and Weems's " Life of Washington," to
which he used to refer many years later. At
this ripe age of fourteen he would write and
cipher with chalk on the cabin walls, or on the
wooden shovel, which he could whittle clean
again, reserving the scarce allowance of paper
for copying extracts from borrowed books. Returning from work, he would go to the cupboard,
take a piece of corn bread, and sit down to
read.

At seventeen he saw his last school days, with
one Swaney, four and one-half miles from the
cabin, and his progress may be guessed from the
tale that he used to deliver discourses against
cruelty to animals, in favor of temperance, and
against the horrors of war. These views go
harmoniously with the story that when he found
the town drunkard freezing by the roadside he
saved his life by carrying him in his arms to the

cabin. In the meantime he continued his own education, taking one step forward by studying the Revised Statutes of Indiana, which he borrowed from the town constable. Of course his father took no joy in these reachings out of his ungainly son, but the new wife was mistress in her home, and she protected Abraham against the interference of Tom, helping the boy to school days and to a quiet corner for study at home. They were friends and confidants, and the stepson's gratitude never ceased. "Education defective" is his complete description of his early life given to the compiler of the Dictionary of Congress, and he hated to speak of it, but much of what light the surrounding obstacles admitted was thankfully credited to his stepmother.

Amid conflicting impressions it seems probable that Abraham, although a strong and effective workman, had no exorbitant love of the axe for its own sake. He enjoyed mounting the stump to make a speech, for which he soon earned local fame, or repeating on Monday the sermon of the Sabbath, or reading texts and delivering discourses to the younger children in the cabin when his parents went alone to hear a preacher. All this was intellectual and unprofitable, and Tom didn't like it. Says the relative Dennis Hanks: "I never could tell whether Abe loved his father very well or not. I don't think he did, for Abe was one of those forward boys. I have seen his father knock him down off the fence when a stranger would ask the way to a neighbor's house. Abe would always have the first word. The old man loved his children." The same facts seem to shine through the statement that Tom's rage grew out of his son's fondness for drawing passers-by into long conversations. The neighbor John Romine says: "Abe was awful lazy. He worked for me; was always reading and thinking; used to get mad at him. He worked for me in 1829, pulling fodder. I say Abe was awful lazy: he would laugh and talk and crack jokes all the time; didn't love work, but did dearly love his pay. . . . Lincoln said to me one day, that his father taught him to work, but never learned him to love it."

His preference for thought, conversation, and observation, working amid difficult surroundings and dealing with things as he found them in a wilderness, did not create spontaneously and at once the style of the Gettysburg address, or of his most profoundly humorous remarks. Much of his early effort was florid, much was coarse, but most of it was vital. Some idea of the form taken by his early love of poetry and humor may be gleaned from these verses by him, written in a book of his own manufacture: —

> " Abraham Lincoln
>   his hand and pen.
> **he** will be good, but
>   god knows When."

Everything about him was elemental, unsifted, and raw. In Gentryville the barbaric aspect of life was disappearing as he reached manhood, but it was still the frontier. Young men and women travelled far to log-rollings, which consisted of piling up timber and burning it for amusement, and to various social gatherings, to which the women in good weather went with their shoes in their hands, the older ones when they reached their destination drinking whiskey toddy while the men drank whiskey straight. Lincoln was always temperate, drinking little with his friends, and nothing at home. Then there were " raisings," or gatherings to build a house in a day ; and wolf-hunts, in which the sportsmen, making a circle miles in diameter, chased the victims toward a chosen centre, marked by a tall pole in the midst of the prairie or clearing. Weddings lasted seldom less than twenty-four hours. The guests assembled in the morning. After some such entertainment as a race for a whiskey bottle there was a mid-day dinner, followed by other games, and a ball at night, after which the bride and groom withdrew, one after the other, followed by jokes and tricks in which Lincoln was unmistak·ably a leader.

It was a superstitious community, and to the very day of his death Lincoln never failed to believe in supernatural portents. If a dog ran directly across the hunter's path, bad luck would follow unless the little fingers were hooked together and vigorously pulled as long as the dog remained in sight; charmed twigs pointed to springs and buried treasure; faith doctors with their mysterious ceremonies wrought cures. If a bird alighted in the window, one of the family would die; a horse breathing on a child gave whooping cough; for good luck rails must be split in the early part of the day or in the light of the moon, roots, such as potatoes, planted in the dark of the moon, but plants which bore fruit above ground in the light of that orb; if a fence was not made in the light of the moon it would sink; and Friday was fatal to every enterprise.

What Lincoln thought of his surroundings at this time can never be known. To a campaign biographer he said, with his usual distaste for this subject, that his early life presented nothing but "the short and simple annals of the poor." Nothing but a temporary, conventional, or politic mood is shown by his remark to a young man introduced to him in 1847: "I do not think you would succeed at splitting rails. That was my occupation at your age, and I do not think I have taken as much pleasure in anything else from that day to this." Nor do we know much of the political opinions left in him by his meditations and his Gentryville reading and talking. One of the earlier accounts shows him fond of singing, without musical ability but with zest, not only hymns but such political reflections as this : —

"Let auld acquaintance be forgot
And never brought to mind,
May Jackson be our President,
And Adams left behind."

Those who owned slaves in the primitive community assumed superiority to those who had none; but questionings about the peculiar institutions were in the air, the contest in favor of excluding slavery having been settled only about the time the Lincolns moved to Indiana, so that its echoes must have resounded in the Gentryville grocery. In 1822, when Lincoln was thirteen, an abolition newspaper was started about one hundred miles from the village, and during his whole boyhood and youth there was plenty to lead his mind, at least occasionally, onto the topic.

The talkative youth presented a pictorial appearance, dressed in coat, trousers, and moccasins of tanned deer hide; for although the habit of wearing garments of fur and wool dyed with the juice of the butternut or white walnut began about the time he reached manhood, and the hides of cattle began to be tanned, for a long time only the women indulged in such luxuries, and Lincoln was not the person to take the lead in elegance. Doubtless he, like his neighbors, looked upon split-log Mitchell, the man whose cabin was made of square hewn timbers, instead of round logs with the bark on, as a good deal of a snob. The most ungainly and crude in the whole collection, Lincoln alone possessed the sacred fire that drove him, not only to every book, and with the rest of the men, gun on arm, to the itinerant preacher and his cabin church; but alone to the court-house, held in a double cabin, in these days when the grand jury sat on a log in the woods and all the petit jurors wore side knives and moccasins. These habits made him a better and better talker at the village store, where his humor, knowledge, and inherited narrative gift were always welcome. His appearance encouraged the humorous point of view. Tall, lanky, sallow, and dark, slightly stooping, with a careless mop of hair, tanned clothes flung on, he was then what a young lawyer described later as " the ungodliest sight I ever saw." Not only humor, but loneliness and melancholy were encouraged by his lack of outer charm, — a sadness perhaps bequeathed to him with the blood of the mother he scarcely knew. Naturally, he became a satirist, and used his gifts of ridicule and rough verse on those by whom he was treated inconsiderately. A family named Grigsby being among the offenders, he wrote a "chronicle" about them, with consequences which showed not only his powers but his prudence. When the chronicle was found by one of the family where the author had carefully dropped it, Billy, the eldest, challenged him to fight with fists. When the combatants and their friends reached the battle-ground, a mile and a half from Gentryville, the magnanimous Lincoln remarked that as he was the superior of Billy in all enumerable respects he would make a fairer contest by delegating his step-brother John Johnson to represent the family. John was speedily on his back, and the astute Lincoln, claiming a foul, hauled Billy off, swung a whiskey bottle over his head, and, as the legend goes, declared that he was the big buck of the lick, able without difficulty to thrash Billy. Billy admitted as much, and offered to produce equality by fighting with pistols, but his opponent intelligently remarked that he did not care to fool away his life on the chances of a single shot.

The other side of his nature, the deep, sympathetic, honest side, which went with the healthy violence of taste and body, comes out in another anecdote of the same period. His younger sister Matilda, against the orders of her mother, secretly

followed early one morning when he was starting
to clear a piece of wood, his axe in his hand.
Softly stealing up behind him the girl sprung
upon his back, threw her arms about his neck, and
brought him backward to the earth.   The falling
axe cut her ankle.   As they were doing what they
could with the wound the frightened Matilda won-
dered how she could escape the mother's detec-
tion, but her brother advised her to confess frankly
to the whole truth, — the first tale we have of the
trait which afterward made him Honest Abe.

A less elevated instance of his desire to help
others is connected with Crawford's school.   There
is conflicting evidence about his orthographical
abilities, but they seem to have surpassed those of
his neighbors, so that he led in the spelling class.
At any rate he could spell "defied," and his schoolmate Kate Roby, who could not, tells a story of
the consequences.   The word "defied" had been
given out by Schoolmaster Crawford, but had been
misspelled several times when it came Miss Roby's
turn.   "Abe stood on the opposite side of the
room," said she in 1865, "and was watching me.
I began d-e-f-, and then I stopped, hesitating
whether to proceed with an *i* or a *y*.   Looking up,
I beheld Abe, a grin covering his face, and pointing with his index finger to his eye.   I took the
hint, spelled the word with an i, and it went
through all right."

There are no real tales of sentimental experiences in these years, but a direction in which he
sometimes dreamed is painted in an interview
with a Springfield editor. It was a rainy day, and
Lincoln, sitting with his feet on the window-sill,
his eyes on the street, watching the rain, suddenly
looked up and said : —

" Did you ever write out a story in your mind?
I did when I was a little codger. One day a
wagon with a lady and two girls and a man broke
down near us, and while they were fixing up, they
cooked in our kitchen. The woman had books
and read us stories, and they were the first I ever
had heard. I took a great fancy to one of the
girls; and when they were gone I thought of her
a great deal, and one day when I was sitting out
in the sun by the house I wrote out a story in
my mind. I thought I took my father's horse
and followed the wagon, and finally I found it,
and they were surprised to see me. I talked with
the girl and persuaded her to elope with me; and
that night I put her on my horse, and we started
off across the prairie. After several hours we
came to a camp; and when we rode up we found
it was the one we had left a few hours before, and
we went in. The next night we tried again, and
the same thing happened — the horse came back
to the same place; and then we concluded that
we ought not to elope. I stayed until I had per-

suaded her father to give her to me. I always meant to write that story out and publish it, and I began once; but I concluded it was not much of a story. But I think that was the beginning of love with me."

CHAPTER II

WHEN Lincoln was nearly twenty-one years of age, his father, discouraged by another epidemic of the milk-sick, found occasion to move. He sold most of what belonged to the various branches of his family, aggregating thirteen persons, and put the rest into one wagon drawn by four oxen, who started off with their load in March, 1830. The driver was Abraham, but he was not content with one occupation. He had saved over $30, and before leaving Gentryville he invested it all in articles which might be of use to the inhabitants of villages through which they were to pass. "A set of knives and forks was the largest item entered on the bill," says Captain Jones, the Gentryville grocer; "the other items were needles, pins, thread, buttons, and other little domestic necessities. When the Lincolns reached their new home, near Decatur, Illinois, Abraham wrote back to my father, stating that he had doubled his money on his purchases by selling them along the road. Unfortunately we did not keep that letter, not thinking how highly we would have prized it years afterward."

After two weeks of this kind of travel through the prairies and scattered villages, the thirteen relatives landed at a point about ten miles west of Decatur, Macon County, Illinois, a spot selected by John Hanks, a relative who already lived there. It was " just before the winter of the deep snow," which is accepted as a dividing line that makes the Lincolns pioneers. They speedily built a log cabin, in which they resided when that first winter in their new home brought them snow three feet deep, followed by rain which froze, after which the mercury remained at twelve below zero for two weeks. It was at Decatur that Lincoln made the first oratorical test of which anything is known. A man came to town and made a speech. John Hanks thereupon remarked that "Abe could beat it." John turned down a box, Lincoln mounted it, and did what John promised. The subject was the navigation of the Sangamon River.

That river saw the beginning of the first eventful trip of Abraham Lincoln's life. After spending the Illinois winter in odd jobs, largely rail-splitting, for his father's benefit, the legal period for his emancipation arrived. After the separation Tom moved at least three times, and although he hereafter counts for little, he will appear later briefly in Abraham's life. The young man's first chance grew out of the fact that Denton Offut, a business man, asked John Hanks to take a boat-load of provisions and stock to New Orleans. John engaged Lincoln and his stepbrother, John Johnson, and Offut was to pay fifty cents a day besides a sum of $60. Lincoln and Hanks started in a canoe down the Sangamon River in March, 1831, and landed at what is now Jamestown, five miles east of Springfield, where they were joined by Johnson, and all three went to Springfield to see Offut. That enterprising person had not prepared a boat, so the three young men constructed it themselves, taking " Congress land " timber and using the machinery of a neighboring mill. In four weeks it was ready, and the venturesome journey was begun. It was full of novelty, full of instruction, fun, and variety. A passing magician offered to cook eggs in Lincoln's hat. The owner hesitated, but finally lent it, and explained that his delay " was out of respect for the eggs, not for my hat." When they reached New Salem, April 19, the boat stranded on Rutledge's mill-dam, and hung helplessly over it for a day and a night. It was the ingenious Lincoln who finally solved the difficulty. He had the goods removed to another boat, and after their craft was empty he bored a hole in the end which projected over the dam, thus allowing the water which had leaked in to run out, and the boat slid over. The company proceeded. At Blue Banks it was necessary to take on board a number of hogs, but these animals proved refractory, turning and rushing past the men who were endeavoring to drive them into the boat. Lincoln therefore suggested that their eyes be sewed shut, and he held the head and Hanks the tail while Offut accomplished the operation. The hogs, not so easily discouraged, stood still, until the navigators carried them one by one to their appointed place.

The many-colored trip down the Mississippi ended early in May in the arrival of the party in New Orleans. As it was Lincoln's first experience in a real city, and as he stayed until June, his mind must have received an avalanche of impressions, but nothing of interest has come down to us except a story, hopelessly exaggerated in the telling, of Lincoln's indignation at seeing a slave auction at which a vigorous and comely mulatto girl who was being sold had her flesh pinched and was made to trot up and down to show her soundness, like a horse. In June the four travellers took a steamboat up the river, disembarking at St. Louis, where Offut remained; Lincoln and his other two companions starting across Illinois on foot. At Edwardsville Hanks branched off toward Springfield, while Lincoln

and Johnson followed the road to Coles County,
to which the father Thomas had meantime moved.
Lincoln stopped there a short time, not doing
anything more important than winning a victory
from a well-known wrestler. In August he returned to New Salem, as he was under engagement to help dispose of a stock of goods which
had been purchased by Offut. Awaiting their
arrival he spent the life of an active but social
village man of comparative leisure, interrupted
by a few stray bits of work. Shortly after his
return he was hanging about the polls on election
day when Schoolmaster Graham, the clerk, wishing
a substitute for his sick assistant, asked Lincoln
if he could write. "Yes," was the reply, " I can
make a few rabbit tracks." He also piloted a family on a flatboat down the rivers to Beardstown.

During his leisure he accomplished at least an
increase of reputation for personal prowess by a
wrestling match with one Jack Armstrong, leader
of a gang of ordinary western toughs, known as
the Clary Grove boys. On an attempt at foul
play Lincoln, waxing indignant, seized Jack in
his long arms and shook him readily. He also
showed his good humor and tact by making him
a friend, and later in life he saved one of the
Armstrong family from the gallows. He also
successfully taught Jack the golden rule in practice. Armstrong applied bad names to a stranger,

who thereupon backed to a woodpile, seized a weapon, and knocked his insulter down. When Jack was preparing for vengeance Lincoln asked him what he would do himself if some one called him unpleasant names.

" Whip him, by ——," said Armstrong.

" Well," said Lincoln, in substance, " this stranger was right on your own principles."

Even after Offut's return and Lincoln's instalment behind the counter of the store, he did not lack leisure. On the advice of Mentor Graham he procured Kirkham's grammar from a man in the neighborhood, and he also studied mathematics. He used to walk miles for a chance to argue at debating clubs. His intelligence, humor, and honesty had already made him popular. The grocery was full alike of his jokes and of his principles. He disliked waiting on women, but he took a man who swore in the store, when women were present, and rubbed smartweed in his eyes until his will was broken. He was also extremely punctilious in weights and change. Political discussion was his delight. In the uncertainty of parties his position cannot be precisely fixed at any one time. He was probably in succession " a whole-hog man," a " nominal Jackson man," and a Whig. The nominal Jackson men often voted with the Whigs, and, as Lincoln said later, he naturally " drifted " into the party along with his immediate associates. In March, 1832, he felt strong enough to announce himself as a candidate for the General Assembly. In accordance with the custom of the locality the youthful politician published a circular, giving his general opinions, astutely putting most emphasis on one which pleased local interest. These handbills were distributed among the voters, after grammatical errors had been corrected, at Lincoln's request, by a friend. A few extracts on the various topics covered, will best speak for themselves.

"Yet, however desirable an object the construction of a railroad through our country may be; however high our imaginations may be heated at thoughts of it — there is always a heart-appalling shock accompanying the amount of its cost, which forces us to shrink from our pleasing anticipations. The probable cost of this contemplated railroad is estimated at $290,000; the bare statement of which, in my opinion, is sufficient to justify the belief that the improvement of the Sangamon River is an object much better suited to our infant resources."

* * * * * * * * *

"It appears that the practice of loaning money at exorbitant rates of interest has already been opened as a field for discussion; so I suppose I may enter upon it without claiming the honor, or risking the danger which may await its first explorer. It seems as though we are never to have an end to this baneful and corroding system, acting almost as prejudicially to the general interests of the community as a direct tax of several thousand dollars annually laid on each county for the benefit of a few individuals only, unless there be a law made fixing the limits of usury. A law for this purpose, I am of opinion, may be made without materially injuring any class of people. In cases of extreme necessity, there could always be means found to cheat the law; while in all other cases it would have its intended effect. I would favor the passage of a law on this subject which might not be very easily evaded. Let it be such, that the labor and difficulty of evading it could only be justified in cases of greatest necessity.

"Upon the subject of education, not presuming to dictate any plan or system respecting it, I can only say that I view it as the most important subject which we as a people can be engaged in. That every man may receive at least a moderate education, and thereby be enabled to read the histories of his own and other countries, by which he may duly appreciate the value of our free institutions, appears to be an object of vital importance, even on this account alone, to say nothing of the advantages and satisfaction to be derived from all being able to read the Scriptures, and other works, both of a religious and moral nature, for themselves."

* * * * * * * * *

"With regard to existing laws, some alterations are thought to be necessary. Many respectable men have suggested that our estray laws, the law respecting the issuing of executions, the road law, and some others, are deficient in their present form, and require alterations. But, considering the great probability that the framers of those laws were wiser than myself, I should prefer not meddling with them, unless they were first attacked by others; in which case I should feel it both a privilege and a duty to take that stand which, in my view, might tend most to the advancement of justice.

"But, fellow-citizens, I shall conclude. Considering the great degree of modesty which should always attend youth, it is probable I have already been more presuming than becomes me. However, upon the subjects of which I have treated, I have spoken as I have thought. I may be wrong in regard to any or all of them; but holding it a sound maxim that it is better only sometimes to be right than at all times to be wrong, so soon as I discover my opinions to be erroneous, I shall be ready to renounce them.

"Every man is said to have his peculiar ambition. Whether it be true or not, I can say, for one, that I have no other so great as that of being truly esteemed of my fellow-men, by rendering myself worthy of their esteem. How far I shall succeed in gratifying this ambition is yet to be developed. I am young, and unknown to many of you. I was born, and have ever remained, in the most humble walks of life. I have no wealthy or popular relations or friends to recommend me. My case is thrown exclusively upon the independent voters of the country; and, if elected, they will have conferred a favor upon me tor which I shall be unremitting in my labors to compensate. But, if the good people in their wisdom shall see fit to keep me in the background, I have been too familiar with disappointments to be very much chagrined.

"Your friend and fellow-citizen,

"A. LINCOLN.

"NEW SALEM, March 9, 1832."

On the navigation question he gave many details. His emphasis of this subject was part of the general enthusiasm of a growing country seeking trade facilities, and, still in the early spring, before the election came on, this enthusiasm was whetted by the trip of the first steamboat which had ever gone down the Sangamon River, a feat which stirred the imagination of all the business men with visions of what might happen now that the stream was proved to be navigable. Lincoln was one of a number of citizens who went to meet and welcome this boat, the *Talisman*, at Beardstown, amid great excitement. Rowan Herndon, who was chosen to pilot the steamer from near Springfield to the Illinois River, which he did at an average speed of four miles a day, took Lincoln as his assistant, and each received $40 for the job, after which Lincoln returned to New Salem.

Offut, however, was led away from that town by other enterprises, and by the summer of 1832 Lincoln was out of a job. He was, therefore, in the humor for anything when the Black Hawk War came along. The chief Black Hawk, in violation of a treaty, had crossed the Mississippi and marched up the Rock River Valley with about five hundred Indians on horseback, while the squaws and children went up the river in canoes. Governor Reynolds of Illinois called for one thousand mounted volunteers to help the United States troops under General Atkinson at Fort Armstrong. There was a company for Sangamon County and Lincoln, seeing nothing better to do, the election being still distant, enlisted. He was soon chosen captain by his comrades. To his first order he received the reply, " Go to the devil, sir." It was not a company amenable to discipline, and Captain Lincoln himself seems to have taken his duties lightly, since for breaking a general order forbidding the discharge of firearms within fifty yards of camp he was put under arrest and stripped of his sword for one day. A slightly heavier penalty was inflicted on him for the fault of his subordinates, who got so drunk on some liquor procured from the officers' quarters with the aid of a tomahawk and four buckets, that they were incompetent when a marching order was given. Lincoln, who was ignorant of the deed, was placed under arrest and carried a wooden sword for two days.

His technical knowledge was naturally slight. Marching with a front of over twenty men he wished to go through a gate. " I could not," he says himself, " remember the proper word of command for getting my company *endwise*, so that it could get through the gate ; so, as we came near the gate, I shouted, ' This company is dismissed for two minutes, when it will fall in again on the other side of the gate.'"

One day a helpless old Indian strayed into the camp with a letter from General Cass. The volunteers, bitterly hating the red men, wished to kill him without investigation, but Lincoln saved his life and discovered that he was genuinely recommended by the general and entirely trustworthy. Another piece of magnanimity grew out of his defeat in a wrestling match with a man named Thompson, who threw him. The friends of Lincoln charged unfairness, but Abe declared that his opponent had acted squarely and proved himself the better man. On slighter evidence, the victor's own, there is a story that a Quaker named Wilson threw Lincoln twice out of three times, and beat him in a race for a five-dollar bill. What is certain is that he was fond of wrestling, very strong, and so competent that he was always backed against any celebrity who happened to be accessible.

As Lincoln was not in any of the engagements of this disgraceful little Indian war, it has little to do with the story of his life. When the volunteers were mustered out, May 27 and 28, he was one of few to reënlist, this time as a private in Captain Elijah Iles's company of Independent Rangers. He was mustered in by General Robert Anderson, who was to command Fort Sumter

D

in the crucial days of 1861. He has left one impression of this war. After a skirmish his company came up in time to help bury five dead.

"I remember just how those men looked, as we rode up the little hill where their camp was. The red light of the morning sun was streaming upon them as they lay heads toward us on the ground. And every man had a round red spot on the top of his head, about as big as a dollar, where the redskins had taken his scalp. It was frightful, but it was grotesque; and the red sunlight seemed to paint everything all over." He paused, as if recalling the picture, and added, "I remember that one man had buckskin breeches on."

Lincoln's company was disbanded, July 10, at Whitewater, Wisconsin, and as his horse had been stolen he walked most of the way to Peoria, Illinois, where he and a companion bought a canoe, paddled down the Illinois River to Havana, sold it, and walked to New Salem. The election was at hand, and Lincoln lost no time in beginning political work of the ordinary kind, including some stump speeches. At the first of these, it is related, he interrupted himself to stop by forcible interference a fight in the audience in which a friend was being worsted by an opponent. He was running essentially as a Whig in a Democratic precinct, and he came in third on a list of twelve. As he says in his autobiography, " This was the only time Abraham was ever defeated on a direct vote of the people." His gift of popularity was proved by the fact that in his own precinct only 13 votes were cast against him, 10 not voting for representative, and the 12 candidates, out of a total vote of 300, standing thus: Abraham Lincoln, 277; John T. Stuart, 182; William Carpenter, 136; John Dawson, 105; E. D. Taylor, 88; Archer D. Herndon, 84; Peter Cartwright, 62; Achilles Morris, 27; Thomas M. Neal, 21; Edward Robeson, 15; Zachariah Peters, 4; Richard Dunston, 4.

This defeat raised the necessity of work again, and Lincoln, after a little thought of utilizing his physical strength as a blacksmith, and an unsuccessful attempt to secure a clerkship in any of the four New Salem stores, went into business in a more independent position by buying from Rowan Herndon his half interest in the store which he owned with William F. Berry. The terms were liberal, Herndon trusting Lincoln's honesty and taking the notes of the two owners. Almost immediately one of the rival merchants, Reuben Radford, by an attack from Clary's Grove, whose boys were so hostile to him that they took a night to smash his doors and windows and damage his goods, was put into a mood for selling out, which he did to William G. Green for a $400 note. At Green's request Lincoln made an inventory and then offered him $650, and the deal went through, as usual in that vicinity, on credit. Notes bought and assigned also brought about the final move, the absorption of the third and last store by Berry and Lincoln.

The consolidated business did not thrive. Berry drank while Lincoln read and studied. One of his branches was law, an interest which had been dormant since his departure from Indiana. "One day," related Lincoln after his first nomination, "a man who was migrating to the west drove up in front of my store with a wagon which contained his family and household plunder. He asked me if I would buy an old barrel for which he had no room in his wagon, and which he said contained nothing of special value. I did not want it, but to oblige him I bought it, and paid him, I think, half a dollar for it. Without further examination, I put it away in the store, and forgot all about it. Some time after, in overhauling things, I came upon the barrel, and emptying it upon the floor to see what it contained, I found at the bottom of the rubbish a complete edition of Blackstone's 'Commentaries.' I began to read those famous works, and I had plenty of time; for during the long summer days, when the farmers were busy with their crops, my customers were few and far between. The more I read, the more intensely interested I became. Never in my whole life was my mind so thoroughly absorbed. I read until I devoured them."

The lack of business prosperity led the partners to take out March 6, 1833, a tavern license, to make it possible, or easier, to retail their liquors. To help perform this labor they hired a clerk, Daniel Green Burner, who has made the following statement about the business: —

" The store building of Berry and Lincoln was a frame building, not very large, one story in height, and contained two rooms. In the little back room Lincoln had a fireplace and a bed. There is where we slept. I clerked in the store through the winter of 1833–34, up to the 1st of March. While I was there they had nothing for sale but liquors. They may have had some groceries before that, but I am certain they had none then. I used to sell whiskey over their counter at six cents a glass — and charged it too. N. A. Garland started a store, and Lincoln wanted Berry to ask his father for a loan, so they could buy out Garland; but Berry refused, saying this was one of the last things he would think of doing."

This transformation into a liquor business did not work either, and Lincoln was glad enough to be appointed postmaster at New Salem, on May 7 of this year 1833, by a Democratic administration, the office being too insignificant to make politics an objection, in Lincoln's own explanation. The mail arrived on horseback once a week, and the new postmaster carried it in his hat until he met the recipients or was able to call at their dwellings. The newspapers he was permitted to open and read as soon as they arrived. All this was pleasant, but not immediately very lucrative, so the postmaster and storekeeper indulged in odd jobs. He split rails and helped at the mill. As Rowan Herndon, with whom he had been living, removed to the country, Lincoln took up at the tavern kept by James Rutledge, who had a daughter named Ann. It was a small log house, covered with clapboards, containing four rooms. He stuck to Blackstone and got hold of Chitty and other law books. He was no observer of times or places. One day an old man, who had given him some of his irregular jobs, saw him on the woodpile, barefoot, in his flax or tow-linen pantaloons, several inches short, probably with one suspender, no vest or coat, calico shirt, and straw hat without a band, his big, rough, gentle face bent over a book.

"What are you reading?" asked the old man.

"I'm not reading, I'm studying," replied Lincoln.

"Studying what?"

"Law, sir."

"Great God Almighty!"

And the old man passed on.

This ungainly young man, with his careless business habits and lounging ways, who slept on the store counter when the tavern was full, was getting on in real preparation for life. He could soon draw deeds, contracts, and mortgages for his neighbors. He frequently got before a justice of the peace, but charged little and often nothing. At the same time he read natural science, a little history, including some Gibbon, and apparently liked to skim Mrs. Lee Hentz's novels, which were popular then, and which he could borrow, though he said later he seldom or never read a work of fiction through. Indeed, reading a thing through was not very frequent with him. Shakespeare and Burns he seems to have early become familiar with in parts, but not to any large extent. In the meantime he did not neglect relaxation, but, being of absolutely sober habits, relieved his spirits by free stories, trials of strength, and miscellaneous amusements such as umpiring at chicken fights, an innocent sporting tendency which was later used against him by Stephen A. Douglas. Behind, in his spirit, was something quite different both from his easy social sport with men and from his legal and political ambition. It was the thought of Ann Rutledge, the daughter at the tavern, who was engaged to another man.

CHAPTER III

WHILE the affairs of the store were growing
steadily worse, Lincoln received an offer which
enabled him to make more money, and showed
the general confidence in his ability and integrity. John Calhoun, the county surveyor,
needing a deputy in the summer of 1833 to help
him in the considerable mass of work created
by the flood of immigration in the prosperous
county of Sangamon, sent a friend to the Salem
postmaster to ask if he would take the place.
Lincoln, who was discovered splitting rails in
the woods, replied that he would see Calhoun
himself. He went to Springfield, told the Democratic surveyor that he was a Whig, and that he
was ignorant of surveying, and was assured by
Calhoun that his acceptance would be no political obligation, and that time for learning would
be allowed. He therefore promised to be ready
as soon as possible, for it was no small lift
in the world to follow a profession which would
pay him $3 a day. He secured all the books on
the subject to be had in the neighborhood, including Flint and Gibson's treatise, received help

from his enthusiastic friend Mentor Graham, and worked intensely day and night for six weeks. At the end of that short time he presented himself to Calhoun, and soon showed that he was sufficiently prepared by rapidly earning a reputation for accurate work. He was employed by the county in surveying roads and by private individuals for farms and probably for some of the numerous paper cities built by speculators. Conditions were still somewhat primitive, and there is a tale that he sometimes used a grapevine instead of a chain.

This lucrative employment came in the nick of time. It saved him from being altogether swamped in the misfortunes of Berry and Lincoln. The firm was getting more and more deeply into debt, and early in 1834 the store, which had been entirely managed for some time by Berry, was sold on credit to brothers named Trent, who failed before their notes became due. Berry died soon after, thus throwing on Lincoln an indebtedness so large that he called it the national debt. He had besides to help his migrating father, now in Coles County, and he had private debts, one of them for a horse, necessary in his surveying. For this animal he had given $50 and had settled all but $10 when he was sued and paid the rest. To the firm's creditors he said that if they would let him alone he would give them all he could make over living expenses, and they consented. Fourteen years after, when he was in the national Congress, he was sending part of his salary to his law partner for this purpose, which was finally accomplished. In all that time only one of the firm creditors annoyed him. One Van Bergen sued him on a note and obtained judgment. The sheriff levied on his surveying instruments, horse, saddle, and bridle, and sold them. James Short, a friend, saying nothing to Lincoln in advance, attended the sheriff's sale, bought the goods for $120, and returned them to Abraham. Lincoln repaid the money with interest, and about thirty years later, when Mr. Short was in pecuniary trouble, the President sent him an appointment as Indian agent.

Lincoln, with his debts on his back, kept industriously ahead. His work left him time to read Paine, Volney, and Voltaire, according to Mr. Herndon, who makes him out quite an argumentative disbeliever. He was evidently very popular with his neighbors, being social, apt, and friendly, always liking to give homely assistance to men or women alike. Jack Armstrong's wife relates that he used to rock the cradle while she prepared the meal, at which he was always welcome when he happened in. In this placid business and sociable life he continued until the next summer, 1834, when he decided to try again for the legislature, this time distinctly as a Whig. He made all the speeches he could until August, when he was elected one of four assemblymen from Sangamon County. He was the youngest member but one of that legislature. The vote was: Dawson, 1390; Lincoln, 1376; Carpenter, 1170; Stuart, 1164. From that time to December 1, when the legislature began, Lincoln, who of course would be unable to do so much surveying, gave special attention to the law, which he had tried spasmodically before, and made the rapid progress due to his energy, his popularity, and the lack of lawyers in the neighborhood.

As the time approached to go to Vandalia, the state capital, seventy-five miles from New Salem, Lincoln borrowed money to buy a comparatively decent suit. It is said that his first candidacy provoked some jests, for he was an ill-clothed and awkward figure even for his surroundings. One witness says: " Governor Yates told me that the first time he saw Lincoln was at New Salem, where he was lying on a cellar door, in the shade, reading. There were many odd-looking specimens of humanity in that region in those days, but Lincoln exceeded all in grotesqueness, oddity, and a queer style of dress; but his conversation showed excellent sense. They went to dinner at Lincoln's boarding place, which was a rough log house, with a puncheon floor and a clapboard roof: the dinner was bread and milk." Even when he appeared at the state capital he did not suggest any effete aristocracy. Vandalia was a big town for him, with three taverns, four doctors, five lawyers, two newspapers, and several stores, in fact all the complexity of a metropolis. Lincoln kept pretty quiet. He observed the large assortment of statesmen with whom he was thrown, but followed his habit of postponing action until he was at home in a new situation. There were in Vandalia many men who afterward became prominent, among them Stephen A. Douglas, who struck Lincoln as "the least man he had ever seen." The representative from Sangamon County voted for the principal bills of the session, chartering a state bank and borrowing half a million dollars for a highway, the beginning of a fever for speculative improvement which a few years later reached a disastrous climax. He naturally did not shine on his committee, that of public accounts and expenditures, a line of thought in which he never became strong, but he did introduce and carry through a bill limiting the jurisdiction of justices of the peace; made a motion to change the rules to prevent amendments to any bill after the third reading, a practice which was eventually adopted three years later; and introduced a resolution in favor of securing to the state a part of the proceeds of public lands within its limits, which was laid on the table.

With this modest and prudent record he returned, in the spring of 1835, to New Salem, and began again to survey, study law, and distribute letters. The first thing of importance that happened to him was not worldly but intimate. He found that Ann Rutledge, the girl of the tavern, was in trouble. Her fiancé had gone away about a year before, and Ann had heard disquieting rumors. When young McNeill settled in New Salem, before Lincoln did, he had shown such business ability that in four years he owned a half interest in a prosperous store and a large farm in the neighborhood. Among the suitors for the beautiful Ann this energetic youth easily won, but as she was only seventeen the marriage was to be postponed. After a long engagement, late in 1833, about the time Lincoln left for Vandalia, McNeill told Ann a secret. His name, he said, was really McNamar, and he had changed it to keep his father's reverses from following him when he ran away from his Eastern home to retrieve the family fortunes. He now wished to go East to look up the relatives whom he was at last able to help, and he sold his interest in the store before starting. On his return, with his father and mother, Ann and he would be married. Ann believed him, but as months passed on and she received no letters she told her secret, and all her friends met the story with convincing scepticism.

Lincoln, finding on his return from Vandalia that months had passed with no news, that Ann was sad and gossip cruel, took heart and asked the girl to be his wife. She consented in the spring to marry him when another year had enabled her to have an autumn and winter season in a Jacksonville academy, and had helped him to make a further start in life.

But Ann never reached the academy. As the spring and summer passed, her memories haunted her. What she felt about Lincoln we do not know. McNamar was on her conscience. Had she wronged him? Was he still faithful? Had she every right to love him in spite of silence? She fell so ill that Lincoln was kept from her presence, and again we can only conjecture what this exclusion means. Finally hope had gone and her new fiancé was allowed to spend an hour with her shortly before her death, which came August 25, 1835.

Lincoln, always tending toward fits of gloom, had his mind almost unsettled by this blow. For the sadness that marked his face through life many reasons have been given by those who knew him best. One of his most intelligent friends believed that constipation was the real cause.

Others find it inherited from his unhappy mother. Others tell of the gloom of pioneer life, the desert spaces, the malaria, the loneliness, the absence of opportunity for a man who feels his powers ready within him.   Whatever the causes, almost all who ever knew Lincoln well believed that the death of Ann Rutledge was an aggravation of the morbid tendency.   She was the loveliest and most lovable woman in New Salem.   Lincoln was deeply fond of her.   In all probability her heart was never fully his, but he had reason to hope it would be.   Then she died, and two months later McNamar's return, with proof of his honesty, gave a final touch to the pioneer tragedy. Lincoln, in one fashion or another, for several years loved rather readily, seeming in a mood to offer his hand and heart whenever a sympathetic relation was established, but in the case of Ann alone was the feeling deep.   He and his friends feared for his sanity.   As long as five or six years after he consulted Dr. Drake, a celebrated Cincinnati doctor, by letter, but the physician refused to give an opinion without a personal interview, and Lincoln was unable to make the trip.   To a fellow-member of the legislature, within two years after the death, the represent-ative from Sangamon said that although he seemed to enjoy life, he was so overcome by depression, whenever he was alone, that he no *l*onger dared to carry a pocket-knife, in spite of his old-time love of whittling. After the first election to the presidency he answered his old friend, Isaac Colgate, who asked if it was true he ran a little wild about the Rutledge matter: " I did really. I ran off the track. It was my first. I loved the woman dearly. She was a handsome girl ; would have made a good, loving wife ; was natural, and quite intellectual, though not highly educated. I did honestly and truly love the girl, and think often, often, of her now." To one of his friends, speaking of Concord Cemetery, seven miles from New Salem, Lincoln said, " My heart is buried there." There was a popular belief that in all weathers he used to sit for hours alone on her grave. McNamar, who saw Lincoln at the post-office, says, " He seemed desolate and sorely distressed ; " — and McNamar, himself, within a year, married another woman.

Apparently it was this experience more than any one other which fixed the habit of reciting lugubrious verse, half-way between doggerel and poetry, which followed him through life, and these effusions represent one side of the man's personal nature with vividness. One of them has been made famous as his favorite, the poem which he recited for some thirty years at every opportunity. Part of it is : —

E

"Oh ! why should the spirit of mortal be proud?
Like a swift-fleeting meteor, a fast-flying cloud,
A flash of the lightning, a break of the wave,
He passeth from life to his rest in the grave.

" The leaves of the oak and the willow shall fade,
Be scattered around, and together be laid ;
And the young and the old, and the low and the high,
Shall moulder to dust, and together shall lie.

" The infant a mother attended and loved ;
The mother that infant's affection who proved ;
The husband that mother and infant who blest, —
Each, all, are away to their dwellings of rest. . . .

"So the multitude goes, like the flower or the weed,
That withers away to let others succeed ;
So the multitude comes, even those we behold,
To repeat every tale that has often been told.

"For we are the same our fathers have been ;
We see the same sights our fathers have seen ;
And drink the same stream, we view the same sun,
And run the same course our fathers have run.

" The thoughts we are thinking our fathers would think ;
From the death we are shrinking our fathers would shrink ;
To the life we are clinging they also would cling ;
But it speeds from us all like a bird on the wing.

"They loved, but the story we cannot unfold ;
They scorned, but the heart of the haughty is cold ;
They grieved, but no wail from their slumber will come ;
They joyed, but the tongue of their gladness is dumb.

"They died, ay, they died ; we things that are now,
That walk on the turf that lies over their brow,
And make in their dwellings a transient abode,
Meet the things that they met on their pilgrimage road.

" Yea, hope and despondency, and pleasure and pain,
Are mingled together in sunshine and rain ;
And the smile and the tear, the song and the dirge,
Still follow each other like surge upon surge.

" 'Tis the wink of an eye, 'tis the draught of a breath,
From the blossom of health to the paleness of death,
From the gilded saloon to the bier and the shroud, —
Oh, why should the spirit of mortal be proud ? "

This brand of melancholy poetic reflection became such a large and settled part of Lincoln's
life that it is, next to his wit, perhaps his most
famous personal trait. Had he possessed the
poetic faculty, it is easy to see what kind of a
poet he would have been. Byron's "dream"
was one of the things he liked, and one of his
prime favorites contained these thoughts : —

" Tell me, ye winged winds
　That round my pathway roar,
　Do ye not know some spot
　Where mortals weep no more ?
　Some lone and pleasant vale,
　Some valley in the west,
　Where, free from toil and pain,
　The weary soul may rest ?
The loud wind dwindled to a whisper low,
And sighed for pity as it answered, No.

"Tell me, thou mighty deep,
  Whose billows round me play,
  Know'st thou some favored spot,
  Some island far away,
  Where weary man may find
  The bliss for which he sighs ;
  Where sorrow never lives
  And friendship never dies?
  The loud waves rolling in perpetual flow
  Stopped for a while and sighed to answer, No.

"And thou, serenest moon,
  That with such holy face
  Dost look upon the Earth
  Asleep in Night's embrace —
  Tell me, in all thy round
  Hast thou not seen some spot
  Where miserable man
  Might find a happier lot?
  Behind a cloud the moon withdrew in woe,
  And a voice sweet but sad responded, No.

"Tell me, my secret soul,
  Oh, tell me, Hope and Faith,
  Is there no resting-place
  From sorrow, sin, and death?
  Is there no happy spot
  Where mortals may be blessed,
  Where grief may find a balm
  And weariness a rest?
  Faith, Hope, and Love, best boon to mortals given,
  Waved their bright wings and whispered, Yes, in
          Heaven."

The melancholy which increased after Ann Rutledge's death, however, is but one side of as enigmatical a character as is known to history. If the great President is ever to be understood as a man, it must be by reconciling wonderful sanity with vagaries almost insane, and it is the wilder and queerer side of his nature that comes to the front for several years after Ann's death. A woman named Mary S. Owens, who had visited New Salem in 1833, returned in 1836. The story of her relation to Lincoln rests mostly on her own evidence, but letters from him are sufficient to give it a singular importance in any attempt to see him intimately. This lady was the object of Lincoln's interest, but she thought him "deficient in those little links which make up the chain of a woman's happiness." She also says, "I thought him lacking in smaller attentions." As a party of friends were riding on horseback one day he failed to draw aside the branch of a tree which the other men had removed for their women companions. Mary remonstrated, and her cavalier replied that he knew she was plenty smart to take care of herself. The rest of the story belongs to a slightly later period.

During this year Lincoln was again a candidate for the legislature. His first important step was the following: —

"New Salem, June 13, 1863.

"To the Editor of The Journal : In your paper of last Saturday I see a communication over the signature of 'Many voters' in which the candidates who are announced in the *Journal* are called upon to 'show their hands.' Agreed. Here's mine : —

"I go for all sharing the privileges of the government who assist in bearing its burdens. Consequently, I go for admitting all whites to the right of suffrage who pay taxes or bear arms (by no means excluding females).

"If elected, I shall consider the whole people of Sangamon my constituents, as well those that oppose as those that support me.

"While acting as their representative, I shall be governed by their will on all subjects upon which I have the means of knowing what their will is ; and upon all others I shall do what my own judgment teaches me will best advance their interests. Whether elected or not, I go for distributing the proceeds of the sales of public lands to the several states to enable our state, in common with others, to dig canals and construct railroads without borrowing money and paying the interest on it.

"If alive on the first Monday in November, I shall vote for Hugh L. White, for President.

"Very respectfully,

"A. Lincoln."

One story of this campaign shows Lincoln's already noticeable political adroitness. One Forquer, who had put on his house the only lightning-rod in Springfield, and the first Lincoln and most of his hearers had ever seen, answered one of the campaign speeches of the candidate from New Salem. Lincoln in his reply said : —

"Mr. Forquer commenced his speech by announcing that the young man would have to be taken down. It is for you, fellow-citizens, not for me, to say whether I am up or down. The gentleman has seen fit to allude to my being a young man; but he forgets that I am older in years than I am in the tricks and trades of politicians. I desire to live, and I desire place and distinction; but I would rather die now, than, like the gentleman, live to see the day that I would change my politics for an office worth three thousand dollars a year, and then feel compelled to erect a lightning-rod to protect a guilty conscience from an offended God."

Lincoln was elected, and his record was much more prominent than it had been during his first term. The three things he proved were that he was a very adroit politician, that he shared a financial insanity which just then pervaded the state, and that he had convictions on slavery. His political address was shown in his leading position among the delegates from his district, called the "Long Nine," from the height of all the members, and its recogni-

tion was proved by the fact that a great scheme
of that body, the removal of the capital, was
left to his engineering. The removal for Vandalia was settled, and Alton, Decatur, Peoria,
Jacksonville, and Illiopolis sought the honor.
The Long Nine, however, by giving their support to other bills only in return for votes for
Springfield, conquered. This success led to com-
plimentary dinners and meetings, and among
the toasts were these: —

"Abraham Lincoln: He has fulfilled the expectations of his friends, and disappointed the hopes of his
enemies."
"A. Lincoln: One of Nature's noblemen."

The interest of the statesmen during this
session, however, was mainly taken up with a
grand scheme for the manufacture of an Illinois boom. Chicago had started on her me-
teoric career, and the legislators were drunk
with the idea of giving the whole state a
similar experience. They planned a canal from
Lake Michigan to the Illinois River and railroads between numerous cities, some of which
owed their existence only to maps. Thirteen
hundred and fifty miles of rail were thus arranged for. Every stream in the state was to
be improved. Unfortunately there were a few

neighborhoods which had no rivers and were not included in the railroad system, but the open-handed Solons met this difficulty by voting $200,000 to be divided among these places. To carry out the rest of the plan they voted the perfectly inadequate sums of $8,000,000 for railroads and $4,000,000 for the canal. Lincoln was on the committee on finance. In the consequences of these dreams he shared at a later session. The frenzy was almost universal, and Stephen A. Douglas was among the most enthusiastic.

As far as Lincoln's career was concerned, however, his most important act was one which passed almost unnoticed, a protest entered March 3, the day before the legislature adjourned. The sentiment in favor of slavery in Illinois, which was peopled largely by settlers from Southern states, had always been considerable. After the separation of Illinois from Indiana, it kept the Indiana act which authorized a sort of slavery by indenture. A serious attempt to open the state to slavery had been made by the legislature no later than the session of 1822–23, and public opinion was very hostile to abolitionists, who were looked upon as pretentious Eastern cranks. It was not the easiest course to take any positive stand on the question, and when Lincoln made this protest the

murder of Lovejoy at Alton was but one year
ahead. The resolutions passed almost unanimously, the protest being signed with but two
names. The resolutions are : —

" Resolved by the General Assembly of the state of
Illinois : That we highly disapprove of the formation of
Abolition societies and of the doctrines promulgated by
them ;

" That the right of property in slaves is sacred to the
slave-holding states by the Federal Constitution, and
that they cannot be deprived of that right without their
consent ;

" That the General Government cannot abolish slavery
in the District of Columbia against the consent of the
citizens of said District, without a manifest breach of
good faith ;

" That the Governor be requested to transmit to the
states of Virginia, Alabama, Mississippi, New York, and
Connecticut, a copy of foregoing report and resolutions."

The record of the protest reads : —

" Resolutions upon the subject of domestic slavery
having passed both branches of the General Assembly
at its present session, the undersigned hereby protest
against the same.

" They believe that the institution of slavery is
founded on both injustice and bad policy, but that the
promulgation of abolition doctrines tends rather to increase than abate its evils.

" They believe that the Congress of the United States

has no power under the Constitution to interfere with the institution of slavery in the different states.

" They believe that the Congress of the United States has the power under the Constitution to abolish slavery in the District of Columbia, but that the power ought not to be exercised unless at the request of the people of the District.

" The difference between these opinions and those contained in the above resolutions, is their reason for entering this protest.

" DAN STONE,
" A. LINCOLN,

" Representatives from the County of Sangamon."

Thus Lincoln put his opinions on record in 1837 in a way that through all the controversy of thirty years he had no need to alter. It was the first striking illustration of his power to say the right thing on great moral issues.

CHAPTER IV

LINCOLN's style about this time was usually pure, but, like those of most men who are to reach a high degree of restrained eloquence, some of his early experiments are florid, as may be seen in an address before the young men's Lyceum of Springfield, January 28, 1838, in which the general tone corresponded to this extract:—

"Shall we expect some transatlantic military giant to step the ocean and crush us at a blow? Never! All the armies of Europe, Asia, and Africa combined, with all the treasure of the earth (our own excepted) in their military chest, with a Bonaparte for a commander, could not by force take a drink from the Ohio or make a track on the Blue Ridge in a trial of a thousand years.

"At what point then is the approach of danger to be expected? I answer, If it ever reach us, it must spring up amongst us; it cannot come from abroad. If destruction be our lot, we must ourselves be its author and finisher. As a nation of freemen we must live through all time, or die by suicide."

A manner of expression much more natural to him is seen in these passages from a letter to Miss Mary Owens, from Vandalia, December 13, 1836:—

"Vandalia, December 13, 1836.

Mary: I have been sick since my arrival, or I should have written sooner.   It is but little difference, however, as I have very little even yet to write.   And more, the longer I can avoid the mortification of looking in the post-office for your letter and not finding it, the better. You see I am mad about that old letter yet.   I don't like very well to risk you again.   I'll try you once more, anyhow.

*   *   *   *   *   *   *   *   *

"You recollect that I mentioned at the outset of this letter that I had been unwell.   That is the fact, though I believe I am about well now; but that, with other things I cannot account for, have conspired, and have gotten my spirits so low that I feel that I would rather be any place in the world than here.   I really cannot endure the thought of staying here ten weeks.   Write back as soon as you get this, and, if possible, say something that will please me, for really I have not been pleased since I left you."

In the short time which he spent at home before the special session, which followed soon after the end of the regular session, Lincoln continued his study of law, and in March he was admitted to the bar in Springfield.   As that town, a great city of over a thousand inhabitants, had been chosen the capital, the ambitious young lawyer-politician determined to cast his fate there.   One fine day he rode into town on a borrowed horse, with a pair of saddle-bags containing two or three law-books and a few pieces of clothing, and landed in the store of a prosperous young merchant friend, Joshua F. Speed, who offered to share his quarters with him.

"What would the furniture for a single bed cost?" asked the newcomer.

"About seventeen dollars," the merchant calculated.

Though that would be cheap, Lincoln admitted, he had not the money to pay. "But if you will credit me until Christmas, and my experiment here as a lawyer is a success, I will pay you then. If I fail in that, I will probably never pay you at all."

Speed proposed to share his double bed.

"Where is your room?" asked Lincoln.

"Upstairs," replied Speed, pointing to stairs which led from the store.

Lincoln picked up his bags, climbed the stairs, put all his worldly goods upon the floor, and returned, a smiling resident of Springfield, saying, "Well, Speed, I've moved."

The kindness which he often won was necessary now. He was taken to board by one William Butler, with whom he stayed several years, probably without pay. A few days after his arrival he formed a law partnership with John T. Stuart, whom he had known in the Black Hawk War, and who had loaned him books some years before.

As Stuart was deeply in politics, Lincoln's active practice began at once. He attended to the office business, drew up most of the pleas, tried the cases, and made all the entries in the books. Something of his business mood may be guessed from this extract from a letter to Stuart:—

"You recollect you told me you had drawn the Chicago Masack money, and sent it to the claimants. A . . . hawk-billed Yankee is here besetting me at every turn I take, saying that Robert Kinzie never received the eighty dollars to which he was entitled. Can you tell anything about the matter? Again, old Mr. Wright, who lives up South Fork somewhere, is teasing me continually about some deeds which he says he left with you, but which I can find nothing of. Can you tell where they are?"

While at work, he occupied the firm office, a room in the court-house, containing a small lounge or bed, a chair with a buffalo robe on it, a hard wooden bench, and a little bookcase. His real headquarters, however, were in Speed's store, a gathering-point of the town philosophers, including men prominent in the legislature, with whom Lincoln had time and opportunity to thrash over all the problems of the day. Springfield was rather more civilized than most towns in Illinois, and Lincoln was thrown in with men who wore better clothes, had better business habits, and knew more about the outside world than most he had formerly met.

His personal feelings, on one side, during these first days in the new town, are left in a letter to Miss Owens: —

"SPRINGFIELD, May 7, 1837.

"FRIEND MARY: I have commenced two letters to send you before this, both of which displeased me before I got half done, and so I tore them up. The first I thought wasn't serious enough, and the second was on the other extreme. I shall send this, turn out as it may.

"This thing of living in Springfield is rather a dull business after all — at least it is so to me. I am quite as lonesome here as (I) ever was anywhere in my life. I have been spoken to by but one woman since I've been here, and should not have been by her if she could have avoided it. I've never been to church yet, and probably shall not be, soon. I stay away because I am conscious I should not know how to behave myself. I am often thinking of what we said of your coming to live at Springfield. I am afraid you would not be satisfied. There is a great deal of flourishing about in carriages here, which would be your doom to see without sharing in it. You would have to be poor without the means of hiding your poverty. Do you believe you could bear that patiently? Whatever woman may cast her lot with mine, should any one ever do so, it is my intention to do all in my power to make her happy and contented, and there is nothing I can imagine that would make me more unhappy than to fail in the effort. I know I should be much happier with you than the way I am, provided I saw no signs of discontent in you.

" What you have said to me may have been in jest or I may have misunderstood it. If so, then let it be forgotten ; if otherwise, I much wish you would think seriously before you decide. For my part I have already decided. What I have said I will most positively abide by, provided you wish it.   My opinion is you had better not do it.   You have not been accustomed to hardship, and it may be more severe than you imagine.   I know you are capable of thinking correctly on any subject : and if you deliberate maturely upon this before you decide, then I am willing to abide your decision.

" You must write me a good long letter after you get this. You have nothing else to do, and though it might not seem interesting to you after you have written it, it would be a good deal of company in this busy wilderness. Tell your sister I don't want to hear any more about selling out and moving.   That gives me the hypo whenever I think of it.

"Yours, etc.,

" A. LINCOLN."

Another letter is : —

" SPRINGFIELD, Aug. 16, 1837.

" FRIEND MARY: You will no doubt think it rather strange that I should write you a letter on the same day on which we parted ; and I can only account for it by supposing that seeing you lately makes me think of you more than usual, while at our late meeting we had but few expressions of thoughts. You must know that I cannot see you or think of you with entire indifference; and yet it may be that you are mistaken in regard to

F

what my real feelings toward you are. If I knew you were not, I should not trouble you with this letter. Perhaps any other man would know enough without further information, but I consider it my peculiar right to plead ignorance and your bounden duty to allow the plea.

"I want in all cases to do right; and most particularly so in all cases with women. I want at this particular time, more than anything else, to do right with you, and if I knew it would be doing right, as I rather suspect it would, to let you alone, I would do it. And for the purpose of making the matter as plain as possible, I now say, that you can now drop the subject, dismiss your thoughts (if you ever had any) from me forever, and leave this letter unanswered, without calling forth one accusing murmur from me. And I will even go farther, and say, that if it will add anything to your comfort or peace of mind to do so, it is my sincere wish that you should. Do not understand by this that I wish to cut your acquaintance. I mean no such a thing. What I do wish is that our further acquaintance shall depend upon yourself. If such further acquaintance would contribute nothing to your happiness, I am sure it would not to mine. If you feel yourself in any degree bound to me, I am now willing to release you, provided you wish it; while, on the other hand, I am willing and even anxious to bind you faster if I can be convinced that it will in any considerable degree add to your happiness. This, indeed, is the whole question with me. Nothing would make me more miserable, nothing more happy, than to know you were so.

"In what I have now said, I think I cannot be misunderstood; and to make myself understood is the sole object of this letter.

"If it suits you best not to answer this — farewell — a long life and a merry one attend you.   But if you conclude to write back, speak as plainly as I do.   There can be neither harm nor danger in saying to me anything you think, just in the manner you think it.

"My respects to your sister.

"Your friend,

"LINCOLN."

As a conclusion to this whole episode, which is one of the most baffling in its bearing on Lincoln's mind and character, we have his own version of it, written April 1, 1838, to his friend, Mrs. O. H. Browning; in a letter which, twenty-five years after, the President warned her against giving to a biographer, on the ground that it contained too much truth.

"SPRINGFIELD, April, 1838.

"DEAR MADAM: Without apologizing for being egotistical, I shall make the history of so much of my life as has elapsed since I saw you the subject of this letter.   And, by the way, I now discover that, in order to give a full and intelligible account of the things I have done and suffered since I saw you, I shall necessarily have to relate some that happened before.

"It was, then, in the autumn of 1836 that a married lady of my acquaintance and who was a great friend of mine, being about to pay a visit to her father and other relatives residing in Kentucky, proposed to me that on her return she would bring a sister of hers with her on condition that I would engage to become her brother-in-law with all convenient despatch. I, of course, accepted the proposal, for you know I could not have done otherwise, had I really been averse to it; but privately, between you and me, I was most confoundedly well pleased with the project. I had seen the said sister some three years before, thought her intelligent and agreeable, and saw no good objection to plodding life through, hand in hand with her. Time passed on, the lady took her journey and in due time returned, sister in company sure enough. This astonished me a little; for it appeared to me that her coming so readily showed she was a trifle too willing; but, on reflection, it occurred to me that she might have been prevailed on by her married sister to come, without anything concerning me ever having been mentioned to her; and so I concluded that, if no other objection presented itself, I would consent to waive this. All this occurred to me on hearing of her arrival in the neighborhood; for, be it remembered, I had not yet seen her, except about three years previous, as above-mentioned. In a few days we had an interview; and, although I had seen her before, she did not look as my imagination had pictured her. I knew she was over-size, but she now appeared a fair match for Falstaff. I knew she was called an 'old maid,' and I felt no doubt of the truth of at least half of the appellation: but now, when I beheld her, I could not for my life avoid thinking of my mother; and this, not from withered features, for her skin was too full of fat to permit of its contracting into wrinkles, but from her want of teeth, weather-beaten appearance in general, and from a kind of notion that ran in my head that nothing could have commenced at the size of infancy and reached her present bulk in less than thirty-five or forty years; and, in short, I was not at all pleased with her. But what could I do? I had told her sister I would take her for better or for worse; and I made a point of honor and conscience in all things to stick to my word, especially if others had been induced to act on it, which in this case I had no doubt they had; for I was now fairly convinced that no other man on earth would have her, and hence the conclusion that they were bent on holding me to my bargain. 'Well,' thought I, 'I have said it, and, be the consequences what they may, it shall not be my fault if I fail to do it.' At once I determined to consider her my wife; and, this done, all my powers of discovery were put to work in search of perfections in her which might be fairly set off against her defects. I tried to imagine her handsome, which, but for her unfortunate corpulency, was actually true. Exclusive of this, no woman that I have ever seen has a finer face. I also tried to convince myself that the mind was much more to be valued than the person; and in this she was not inferior, as I could discover, to any with whom I had been acquainted.

"Shortly after this, without coming to any positive understanding with her, I set out for Vandalia, when and where you first saw me. During my stay there I had letters from her which did not change my opinion of her intellect or intention, but on the contrary confirmed it in both.

"All this while, although I was fixed, 'firm as the surge-repelling rock,' in my resolution, I found I was continually repenting the rashness which had led me to make it. Through life, I have been in no bondage, either real or imaginary, from the thraldom of which 1 so much desired to be free. After my return home, I saw nothing to change my opinions of her in any particular. She was the same, and so was I. I now spent my time in planning how I might get along through life after my contemplated change of circumstances should have taken place, and how I might procrastinate the evil day for a time, which I really dreaded as much, perhaps more, than an Irishman does the halter.

"After all my suffering upon this deeply interesting subject, here I am, wholly, unexpectedly, completely, out of the 'scrape'; and now I want to know if you can guess how I got out of it — out, clear, in every sense of the term; no violation of word, honor, or conscience. I don't believe you can guess, and so I might as well tell you at once. As the lawyer says, it was done in the manner following, to wit : After I had delayed the matter as long as I thought I could in honor do (which, by the way, had brought me round into the last fall), I concluded I might as well bring it to a consummation without further delay; and so I mustered my resolution, and made the proposal to her direct; but, shocking to relate, she answered, No. At first I supposed she did it through an affectation of modesty, which I thought but ill became her under the peculiar circumstances of her case; but on my renewal of the charge, I found she repelled it with greater firmness than before. I tried it again and again, but with the same success, or rather with the same want of success.

"I finally was forced to give it up; at which I very unexpectedly found myself mortified almost beyond endurance. I was mortified, it seemed to me, in a hundred different ways. My vanity was deeply wounded by the reflection that I had been too stupid to discover her intentions, and at the same time never doubting that I understood them perfectly; and also that she, whom I had taught myself to believe nobody else would have, had actually rejected me with all my fancied greatness. And, to cap the whole, I then for the first time began to suspect that I was really a little in love with her. But let it all go. I'll try and outlive it. Others have been made fools of by the girls: but this can never with truth be said of me. I most emphatically, in this instance, made a fool of myself. I have now come to the conclusion never again to think of marrying, and for this reason: I can never be satisfied with any one who would be blockhead enough to have me.

"When you receive this, write me a long yarn about something to amuse me. Give my respects to Mr. Browning.

"Your sincere friend,

"A. LINCOLN."

Although Lincoln's legislative career during these Springfield years has left no very salient points, it strengthened him with his party. The special session of 1837 had to face a panic brought on by the wild deeds of the year before. Loans were made and work begun on the roads and canal. By the time the election for the regular session of 1838 was at hand, the improvement craze was giving place to a more cautious spirit, but the dreamers had not yet abandoned their schemes.   Lincoln was elected and put on the finance committee and the committee on counties. His standing with the Whigs was shown in his nomination for speaker, and although the party was in a minority he came within one vote of election.   The legislature voted $800,000 more, although the hearts of the promoters had begun to sink.   Lincoln defended the venture until the inevitable outcome forced him to admit that he was no financier.   In the session of 1839, which was occupied with discussing means of paying the appalling debt, Lincoln suggested a scheme providing for the issue of bonds for the payment of interest due by the state, and for the appropriation of a special portion of the state taxes to meet the obligation thus incurred, but his suggestions were not accepted.   So great was the burden that there was a decided movement for repudiation. Payment of interest for that year, however, was gained by a measure which forced Fund Commissioners to decide what part of the debt was legal. Suspension of specie payment by the state banks had been made legal up to " the adjournment of the next session of the legislature." This provision led to a hard fight over adjournment, in which at one point an unparliamentary victory was won by the Whigs, some of whom, seeing all ordinary methods exhausted and a vote about to be forced by the Democratic majority, left the hall,

Lincoln and two others jumping from the windows of the church in which the legislature sat.
He always disliked any reference to this irregular
road to a victory by which the Whigs were finally
able to give the state banks a new lease of life.
They lasted but two years, however, and with their
fall ended the improvement schemes, leaving behind nothing but a few miles of embankment, a
few abutments, and an enormous load of debt.

In 1840 Lincoln was again the Whig nominee
for speaker, and was again defeated. On his political and social methods during these years a few
of the remaining stories throw a rather vivid light.
He had naturally learned to make the most of his
lowly origin when speaking from the stump. Once
when a Democratic orator, Colonel Dick Taylor,
was attacking the Whigs for aristocracy, Lincoln
seized his coat, tore it open, and showed a shirt-
front so profusely adorned that the owner stood
hopelessly convicted of pretentions unbecoming a
Western American. In another field Lincoln and
others showed equal decision. A shoemaker, who
used to beat his wife in drunken fits, was, after sufficient warning, tied to a pump and stripped of his
shirt, his spouse was supplied with a good limb,
and told to "light in." Alone Lincoln settled one
controversy which took place while he was in his
room above Speed's store.   In that gathering
place E. D. Baker, Lincoln's Whig friend, put

such acerbity into his description of Democrats
in general that a member of the abused party began a personal chastisement.   Lincoln's long legs
were seen dropping from the aperture above, followed by the rest of his body.   As soon as he
reached the ground floor he seized a water-pitcher
and offered to break it over the head of the first
man who interfered with Baker, explaining immediately that America was a land of free speech.
The softer side of his nature comes out in the tale
that after he had mercilessly ridiculed an opponent, mimicking his personal peculiarities, his conscience smote him for going too far, and he hunted
his victim up to apologize.   It was in a letter of
this period that he says to Stuart, "I am, as you
know, opposed to political removals to make
places for our friends."

While his political and legal progress was
rapid, his tendency to offer himself in marriage
on slight provocation was preparing the way for
trouble.   Sarah Rickard, sister of Mrs. William
Butler, says that Lincoln proposed to her in the
summer of 1840, but she, being but sixteen, looked
upon him only as an elder brother.   In 1839 Mary
Todd, aged twenty-one, came to her sister's house
in Springfield, and speedily became popular with
that city's swains, among them Lincoln, to whom
she became engaged.   Douglas was among her
friends, and of the many reports one says that

she rejected him because she believed more firmly in his rival's future, another and less probable one that at one time only a respect for her engagement kept her from marrying "the Little Giant," as Douglas was soon to be known to the world.

One evening, according to Herndon, who was then a clerk in Speed's store, Lincoln read Speed a letter to Miss Todd, telling her he did not love her enough to marry her and asked Speed to deliver it. Speed, who was the most intimate friend Lincoln ever had, threw it into the fire and said the message ought to be delivered orally. Lincoln obeyed, but when Mary burst into tears and said something about the deceiver being deceived, her fiancé wept also, caught her in his arms, kissed her, and allowed things to drift on toward marriage, which was fixed for January 1, 1841. According to Herndon's story, which has been doubted, but not essentially shaken, Lincoln failed to appear when all the preparations for the marriage had been made, but was found at daybreak in so distraught a state that friends watched over him and kept from him all knives, razors, and other weapons with which he might have ended his troubles. One story is that he had just fallen in love with Miss Matilda Edwards. At any rate, three weeks later, on the 23d of January, he wrote to his partner Stuart:—

"I am now the most miserable man living. If what I feel were equally distributed to the whole human family, there would not be one cheerful face on earth. Whether I shall ever be better, I cannot tell; I awfully forbode I shall not. To remain as I am is impossible. I must die or be better, as it appears to me. . . . I fear I shall be unable to attend any business here, and a change of scene might help me. If I could be myself, I would rather remain at home with Judge Logan. I can write no more."

Herndon tells of a few lines sent by Lincoln at this period to the *Sangamon Journal* under the title "Suicide," and later cut out of the files. According to Herndon also, Miss Todd released her fiancé from his engagement by letter a few days after the incidents of what Lincoln called "that fatal first of January, 1841."

Whatever may have been the degree of these perturbations the victim of them was so much in active life that he was in his seat in the legislature January 1 and 2, and most of the time to the close of the session March 1; and on April 14, 1841, the firm of Stuart and Lincoln was dissolved and that of Logan and Lincoln established, the senior partner being Stephen T. Logan, an ex-Judge of the Circuit Court of the United States, with the reputation of being the best *nisi prius* lawyer in Illinois. He was a man of studious and saving habits, devoted to the technical aspect of his profession, methodical, and in most respects the opposite of Lincoln. Logan wrote in the regular formal legal style, whereas his partner's manner may be illustrated by this letter to a client:—

"As to the real estate we cannot attend to it. We are not real estate agents, we are lawyers. We recommend that you give the charge of it to Mr. Isaac S. Britton, a trustworthy man, and one whom the Lord made on purpose for such business."

If his business activity did not cease during these trying months, no more did his humor, which could be at the expense of his own misfortunes. It is in this session that he said in a speech:—

"The gentlemen had accused old women of being partial to the number nine; but this, he presumed, was without foundation. A few years since, it would be recollected by the House, that the delegation from this county was dubbed by way of eminence 'The Long Nine,' and, by way of further distinction, he had been called 'The Longest of the Nine.' 'Now,' said Mr. Lincoln, 'I desire to say to my friend from Monroe (Mr. Bissell), that if any woman, old or young, ever thought there was any particular charm in this distinguished specimen of number nine, I have as yet been so unfortunate as not to have discovered it."

It was during the same session that he had the

first noticeable issue with his famous rival, on Douglas's bill for " reforming " the judiciary, which was merely a scheme to turn out the judges and appoint others for partisan purposes. It passed the legislature, in spite of the protest of Lincoln and others, but seven years after, Governor Ford, a Democratic leader, said that it was both wrong and impolitic.

However, while there are many signs that no absolute gap in his political and legal activities was made by his inner troubles, before or after the fatal first of January, they certainly weighed heavily on his spirit. In the summer Speed asked him for a visit at Louisville, Kentucky, his old home, and Lincoln was much helped by the change. On his return he wrote a letter to Miss Mary Speed, in which occurs this significant passage : —

" By the way, a fine example was presented on board the boat for contemplating the effect of condition upon human happiness. A gentleman had purchased twelve negroes in different parts of Kentucky, and was taking them to a farm in the South. They were chained six and six together. A small iron clevis was around the left wrist of each, and this fastened to the main chain by a shorter one, at a convenient distance from the others, so that the negroes were strung together precisely like so many fish upon a trot-line. In this condition they were being separated forever from the scenes

of their childhood, their friends, their fathers and
mothers, and brothers and sisters, and many of them
from their wives and children, and going into perpetual
slavery, where the lash of the master is proverbially
more ruthless and unrelenting than any other where;
and yet amid all these distressing circumstances, as we
would think them, they were the most cheerful and
apparently happy creatures on board. One whose
offence for which he had been sold was an over-fondness
for his wife, played the fiddle almost continually, and
the others danced, sang, cracked jokes, and played
various games with cards from day to day. How true
it is that ' God tempers the wind to the shorn lamb,' or
in other words, that he renders the worst of human conditions tolerable, while he permits the best to be nothing
better than tolerable. To return to the narrative.
When we reached Springfield I stayed but one day,
when I started on this tedious circuit where I now am.
Do you remember my going to the city, while I was in
Kentucky, to have a tooth extracted, and making a
failure of it? Well, that same old tooth got to paining
me so much that about a week since I had it torn out,
bringing with it a bit of the jawbone, the consequence
of which is that my mouth is now so sore that I can
neither talk nor eat.''

He was being talked about for governor, but
believed it unadvisable to run for the office, as
shown in a semi-official announcement in the
Sangamon Journal, the editorial columns of
which were always open to him : —

"His talents and services endear him to the Whig party ; but we do not believe he desires the nomination. He has already made great sacrifices in maintaining his party principles, and before his political friends asked him to make additional sacrifices, the subject should be well considered. The office for governor, which would of necessity interfere with the practice of his profession, would poorly compensate him for the loss of four of the best years of his life."

He therefore kept on with the law, but his mood did not become exactly gay. In February Speed, who had become engaged in the summer, was to be married, and Lincoln's comments are full of light on his own frame of mind. He warns his friend just before the wedding that a period of depression is likely to follow, due first to probable bad weather on the journey, second to "the absence of all business and conversation of friends which might direct his mind and give it occasional rest from the intensity of thought which will sometimes wear the sweetest idea threadbare, and turn it to the bitterness of death." It is such thoughts as this that have led to the observation that Lincoln was by temperament a poet of meditation and melancholy.

On February 13, he wrote : —

"If you went through the ceremony calmly or even with sufficient composure not to excite alarm in any present, you are safe beyond question, and in two or three months, to say the most, will be the happiest of men."

On the 25th, he wrote : —

" I shall be very lonesome without you.   How miserably things seem to be arranged in this world!   If we have no friends we have no pleasure, and if we have them we are sure to lose them, and be doubly pained by the loss."

March 27, he says :—

" It cannot be told how it thrills me with joy to hear you say you are 'far happier than you ever expected to be'.   That much, I know, is enough.   I know you too well to suppose your expectations were not, at least sometimes, extravagant, and if the reality exceeds them all, I say 'Enough, dear Lord.'   I am not going beyond the truth when I tell you that the short space it took me to read your last letter gave me more pleasure than the total sum of all I have enjoyed since that fatal first of January, 1841.   Since then it seems to me I should have been entirely happy but for the never-absent idea that there is one still unhappy whom I have contributed to make so.   That kills my soul.   I cannot but reproach myself for even wishing to be happy while she is otherwise.   She accompanied a large party on the railroad cars to Jacksonville last Monday, and on her return spoke, so that I heard of it, of having enjoyed the trip exceedingly.   God be praised for that."

Early in this year, 1842, he entered into what was known as the Washington movement, to

G

suppress the evils of intemperance. He had always been singularly abstemious for a frontier politician, but he gained nothing with the church people by championing the good cause, but rather hostility, for his frankness led in one speech to his statement that those who had never fallen victims to the vice were spared more by lack of appetite than by any superiority, and that taken as a class drunkards would compare favorably in head and heart with any other.

His frame of mind as summer came on is recorded by himself in a letter of July 4, to Speed : —

"I must gain confidence in my own ability to keep my resolves when they are made. In that ability I once prided myself as the only chief gem of my character; that gem I lost, how and where you know too well. I have not regained it; and until I do I cannot trust myself in any matter of much importance. I believe now that had you understood my case at the time as well as I understood yours afterward, by the aid you would have given me I should have sailed through clear; but that does not now afford me sufficient confidence to begin that or the like of that again. . . . I always was superstitious; I believe God made me one of the instruments of bringing Fanny and you together, which union I have no doubt he had foreordained. Whatever He designs He will do for me yet. 'Stand still and see the salvation of the Lord,' is my text just now. If, as you say, you have told Fanny all, I have no objection to her seeing this letter, but for its reference to our friend here; let her seeing it depend upon whether she has ever known anything of my affairs; and if she has not, do not let her. I do not think I can come to Kentucky this season. I am so poor and make so little headway in the world that I drop back in a month of idleness as much as I gain in a year's sowing."

On October 5, he wrote to Speed:—

"I want to ask you a close question—Are you now, in *feeling* as well as in judgment, glad you are married as you are? From anybody but me this would be an impudent question, not to be tolerated; but I know you will pardon it in me. Please answer it quickly, as I am impatient to know."

He was contemplating marriage again. Just how long he had been wavering we do not know. During the summer friends had brought the former fiancés together, and they immediately saw much of each other. One result was a duel, to which Lincoln, in later years, disliked any reference. A Democratic politician, named James Shields, was ridiculed by Lincoln in a letter to a Springfield paper, signed "Aunt Rebecca." Miss Todd and a woman friend then tried their hands, under the same signature, in a similar letter, followed a few days later by verses on the subject signed "Cathleen." Shields was furious, and Lincoln, to protect the women, gave himself out as the author. The consequence was a challenge.

Lincoln named the bottom land in Missouri, opposite Alton, as the scene, and set the following conditions:—

"First. Weapons: Cavalry broadswords of the largest size, precisely equal in all respects, and such as now used by the cavalry company at Jacksonville.

" Second. Position: A plank ten feet long, and from nine to twelve inches broad, to be firmly fixed on edge on the ground, as the line between us, which neither is to pass his foot over on forfeit of his life. Next, a line drawn on the ground on either side of said plank and parallel with it, each at the distance of the whole length of the sword and three feet additional from the plank; and the passing of his own such line by either party during the fight shall be deemed a surrender of the contest."

Lincoln and his second, E. H. Merryman, drove to Alton in a buggy, and the party, on a horse ferry, crossed the river to a sand-bar. When they reached the rendezvous they were joined by unexpected friends, who pacified them and led them home in quiet. On one of the very rare occasions when he was willing to mention this affair at all, Lincoln said to a friend, who asked why he chose broadswords: " To tell you the truth, Linder, I didn't want to kill Shields, and felt sure I could disarm him, having had about a month to learn the broadsword exercise; and, furthermore, I didn't want the damned fellow to kill me, which I rather think he would have done if we had selected pistols."

On the morning of November 4, 1842, Lincoln went to the room of James H. Matheney and asked him to be his best man at a marriage not yet announced, but to be celebrated that night. Miss Todd at the same time asked of a friend a similar favor. The license was obtained, a minister summoned, and in the presence of a few friends the deed was done. While the groom was dressing at Butler's house, according to Herndon, a small Butler boy asked him where he was going. "To hell, I suppose," was the reply. Another story goes that among the guests was Thomas C. Brown, one of the judges of the Supreme Court, a man who represented a somewhat earlier stage of Illinois civilization. When the groom, putting on the ring, repeated, "with this ring I thee endow with all my goods and chattels, lands and tenements," Judge Brown, standing close by the bridal couple, witnessing such a proceeding for the first time, exclaimed, "God Almighty, Lincoln, the statute fixes all that!" Thus, in a life containing more mystery than that of any equally celebrated modern, a mysterious wedding was accomplished.

CHAPTER V

A FEW years after her marriage Mrs. Lincoln
said to Ward H. Lamon, who had remarked
that her husband was a great favorite in the
eastern part of the state: " Yes, he is a great
favorite everywhere. He is to be President of
the United States some day. If I had not
thought so, I would never have married him,
for you can see he is not pretty. But look at
him. Doesn't he look as if he would make a
magnificent President? "

Lincoln was in politics almost constantly for
several years. The spring after his marriage,
March 1, 1843, however, he offered to a Whig
meeting at Springfield a series of resolutions of
which the following are especially significant;
in spite of the fact that his ideas on tariff and
finance were never very deeply pondered: —

" *Resolved*, That a tariff of duties on imported goods,
producing sufficient revenue for the payment of the
necessary expenditures of the National Government,
and so adjusted as to protect American industry, is
indispensably necessary to the prosperity of the American people.

"*Resolved*, That we are opposed to direct taxation for the support of the National Government.

"*Resolved*, That a national bank, properly restricted, is highly necessary and proper to the establishment and maintenance of a sound currency, and for the cheap and safe collection, keeping, and disbursing of public revenue."

At this time he was endeavoring to get to Congress. On the 24th of the same month he wrote to Speed: —

"DEAR SPEED: We had a meeting of the Whigs of the county here on last Monday to appoint delegates to a district convention; and Baker beat me, and got the delegation instructed to go for him. The meeting, in spite of my attempt to decline it, appointed me one of the delegates; so that in getting Baker the nomination I shall be fixed a good deal like a fellow who is made a groomsman to a man that has cut him out and is marrying his own dear "gal." About the prospects of your having a namesake at our town, can't say exactly yet.

"A. LINCOLN."

Logan also wanted to go to Congress that year, and political rivalry led to the severance of a partnership which had been a valuable training for the junior member. With W. H. Herndon was formed the firm of Lincoln and Herndon, which was dissolved only by the President's death.

Lincoln believed, as is shown by his correspondence, that his expected defeat by Edward H. Baker, who finally missed the prize that fell to Colonel J. J. Hardin, was due largely to his being suspected of deism. Some years earlier, full of Volney's " Ruins " and Paine's " Age of Reason," he had prepared an extended argument against the inspiration of the Bible, which one of his cautious friends deposited in the stove. What his belief was can never be indubitably known, partly because in varying moods it probably wavered, partly because prudence compelled him to make reasonable concessions to circumstance. He once asked Herndon to erase the word " God " from the draft of a speech, because it suggested the existence of a more personal power than Lincoln believed in. He did not believe in eternal punishment and never joined a church. During his presidency a convention of preachers asked him to recommend to Congress an amendment to the Constitution recognizing the existence of God, and the first draft of his message called attention to the subject, but he struck out the clause in correcting the proof. His creed, as far as it can be gathered, seems to have been very much like Hamlet's, and he was fond of quoting, " there's a divinity that shapes our ends, rough-hew them how we will." From the days when he imbibed a belief in luck and omens from his environment to the time when he took his son Robert to Terre Haute to be cured by a mad-stone of the bite of a dog, down to the war when he forbade a movement on Sunday because Bull Run had been fought on the Sabbath, he was still foreseeing good and evil fortune, private and public. Superstition, faith, and doubt were inextricably mixed up in him.

Infidelity was again urged the next time he was a candidate. In 1844 he refused to contest the nomination with Baker, but in 1846, by the convention which met on May 1, he was nominated. That an agreement had been made between Hardin, Baker, Lincoln, and Logan, that each should have a term in Congress, is almost proved by Lincoln's correspondence, and such was the outcome, Logan being nominated and defeated in 1838. After being a presidential elector for Clay and stumping the state in 1844, Lincoln received the nomination for Congress in 1846, and ran against a famous Methodist preacher named Peter Cartwright. Although the Democrats attacked the Whig candidate on religious grounds, Lincoln was elected, the only Whig in the Illinois delegation. The district gave him 1511 as against 914 for Clay in the preceding presidential campaign, and Sangamon County gave him the largest majority received by any candidate from 1836 to 1850

inclusive. His correspondence is sufficient evidence of the care and shrewdness with which he
worked to bring about this victory. One story
illustrates the faculty for which he was famous, of
foreseeing political results. During the campaign
a Democratic friend promised him his vote if it
seemed absolutely necessary. A short time before the election Lincoln answered, " I have got
the preacher and don't want your vote." To Speed,
soon after the victory, he wrote, " Being elected to
Congress, though I am very grateful to our friends
for having done it, has not pleased me as much as
I expected."

Before following Lincoln to Washington, where
he took his seat in December, 1847, we may pause
to notice his spiritual estate as exhibited by two
modest effusions of his muse. When he was
stumping for Clay he crossed into Indiana and re-
visited his old home. "That part of the country
is, within itself, as unpoetical as any spot on earth;"
he wrote, "but still, seeing it and its objects and
inhabitants aroused feelings in me which were certainly poetry; though whether my expression of
these feelings is poetry is quite another question."
Here is a sample : —

> " Near twenty years have passed away
>   Since here I bid farewell
> To woods and fields, and scenes of play,
>   And playmates loved so well.

" Where many were, but few remain
    Of old familiar things ;
  But seeing them, to mind again
    The lost and absent brings.

" The friends I left that parting day,
    How changed, as time has sped !
  Young childhood grown, strong manhood gray,
    And half of all are dead.

" I hear the loved survivors tell
    How naught from death could save,
  Till every sound appears a knell,
    And every spot a grave.

" I range the fields with pensive tread,
    And pace the hollow rooms,
  And feel (companion of the dead)
    I'm living in the tombs."

In Gentryville he found his old schoolfellow,
Matthew Gentry, in a state of hopeless insanity,
and was inspired to put his feelings into verse, of
which this a fragment: —

  " And when at length the drear and long
    Time soothed thy fiercer woes,
  How plaintively thy mournful song
    Upon the still night rose !

  " I've heard it oft as if I dreamed,
    Far distant, sweet and lone,
  The funeral dirge it ever seemed
    Of reason dead and gone.

> " Now fare thee well !   More thou the cause
>   Than subject now of woe.
>   All mental pangs by time's kind laws
>   Hast lost the power to know.
>
> " O death ! thou awe-inspiring prince
>   That keep'st the world in fear,
>   Why dost thou tear more blest ones hence,
>   And leave him lingering here ? "

In sending this to a friend, Lincoln lightens it a trifle with the remark, " If I should ever send another, the subject will be a ' Bear Hunt.' "

Mrs. Lincoln accompanied her husband to Washington, with their two children. A few days after the opening, Lincoln did the most conspicuous thing done by him during the session. President Polk, who had tricked the nation into the war with Mexico by various misrepresentations, had said in his message of May 11, 1846, that Mexico had invaded our territory and shed the blood of our citizens on our soil, and Lincoln, representing Whig hostility to the war, introduced resolutions calling upon the President to name the exact "spot" where these outrages occurred. Of course Polk paid no attention to the request, but the " spot resolutions," expressing a general disbelief in the President's honesty, attracted considerable attention.

About three weeks after the introduction of these resolutions, Lincoln wrote to Herndon, January 8,

1848: "As to speech-making, by way of getting the hang of the House, I made a little speech two or three days ago on a post-office question of no general interest. I find speaking here and elsewhere about the same thing. I was about as badly scared, and no worse, as I am when I speak in court. I expect to make one within a a week or two in which I hope to succeed well enough to wish you to see it." Four days later he called up his "spot resolutions," and made a long speech upon them. His attitude on the Mexican War for some time cost him much, but he never wavered. To Herndon, a very practical man, who remonstrated, he wrote, " Would you have voted what you felt and knew to be a lie? " He, like most of the Whigs, voted for the supplies, but honestly proclaimed his belief that the war itself was unjust. Shrewd and calculating as he was, he was a man of emotional, deep conviction. How he could feel is indicated in a brief note to his partner, written hastily on impulse, February 2, 1848, to mention a speech by Mr. Stephens of Georgia. " My old withered dry eyes are full of tears yet." He was in his fortieth year, but his sorrowful nature looked upon itself as already old. Soon after he wrote to Herndon: " I suppose I am now one of the old men; and I declare, on my veracity, which I think is good with you, that nothing could afford me more satisfaction than to learn that you and others of my young friends at home are doing battle in the contest, and endearing themselves to the people, and taking a stand far above any I have been able to take in their admiration."

In the spring he worked for General Taylor's nomination by the Whigs and later for his election, making in the House an oration which has become famous for its closing attack on the Democratic candidate, General Cass, a rough bit of sarcasm, full of stump vigor, but in no way distinguished. Here is one passage:—

"Mr. Polk himself was 'Young Hickory,' 'Little Hickory,' or something so; and even now your campaign paper here is proclaiming that Cass and Butler are of the 'Hickory stripe.' No, sir, you dare not give it up. Like a horde of hungry ticks, you have stuck to the tail of the Hermitage lion to the end of his life; and you are still sticking to it, and drawing a loathsome sustenance from it, after he is dead. A fellow once advertised that he had made a discovery by which he could make a new man out of an old one and have enough of the stuff left to make a little yellow dog. Just such a discovery has General Jackson's popularity been to you. You not only twice made Presidents of him out of it, but you have enough of the stuff left to make Presidents of several comparatively small men since; and it is your chief reliance now to make still another."

The most important question on which he put himself on record was slavery. The principle of the Wilmot Proviso — that slavery was to be prohibited in thereafter acquired territory — was then being fought over in various forms in Congress, and Lincoln has more than once said that he voted in favor of it "about forty-two times," although he took little part in the discussion. As Daniel Webster and the branch of the Whigs of which he was the head were going to pieces over this question, Lincoln's clearness is worthy of emphasis. On this fundamental issue his convictions seem to have been firm from the beginning. What he thought at once just and practicable under the actual conditions is shown by a bill which he himself introduced to prohibit the slave-trade in the District of Columbia. It forbade bringing slaves into the District, except as household servants by government officials who were citizens of slave states, or selling them to be taken out of the District. It provided for the gradual freeing of children thereafter born in slavery, and for compensation; it recognized the Fugitive Slave Law, and it was to be submitted to popular vote in the District. Altogether it was much like his attitude in 1862. In spite of its moderation it received some abolitionist support, but was soon pushed aside.

A number of small matters connected with the term in Washington are of decided interest. To the compiler of the " Dictionary of Congress,"

Lincoln gave the following notes, which show what he deemed the main points in his career up to this time: " Born February 12, 1809, in Hardin County, Kentucky, education defective, profession, a lawyer. Have been a captain of volunteers in the Black Hawk War. Postmaster at a very small office. Four times a member of the Illinois legislature, and was a member of the Lower House of Congress."

A fragment written by him in the summer of 1848 states what he thought ought to be said by General Taylor. It doubtless expresses partly policy and partly principle, but as it touches several of the most important questions of the day it is a valuable witness to the state of Lincoln's political beliefs : —

" The question of a national bank is at rest. Were I President, I should not urge its reagitation upon Congress; but should Congress see fit to pass an act to establish such an institution, I should not arrest it by the veto, unless I should consider it subject to some constitutional objection from which I believe the two former banks to have been free.

" It appears to me that the national debt created by the war renders a modification of the existing tariff indispensable; and when it shall be modified I should be pleased to see it adjusted with a due reference to the protection of our home industry. The particulars, it appears to me, must and should be left to the untrammelled discretion of Congress.

"As to the Mexican War, I still think the defensive line policy the best to terminate it. In a final treaty of peace, we shall probably be under a sort of necessity of taking some territory; but it is my desire that we shall not acquire any extending so far south as to enlarge and aggravate the distracting question of slavery. Should I come into the presidency before these questions shall be settled, I should act in relation to them in accordance with the views here expressed.

"Finally, were I President, I should desire the legislation of the country to rest with Congress, uninfluenced by the executive in its origin or progress, and undisturbed by the veto unless in very special and clear cases."

During his term in Congress he was not only sending part of his salary to Herndon to pay the old debts of Lincoln and Berry, but he had occasional other calls for money. December 12, 1848, he wrote to his father a letter which, though kind, indicates what the son thought of his parent's business ability

"WASHINGTON, Dec. 24, 1848.

"MY DEAR FATHER: Your letter of the 7th was received night before last. I very cheerfully send you the twenty dollars, which sum you say is necessary to save your land from sale. It is singular that you should have forgotten a judgment against you; and it is more singular that the plaintiff should have let you forget it so long; particularly as I suppose you always had property enough to satisfy a judgment of that amount. Be-

H

fore you pay it, it would be well to be sure you have not paid, or at least, that you cannot prove you have paid it.

"Give my love to mother and all the connections.

"Affectionately your son,

"A. LINCOLN."

.On his way to Springfield from Washington, Lincoln, stopping at Niagara, was so much impressed that he has left some notes for a lecture, which illustrate the truth that flights into the poetic aspects of science and nature were not his strongest gifts. The vessel on which his journey home was continued got stranded on a sand-bar, and the captain floated it by forcing loose planks, empty barrels, and boxes under the sides of the boat. Inspired by this principle Lincoln borrowed tools from a mechanic in Springfield, made a model, and secured a patent which was never used. His application read: —

"What I claim as my invention, and desire to secure by letters patent, is the combination of expansible buoyant chambers placed at the sides of a vessel with the main shaft or shafts by means of the sliding spars, which pass down through the buoyant chambers and are made fast to their bottoms and the series of ropes and pulleys or their equivalents in such a manner that by turning the main shaft or shafts in one direction the buoyant chambers will be forced downward into the water, and at the same time expanded and filled with air for buoying up the vessel by the displacement of water, and by turning the shafts in an opposite direction the buoyant chambers will be contracted into a small space and secured against injury.

" A. LINCOLN."

Far more significant, however, than anything else connected with his experience in Washington except slavery, is his attitude toward public office. Although the facts on this subject will not please purists, they play so large a part in any sincere estimate of Lincoln, — and, to a sound mind, so honorable a part, — that the main points, as unmistakably set forth in that mine of information, his correspondence, should be seriously dwelt upon. Larger and harder problems about the proper relation of practical and immediate to ideal and distant considerations arose in the war, but the point of view which always governed him was as settled twenty years earlier. He writes to the Secretary of the Treasury that as the Whigs of Illinois hold him and Colonel Baker, their only members of Congress, responsible to some extent for appointments of Illinois citizens, they ask to be heard whenever such an appointment is contemplated. To the Secretary of State he sends the papers of one applicant. " Mr. Bond I know to be personally every way worthy of the office . . . and I solicit for his claims a full and fair consideration." He then adds that in his individual judgment the appointment of another man would be much better. There are a number of letters, almost exactly the same in language, stating that certain incumbents, who have filled their offices excellently, are decided partisans. In most cases he carefully states that he will express no opinion on the validity of partisanship as a ground of removal, but that if it is accepted as such the rule should be general, and the particular individual designated no exception. One of these notes has the personal interest of relating to the friend from whom Lincoln had so long received free board. " I recommend that William Butler be appointed pension agent when the place shall be vacant. Mr. Hurst, the present incumbent, I believe has performed the duties very well. He is a decided partisan, and, I believe, expects to be removed. Whether he shall, I submit to the department." Of another he says: " I have already said he has done the duties of the office well, and I now add he is a gentleman in the true sense. Still, he submits to be the instrument of his party to injure us. His high character enables him to do it more effectually." The two following letters speak for themselves : —

"CONFIDENTIAL.

"SPRINGFIELD, ILLINOIS, May 25, 1849.

"HON. E. EMBREE,

"*Dear Sir:* I am about to ask a favor of you, — one which I hope will not cost you much. I understand the General Land Office is about to be given to Illinois, and that Mr. Ewing desires Justin Butterfield, of Chicago, to be the man. I give you my word, the appointment of Mr. Butterfield will be an egregious political blunder. It will give offence to the whole Whig party here, and be worse than a dead loss to the administration of so much of its patronage. Now, if you can conscientiously do so, I wish you to write General Taylor at once, saying that either I, or the man I recommend, should in your opinion be appointed to that office, if any one from Illinois shall be. I restrict my request to Illinois because you may have a man from your own state, and I do not ask to interfere with that.

"Your friend as ever,

"A. LINCOLN."

"SPRINGFIELD, June 5, 1849.

"*Dear William:* Your two letters were received last night. I have a great many letters to write, and so cannot write very long ones. There must be some mistake about Walter Davis saying I promised him the post-office. I did not so promise him. I did tell him that if the distribution of the offices should fall into my hands, he should have something; and if I shall be convinced he has said any more than this, I shall be disappointed. I said this much to him because, as I

understand, he is of good character, is one of the young
men, is of the mechanics, and always faithful and never
troublesome; a Whig, and is poor, with the support of
a widow mother thrown almost exclusively on him by
the death of his brother. If these are wrong reasons,
then I have been wrong; but I have certainly not been
selfish in it, because in my greatest need of friends he
was against me, and for Baker.

" Yours as ever,
" A. LINCOLN.

" P.S. — Let the above be confidential."

Lincoln went into the fight for the General
Land Office actively, received support in many
directions, but failed. The administration offered to make him either governor or secretary
of Oregon, and he made a special trip to Washington, just after the expiration of his term, to
discuss the subject. He was rather inclined to
accept, feeling that his attitude toward the Mexican War had probably ruined him politically, but
the opposition of Mrs. Lincoln led him to decline
and settle down to active practice in the law.

CHAPTER VI

LINCOLN AS A LAWYER

WITH little hope of a political future, gloom at home, and a constant, grim determination to make the best of what fate allowed him, Lincoln settled quietly into the routine of Springfield and circuit practice. A Chicago lawyer, named Grant Goodrich, with a good business, offered him a partnership, which he declined on the ground that, as he already tended toward consumption, hard study and confinement would kill him. He therefore undertook his part of the work of Lincoln and Herndon, spending half of the year at home, and half around the state, following Judge Davis, and there is every reason to believe that the travelling life was more agreeable. On Saturday nights it was customary for the judges and lawyers who lived within reach to go home, but of this opportunity Lincoln seldom or never availed himself, preferring to spend his Sundays chatting at the tavern.

In the Springfield office he spent a good deal of his time on Euclid, poetry, and history, and more on the newspapers, conversation, and stories, somewhat to the annoyance of his more methodical partner, who failed to enjoy Lincoln's habit of reading the papers aloud when they two were alone. Law was not neglected by him, however, especially when a case was at hand, and he often studied late into the night, making such progress, through his fundamental clearness of understanding, that his reputation increased very rapidly, even for legal arguments to the court, but particularly for jury trials, where his colloquial, honest, and racy manner had its full opportunity. His speech was never technical or pompous, but always familiar. He "reckoned it would be fair to let in that," and if the court overruled him he said, " Well, I reckon I must be wrong." He was leisurely, and when Herndon suggested that he was too slow in speech and manner he turned his long jackknife in a circle, and then a small penknife with the same speed at the circumference, to show that the one which took longest in completing the circle had travelled farthest, and he in turn advised the younger partner never to aim over the heads of the people he was talking to. It is significant that during his presidency he told Mr. Colfax that in all his time at the bar he never found an opponent's case stronger than he expected, and usually found it weaker.

With an earnest, honest, and simple mind, and little aptitude for technicalities, his strength naturally lay in cases where the fundamental right

was clear. He frequently advised the dropping
of cases which could only be won by technical
adroitness. Once when Herndon, who reveals
his own elastic standards with unhesitating frankness, had drawn a fictitious plea, and explained
to his partner that, although it was not sound, he
had overheard remarks of the opposing counsel
which showed that they would not be able to dis-
prove it, Lincoln advised its withdrawal. After
he had won in the prosecution of a murder trial,
he was for a long time haunted by a bare doubt
of the prisoner's sanity. He induced his young
friend Lamon, when they had been retained on
the same case, to return part of a joint fee agreed
upon in advance, because he thought afterward
that it was excessive. In a suit against a railroad
company, before judgment was pronounced, he
arose to point out that his opponents had failed
to prove all that was justly due them in offset, and
the amount which he explained might have been
found was allowed in the judgment. However,
he was not beyond provocation. When the Illinois Central contested a bill of $2000, Lincoln
sued for $5000 and won.

These characteristics became widely known.
As he for years went over the whole circuit, he
was always among friends, never facing a jury
without seeing familiar countenances before him.
To the popularity brought him by his honesty

and simplicity, his breezy spirits added much.
He would enter the court-room with some such
exclamation as, " Well, here I am, ain't you glad
to see me ? " The well-known smallness of his fees,
which kept him always poor, his constant habit
of never suing, and his willingness to give help
in any just cause, also helped him win the general
heart. He was invariably kind to young lawyers,
and he never objected to any reasonable request
by opposing counsel. The easy, untechnical
character of the law in Illinois in those days was
just what his character needed. When he read,
he took no notes, because he understood the principles, and they were all he cared to remember.
So in court he easily remembered the testimony
as far as it bore on the real issue, for his attention
never strayed from that. He did not know a
great number of precedents, but he could reason
logically and persuasively from sound general
principles. His standing on technical details is
probably correctly indicated by a story told by a
lawyer who asked him, in 1855, if they could in-
terpose the same defence to an action upon the
judgment of another state that they could to the
original claim. Lincoln's answer was " Yes."
At another time the same man asked him if, in an
attachment suit, a service of the attachment writ
on the defendant had the force of a summons.
" Damfino," said Lincoln.

Nevertheless, "any one," as Leonard Swett says, "who took Lincoln for a simple-minded man would very soon wake up on his back, in a ditch." He nearly always stuck to simple, central truths, but he could, when necessary, use a kind of adroitness of his own, although it was not very technical. One of his companions tells this story:—

"During my first attendance at court in Menard County, some thirty young men had been indicted for playing cards, and Lincoln and I were employed in their defence. The prosecuting attorney, in framing the indictments, alternately charged the defendants with playing a certain game of cards called 'seven-up,' and in the next bill charged them with playing cards at a certain game called 'old sledge.' Four defendants were indicted in each bill. The prosecutor, being entirely unacquainted with games at cards, did not know the fact that both 'seven-up' and 'old sledge' were one and the same. Upon the trial on the bills describing the game as 'seven-up' our witnesses would swear that the game played was 'old sledge,' and vice versa on the bills alleging the latter. The result was an acquittal in every case under the instructions of the court. The prosecutor never found out the dodge until the trials were over, and immense fun and rejoicing were indulged in at the result."

Judge Davis, an unusually good witness, on account of his ability and his intimacy with Lincoln, says that he was "hurtful in denunciation and merciless in castigation." One of his most eloquent onslaughts was in the Wright case, where he attacked a pension agent for cheating a poor widow. Lincoln, who was himself surety for her costs, gave such a picture of her husband's hardships, the sufferings of the soldiers at Valley Forge, and the heartless extortion of the agent, that the jury was in tears, and the verdict was entirely in favor of the widow. Lincoln's notes for this argument could hardly be surpassed for individuality. They were: "No contract. — Not professional services. — Unreasonable charge. — Money retained by Def't not given by Pl'ff. — Revolutionary War. — Describe Valley Forge privations. — Ice. — Soldier's bleeding feet. — Pl'ff's husband. — Soldier leaving home for army. — Skin Def't. — Close." That he did skin the defendant there is no doubt.

Besides this ability in castigation Judge Davis also credits him with a large power in comparison, which he seldom failed to use in legal arguments, and this power was often brought out in his favorite narrative form. " The ability,"

Judge Davis says, "however, which some eminent lawyers possess, of explaining away the bad points of a cause by ingenious sophistry, was denied him." Among the number of stories which illustrate this characteristic honesty, one of the most definite tells of the trial of a man for homicide committed at Sandorus, Illinois. When the facts were brought before the petit jury it was clearly developed that the indictment ought to have been for murder instead of for manslaughter. The two lawyers associated with Lincoln in the defence wished to try for an acquittal. Leonard Swett made an effective speech one evening, in which he brought much pathos out of several small children and the wife about to be confined. Lincoln, following on the same side the next day, damaged by the honesty of his mental processes the effect made by Swett. He disagreed with the pathos argument and said that was not to be weighed by the jury. His client, found guilty, was sent to the penitentiary for three years, and Lincoln, who believed that he had committed murder, induced the Government to pardon him a short time after.

Judge Davis frequently had Lincoln hold court for him, sometimes for an hour or two, sometimes a day or more, occasionally even for a long time, and it is said that two cases were afterward reversed for this reason. Stories with more point than probability relate that the temporary judge used to leave the bench to entertain the crowd with stories, and that he once granted a new trial on the ground of the incompetency of the court. Another tale, probably true, is thus told by one of his colleagues:

"Several of us lawyers in the eastern end of the circuit annoyed Lincoln once while he was holding court for Davis by attempting to defend against a note to which there were many makers. We had no legal, but a good moral defence, but what we wanted most of all was to stave it off till the next term of court, by one expedient or another. We bothered 'the court' about it till late on Saturday, the day of adjournment. He adjourned for supper with nothing left but this case to dispose of. After supper he heard our twaddle for nearly an hour, and then made this odd entry: 'L. D. Chaddon *vs.* J. D. Beasley *et al* April Term, 1856. Champaign County Court. Plea in abatement by B. Z. Green, a defendant not served, filed Saturday at eleven o'clock A.M., April 24, 1856, stricken from the files by order of court. Demurrer to declaration, if there ever was one, overruled. Defendants who are served now, at eight o'clock, P.M. of the last day of the term, ask to plead to the merits, which is denied by the court on the ground that the offer comes too late, and

therefore, as by *nil dicet*, judgment is rendered
for Pl'ff. Clerk assess damages. A. Lincoln,
Judge *pro tem.*'"

One of the lawyers, on recovering from his
astonishment, inquired, "Well, Lincoln, how can
we get this case up again?" Lincoln eyed him
a moment, and then answered, "You have all
been so 'mighty smart about this case, you can
find out how to take it up again yourselves."

Another direction in which Lincoln managed
to extract amusement from life, in spite of the
fact that he was unable to proceed in his chosen
direction, is indicated by Lamon's story of a time
when he also was practising in Illinois. Called
suddenly into court from an improvised wrestling
match outside, Lamon arose to address the judge,
unconscious of a large rent in his trousers. The
fun-loving country attorneys quickly circulated a
paper begging subscriptions to correct the worthy
youth's apparel. Each member to whom the
paper came added some absurd contribution, but
when it reached Lincoln, he wrote on it, "I can
contribute nothing to the *end in view.*"

In Springfield, however, the natural social
gayety of his existence, which under any circumstances had a background of melancholy, was
lessened by unhappy home surroundings. Lincoln's usual hour for reaching the office was nine,
but sometimes Herndon, who arrived earlier,

found his partner already there, which meant something unpleasant in the family, and the only morning salutation then vouchsafed by the senior was a grunt. Herndon also declares that Lincoln feed a maid to endure the peculiarities of his wife, and that, although his home was but a few squares away, he lunched at the office on crackers and cheese and frequently remained long after dark.

An easy carelessness reigned in the office. On one large envelope Lincoln had written, "When you can't find *it* anywhere else look into this." Another receptacle was still more devoted to general utility, his big silk plug hat, which he used now for law as he had formerly for mail. He once apologized to a lawyer for not having answered a letter, on the ground that he put it in his old hat and bought a new one. The papers and other material in the office were strewn anywhere, and a law student who endeavored to clean up the place found that some seeds brought back by Lincoln from Washington had sprouted in the accumulated dirt. In this easy atmosphere the head of the firm divided his time between discussing, telling stories, often repeating a new one several times to newcomers in as many hours with the same zest, and spells of hard work. One observer says, " As for Lincoln, he had three different moods, if I may so express myself; first, a *business* mood, when he gave strict and close attention to business, and banished all idea of hilarity; *i.e.* in counselling or in trying cases, there was no trace of the joker; second, his *melancholy* moods, when his whole nature was immersed in *Cimmerian* darkness; third, his *don't-care-whether-school-keeps-or-not* mood; when no irresponsible 'small boy' could be so apparently careless, or reckless of consequences."

At home he was an indulgent parent, seemingly unwilling to cross his children in anything. He is described as fond of playing with kittens, taking walks with the children, working about the house, or lying on the floor reading, but caring nothing for food or drink, or for some aspects of natural beauty, such as flowers and trees. He would often slip away by himself to a theatre or concert, especially if the entertainment was light, and he enjoyed particularly minstrels and a little magic-lantern show intended for children. He would stop in the street to analyze any machine he saw, from an omnibus to a clock, turning onto mechanical and intellectual problems the same spirit of analytic interest. "While we were travelling in ante-railway days," says Henry C. Whitney, "on the circuit, and would stop at a farmhouse for dinner, Lincoln would improve the leisure in hunting up some farming implement, machine, or tool, and he would carefully examine it all over, first generally and then critically; he would 'sight' it to determine if it was straight or warped; if he could make a practical test of it, he would do that; he would turn it over or around and stoop down, or lie down, if necessary, to look under it; he would examine it closely, then stand off and examine it at a little distance; he would shake it, lift it, roll it about, up-end it, overset it, and thus ascertain every quality and utility which inhered in it, so far as acute and patient investigation could do it. He was equally inquisitive in regard to matters which obtruded on his attention in the moral world; he would bore to the centre of any moral proposition, and carefully analyze and dissect every layer and every atom of which it was composed, nor would he give over the search till completely satisfied that there was nothing more to know, or be learned about it."

"His home," says Whitney, "was very ordinary and isolated; there was little external indication of life or movement there: Lincoln was occasionally seen to be walking to and fro, on the sidewalk, with a child in his arms, or hauling one in a little child's go-cart; or, in the morning, at irregular hours, might be seen to come furtively out of the house, or from his little barn, and walk in solitary mood up-town, where he would drop into the circuit clerk's office — or at a store where citizens congregated — or anywhere that he could find somebody to listen to his stories; he would sometimes turn up at his own office, and, not infrequently, at the law library of the State House; in the latter part of the day, he would go home and drive up and milk his cow, feed his horse, clean out his very humble stable, chop some wood; and his day's work was done, unless, as was quite common, he again went up-town, to pass the evening in some grocery store, or other citizens' *rendezvous*, engaged in his usual avocation of telling stories; or, perhaps, wandering alone, aimlessly, in the unfrequented streets, clothed in melancholy, and his mind turned completely within itself, in deep reflection.

" His stable stands yet, or did recently, just as he left it thirty years ago, barring the ravages of time; it is primitive and uninteresting, save by its reminiscences; it is of boards nailed up endwise — no battens — only about six and one-half feet to the eaves — the roof with the least pitch possible to carry off the water at all; only one apartment, where his horse — old Tom — his cow — his old open buggy — his hay and feed were all together. He was his own wood-chopper, hostler, stable-boy and cow-boy, clear down to, and even beyond, the time that he was President-elect of the United States.

" Of course I do not mean that he did no business in his profession at Springfield; but in Lincoln's day there, courts did not sit often, and preparation for trials was not very elaborate; he had much leisure, and that was passed much as I have defined. The tendencies of his mind alternated between deep, earnest, solitary reflection, at which times he wanted no contact or communication with others, and light, frivolous, frolicsome moods, when he wanted an audience, but was utterly regardless of its size, quality, or character."

In winter an old gray shawl was wrapped about his neck. His hat had no nap, his boots were unblacked, his clothes unbrushed, he carried a dilapidated carpet-bag for legal papers, a faded green umbrella with the knob gone, a string tied about the middle, and the name "A. Lincoln" cut out of white muslin in large letters and sewed in the inside. He always wore short trousers and usually a short circular blue cloak, which he got in Washington in 1849, and kept for ten years, which, like his vest, hung very loosely on his frame. He slept in a warm yellow flannel shirt, which came half-way between his knees and his ankles. The changes which gradually took place in his dress, which reached its greatest elegance in his presidency, were slight and marked no decrease in his own innocence about appearances, the improvements being usually suggested to him by his wife and friends.

Lying on the floor in his shirt-sleeves was a favorite attitude for reading. As he had no library, and the parlor, with its sofa, six haircloth chairs, and marble table, strewn with gift books in blue and gilt, expressed not his spirit but his wife's, he often chose the hall for his recumbent study; and if women happened to call Lincoln would go to the door attired as he was and promise that he "would trot the women folks out." It is alleged that for such practices, and possibly also for obtaining butter at the table with his own knife, Mrs. Lincoln found opportunities to punish him.

Of his attitude toward hardship Leonard Swett says: "I rode the Eighth Judicial Circuit with him for eleven years, and in the allotment between him and the large Judge Davis, in the scanty provision of those times, as a rule I slept with him. Beds were always too short, coffee in the morning burned or otherwise bad, food often indifferent, roads simply trails, streams without bridges and often swollen, and had to be swam, sloughs often muddy and almost impassable, and we had to help the horses, when the wagon mired down, with fence-rails for pries, and yet I never heard Lincoln complain of anything."

Mr. Whitney says: "At Danville, the county seat of Vermilion County, the judge and Lincoln and I used to occupy the ladies' parlor of the old McCormick House, changed to a bed-room during court, the former occupying a three-quarter bed, and Lincoln and I occupying the other one, jointly. This parlor was an 'annex' to the main building, and one door opened out directly on the sidewalk, and as the Fall term was held in cold weather, we had a hearth wood fire to heat our room. One morning, I was awakened early — before daylight — by my companion sitting up in bed, his figure dimly visible by the ghostly firelight, and talking the wildest and most incoherent nonsense all to himself. A stranger to Lincoln would have supposed he had suddenly gone insane. Of course I knew Lincoln and his idiosyncrasies, and felt no alarm, so I listened and laughed. After he had gone on in this way for, say, five minutes, while I was awake, and I know not how long *before* I was awake, he sprang out of bed, hurriedly washed, and jumped into his clothes, put some wood on the fire, and then sat in front of it, moodily, dejectedly, in a most sombre and gloomy spell, till the breakfast bell rang, when he started, as if from sleep, and went with us to breakfast."

Of the influence of this circuit life on Lincoln's natural bent toward story-telling he himself said to Chauncey M. Depew that, " Riding the circuit for many years and stopping at country taverns where were gathered the lawyers, jurymen, wit-

nesses, and clients, they would sit up all night nar-
rating to each other their life adventures; and
that the things which happened to an original
people, in a new country, surrounded by novel
conditions, and told with the descriptive power
and exaggeration which characterized such men,
supplied him with an exhaustless fund of anecdote
which could be made applicable for enforcing or
refuting an argument better than all the invented
stories of the world." To the same Mr. Depew,
himself so well known as a story-teller, Lincoln
said : —

" They say I tell a great many stories; I reckon
I do, but I have found in the course of a long experience that common people "—and repeating it
— " common people, take them as they run, are
more easily influenced and informed through the
medium of a broad illustration than in any other
way, and as to what the hypercritical few may
think, I don't care. . . . I have originated but two
stories in my life, but I tell tolerably well other
people's stories." In Mr. Depew's opinion Lincoln's appreciation of humor was wonderful, but
his estimate of it was not very critical. Certainly
it was not captious. Fineness and coarseness, col-
loquialism and sublimity, were mixed in him in a
fashion seldom rivalled. Intelligent observers
have compared him to Socrates, but Leonard
Swett gives a more vivid impression when he

says, " No one who knew him ever knew another man like him."

To this period, stretching from his term in Washington to the return of political activity after the repeal of the Missouri Compromise, belongs one short letter to his brother which shows what feeling was left in him for his father, and also gives one side of the case in the discussion, never to be settled, about his religion. Toward his father, of whom he said to Swett that his father wished him to have a good education, but that his idea of a good education was that he should cipher clear through the old arithmetic in the house, — toward this enlightened parent Lincoln's attitude remained just and cold.   Certainly the religion which he deals out to him will not have the sound of intimate reality to every reader.   The letter, which is dated January 12, 1851, reads : —

" You already know I desire that neither Father or Mother shall be in want of any comfort either in health or sickness while they live; and I feel sure you have not failed to use my name, if necessary, to procure a doctor, or anything else for Father in his present sickness.   My business is such that I could hardly leave home now, if it were not, as it is, that my own wife is sick abed (it is a case of baby-sickness, and I suppose is not dangerous).   I sincerely hope Father may yet recover his health; but at all events tell him to remember to call upon and confide in our great, and good, and merciful Maker, who will not turn away from him in any extremity. He notes the fall of a sparrow, and numbers the hairs of our heads; and He will not forget the dying man who puts his trust in Him. Say to him that if we could meet now, it is doubtful whether it would not be more painful than pleasant; but that if it be his lot to go now he will soon have a joyous meeting with many loved ones gone before, and where the rest of us, through the help of God, hope ere long to join them."

Of all the details of this period of legal practice, however, the most dramatic incident is one of the last, belonging to the summer of 1857 after his new political activity was well under way, and connected with a visit to Cincinnati on the case of McCormick *vs.* Manny. There he was not only treated with rude contempt by a more prominent lawyer, who looked upon him as a backwoodsman, but the somewhat imaginative account adds that this lawyer even spoke scornfully, within his hearing, of the ridiculous appearance of the apparition from Illinois. At any rate, there seems to be little doubt that Lincoln was wounded. Five years later he made his insulter Secretary of War, and thereby was able to add to this first experience numberless other proofs of magnanimous patience in enduring the brutal absence of decent personal feeling in Edwin M. Stanton. He could say of a certain singer in a light-hearted way, "She is the only woman that ever appreciated me enough to pay me a compliment," and make other similar jests at his own grotesqueness, but enough is known of his real sensitiveness to suggest what deep strength was required to take all the rough treatment he received from Stanton and so many others with that distant, kind, patient reasonableness that seems more wonderful the more it is thought of. His was the highest dignity. He was unhappy, kind, and alone. Most of his friends speak as if they did not feel they really knew him, and Swett once said, "You cannot tell what Lincoln is going to do, until he does it."

CHAPTER VII

LINCOLN's return to political activity was caused by the same changes that created the Republican party and the Civil War. During his comparative quiescence he had not lost the leadership of the Illinois Whigs, and he took what steps the political situation demanded. In the campaign of 1852 he made a few speeches in favor of Scott, but at that time both parties avoided the real issue, pretending to think the "compromise" of 1850 final — that compromise which gave the South everything, provided for a stricter fugitive slave law, removed the barriers to slavery, repealed the Missouri Compromise by taking the whole subject out of the control of Congress, and yet received the support of Daniel Webster, marked by his great and notorious speech of the 7th of March. Lincoln was interested, especially after the Missouri Compromise was in 1854 openly declared repealed, and even when he was not actively speaking he was thinking. He read all the best speeches of Giddings, Phillips, Sumner, Seward, and Parker, as well as controversial and historical books upon the subject, and he contributed editorial writings

to the *Springfield Journal* at intervals until 1860.
That he was also alive to the game of politics is
indicated by Herndon's story of his trick, endorsed by Lincoln, by which a pro-slavery paper
was induced to publish an article so extreme as
to be damaging to its own cause, after which
the anti-slavery people who had got it printed
turned in and denounced it. To find his genuine feelings on slavery wholly disconnected from
any political considerations it is safest to turn to
a letter to his only intimate friend, Speed, August
25, 1855. Speed had written to Lincoln protest-
ing against his opinions, and Lincoln explains at
length that, while he would not interfere, against
the law, with the property of Speed or any other
slaveholder, he thinks the vital difference between them is that his friend looks upon this
property as on any other, while he himself sees
it as a deep wrong that must be endured but not
allowed to spread. "In 1841 you and I had
together a tedious low-water trip on a steamboat
from Louisville to St. Louis. You may remember as well as I do that from Louisville to the
mouth of the Ohio there were on board ten or a
dozen slaves shackled together with irons. That
sight was a constant torture to me." On the
great issue of the day he remarks, "You say
that if Kansas fairly votes herself a free state,
as a Christian you will rejoice at it. All decent

slaveholders talk that way, and I don't doubt their candor, but they never vote that way." He indignantly denies any sympathy with the Know-Nothing or American party, which consisted of crusaders against Catholics and foreigners, and exclaims that if such ideas should ever get control he would rather emigrate to some country, like Russia, where despotism could be taken pure, with no hypocritical talk about freedom and equality. As late as the Douglas campaign, May 15, 1858, he wrote to E. B. Washburne that the principal danger of defeat came from the American party.

It was fortunate for Lincoln that one of the sharpest blows to the excesses of the slavery party was given by the Democratic leader from his own state. Senator Douglas in 1854 took part in the conflict on the status of slavery in the region which is now Kansas and Nebraska, then seeking admission as territories. He introduced his " Kansas-Nebraska Bill," which, establishing those territories, expressly declared the Missouri Compromise inoperative in them, and an amendment soon declared that compromise inconsistent with the legislation of 1850, which denied any right of intervention by Congress with slavery in territories. This amendment now added the word *states* to territories in restricting the powers of Congress to interfere. A clause intended to

soften this blow at the North stated that the intention was to leave the people of any territory
or state free to regulate slavery in its own way,
and this was the doctrine of "popular sovereignty,"
so soon to be fought out between Douglas and
Lincoln.

When Douglas began to defend himself in Illinois, where his concessions to the South had aroused
much Democratic hostility, Lincoln was at once
chosen by the opponents of slavery as the proper
champion to meet the Little Giant.　He made
such an effective answer to Douglas at the great
state fair in October that the abolitionists, under
the lead of Owen Lovejoy, announced a meeting
for that evening with the purpose of getting Lincoln to speak and commit himself to extreme
views.　On the advice of his partner, however,
who was as cautious as he was abolitionist, Lincoln found he had business which compelled him
to drive hastily out of town that afternoon.　Two
principles evidently contended within him from
this time forward.　He was always a conservative
and practical politician, but he was always a man
of conviction and courage, and he was now keenly
wrought up over slavery.　In his days in Congress
he had sometimes been invited to the Saturday
breakfasts of the great Daniel Webster, to meet
the "solid men of Boston," but none of the spirit
of concession to property interests that ruined

Webster had ever poisoned Lincoln. The moral reality of the problem was always alive and burning in him, and when he refused to go faster than a certain pace it was with a view to final victory and not to surrender. He knew that if no mistakes were made the natural course of events would stamp out the evil through the increasing power of the North. To the efforts of the South to offset this inevitable outcome by forcing slavery into those states and territories in which the majority wished to exclude it, he was deeply opposed, and that was to be the vital issue of the immediate future. "He grew because we watered him," said Wendell Phillips, the famous abolitionist orator, speaking one of the numberless calumnies of his sect against Lincoln. From the outbreak of the controversy to its end he was for final extinction of the evil, and he waited only for means. He knew what could be done in a land governed by popular opinion and what could not, and Phillips and his friends watered him only indirectly as they prepared the public.

In the winter of 1854–55 he was elected against his will to the Illinois legislature, but resigned, that there might be no doubt about his eligibility for the United States Senate. A little wave of reaction elected a Democrat in his place. When the legislature came to vote for Senator in February, Lincoln had 45 on the first ballot, Shields

41, Trumbull 5, with a few scattering. A few ballots showed that Lincoln could not be elected, he being supposed to be too much tainted with abolitionism, and then he induced his followers, against their will, to elect Trumbull, a Democrat, but known to be opposed to the Kansas-Nebraska policy of Senator Douglas.

In the convention held in 1856 by the newly born Republican party, which came into being in 1854 to concentrate the anti-slavery elements of the other organizations, John C. Fremont was nominated for President and William L. Dayton for Vice-President, Dayton receiving on the first ballot 259 votes to Lincoln's 110, a result which speaks much for the Illinois leader's general reputation before the Douglas debates attracted national attention. At the head of the electoral ticket in the state he made some imperfectly reported but sufficiently pronounced speeches. An earlier one at Bloomingdale May 29, at a state convention of the "opponents of anti-Nebraska legislation" is well known through its effect on the hearers, and a rather good report of this "Lincoln's lost speech" has recently been made public. It was fervid and fearless. The contrast between his feelings and the Springfield atmosphere is shown by the fact that when Herndon and Lincoln tried to get up a mass-meeting to endorse the action of this convention, only one

other man attended. During the following cam·
paign at Galena, in August, Lincoln said, "We
do not want to dissolve the Union; you shall not."
December 10, after the election, he said: "Our
government rests in public opinion. Whoever
can change public opinion can change the government practically just so much. Public opinion,
on any subject, always has a 'central idea' from
which all its minor thoughts radiate. That 'central idea' in our political public opinion at the
beginning was, and until recently has continued
to be, 'the equality of men.' The late presidential election was a struggle by one party to discard that central idea and to substitute for it the
opposite idea that slavery is right in the abstract.
. . . To us it is left to know that the majority of
the people have not yet declared for it, and to
hope they never will. All of us who did not vote
for Mr. Buchanan, taken together, are a majority
of 400,000. But in the late contest we were divided between Fremont and Fillmore. Can we
not come together for the future?"

Buchanan's election was immediately followed
by a judicial decision which helped solidify the
friends of freedom. This was the famous Dred
Scott case, in which the Supreme Court of the
United States decided that the state court of
Missouri could determine for itself whether a
slave from that state, who had lived in freedom

K

elsewhere, could afterward be held in slavery by his master in Missouri, and that temporary residence in a free state did not give him freedom. In thus refusing to interfere, the federal court practically decided what Lincoln summed up fairly when he said that it was "singular that the courts would hold that a man never lost his right to his property that had been stolen from him, but that he instantly lost the right to himself if he was stolen." This case was argued for the slave at the first hearing by Montgomery Blair, afterward a member of Lincoln's cabinet, and at the second hearing by Blair and George Ticknor Curtis. So intense was the feeling about the whole subject at issue that the judges instead of ordinary opinions wrote elaborate essays on all branches of the slavery topic, which did much to fan the already raging flames. Chief Justice Taney's majority opinion, going to the extreme of the pro-slavery position, soon after furnished Lincoln with many of his points of attack, including the principle, not before the court, that slavery could be excluded from a territory neither by Congress nor by a territorial legislature.

This obiter theory was accepted and defended by Douglas, whose most difficult task was to make it fit into his own doctrine of popular sovereignty. In a speech at Springfield, June

12, 1857, he covered the opinions of Taney and the other concurring judges with florid eulogy. He accepted the positions that a negro descended from slave parents could not be a citizen of the United States, and that the Missouri Compromise, being unconstitutional and void even before it was repealed by the Nebraska act, did not extinguish a master's right to his slave in the territory covered by it. He then proceeded: "While the right continues in full force under the guarantees of the Constitution, and cannot be divested or alienated by an act of Congress, it necessarily remains a barren and a worthless right, unless sustained, protected, and enforced by appropriate police regulations and local legislation, prescribing adequate remedies for its violation." As this legislation would depend on the will of the voters in the territory, Douglas pretended that he had saved the principle of popular sovereignty.

Lincoln answered this speech at Springfield, June 27, covering points which were fully fought out in the later debates, and saying in answer to Douglas's appeal to the strong race prejudice in Illinois, these well-known sentences: "I protest against the counterfeit logic which concludes that because I do not want a black woman for a slave I must necessarily want her

for a wife. I need not have her for either. I
can just leave her alone. In some respects she
certainly is not my equal; but in her natural
right to eat the bread she earns with her own
hands, without asking leave of any one else,
she is my equal and the equal of all others."
This last sentence was praised by a friend, and
Lincoln said, " Then I will get it off again,"
which he did. When he made a good point he
habitually stuck to it.

The slavery issue had led at its height in
Kansas to civil war, just as in Congress it led
to a barbarous assault on Charles Sumner
as he sat quietly in his chair. Although this
physical warfare ceased in the fall of 1856, the
situation then was still watched with the utmost
anxiety from all over the country; Kansas was
still the centre of the slavery conflict, and
the two factions, Northern and Southern emi-
grants, stood ready for more trouble at any
moment. By the use of United States troops,
in October, 1857, Governor Walker secured
a fair election, and the Republicans' delegate
was elected to Congress by more than two
to one. Nevertheless a fraudulently conducted
convention at Lecompton drew up a constitution practically committing the state to slavery,
but this, after a fraudulent election, was rejected, overwhelmingly, at a second and honest

vote. Buchanan then determined to secure the
adoption of the constitution against the will of
the people, which decision brought out the lion
in Douglas. The Little Giant told the President that if that constitution was recommended
in the annual message he would denounce it.
Buchanan warned him that in opposing the
administration he would be crushed, but Douglas, who although shifty was not cowardly,
made an insolent reply, and immediately began
to defend his position before the country, saying in the South, December 9, 1857: "If Kansas wants a slave constitution she has a right
to it; if she wants a free state constitution she
has a right to it. It is none of my business
which way the slavery clause is decided. I care
not whether the slavery clause is voted down
or voted up." He declared that he would resist any violation of the principle of free government to the last. A fraudulent election was
held and the slavery constitution endorsed by
Buchanan and the Senate, but it was rejected
by the House. Another attempt in the same
direction, though a little less flagrant, called
the English bill, was resisted by Douglas, passed
by both Houses, signed by the President, and
rejected almost unanimously by Kansas. With
this record Douglas was endorsed in April by
the Illinois Democratic State Committee, which

meant that he would be their candidate for the Senate again in the fall. In the Republican State Convention of June 16, 1858, it was resolved that Abraham Lincoln was the first and only choice for United States Senator to fill the vacancy about to be created by the expiration of Douglas's term.

The speech of acknowledgment made by Lincoln was believed by him at the time, and proved later by events, to be one of the most important utterances of his career. Knowing that he would probably be the candidate of his party he meditated his words for weeks, jotting down on stray envelopes and bits of paper any phrase with which he was favorably struck, and then finally arranging the whole, so that when the expected hour came his speech was not only written and deeply considered, but committed to memory. The day before reciting it publicly he read it to a few friends. All except Herndon looked upon the following sentences as little short of fatal: " We are now far into the fifth year since a policy was initiated with the avowed object and confident purpose of putting an end to slavery agitation. Under the operation of that policy it has not only not ceased, but has constantly augmented. In my opinion, it will not cease until a crisis shall have been reached and passed. ' A house divided against itself cannot stand.' I believe this government cannot endure permanently half slave and half free. I do not expect the Union to be dissolved. I do not expect the house to fall — but I do expect it will cease to be divided. It will become all one thing or all the other. Either the opponents of slavery will arrest the further spread of it, and place it where the public mind shall rest in the belief that it is in the course of ultimate extinction; or its advocates will push it forward, till it shall become alike lawful in all the states, old as well as new, — North as well as South."

To the protests of his friends that so bold a statement would wreck him, Lincoln replied, with firmness, that if he had to erase all of his life except one poor record, he would choose to save that speech, and that he would rather be defeated with the 'house divided against itself' in the speech, than victorious without it. This determination has been interpreted by some as all principle, by others as keen policy, which saw that the man who was to have the support of the Republicans must take an early stand on a position that was inevitable. It would be at least as consistent with the general trend of Lincoln's nature if policy and principle were not seen as separate by him in this case, but as one and the same. He is reported to have declared to protestors that it would some day be recognized as

the wisest thing he ever said. He believed that
it was true. It was a truth also that was alive.
Not improbably he believed that it would be a
more distinct issue in 1860 than it was then.
Very probably he thought, as Douglas was the
inventor of the temporizing doctrine of popular
sovereignty, that if there was any way to beat him
it was by confronting him boldly. Lincoln was
deeply honest, but his honesty was not foolish.
The time when he spoke was usually the time
when it was wisest to speak.

His speech went on to make more distinct
what he meant. After going over the legislation
of 1850, the Nebraska Bill, and the Dred Scott
doctrine, he said that all that was needed was a
decision by the Supreme Court that the Constitution of the United States does not permit a state
to exclude slavery from its limits. "We shall lie
down pleasantly dreaming that the people of
Missouri are on the verge of making their state
free ; and we shall awake to the reality instead,
that the Supreme Court has made Illinois a slave
state."

One important point was the considerable
Republican support of Douglas. Lincoln urged
that the cause must be intrusted to its real
friends, those who cared for the result, not to
those who, like Douglas, were indifferent whether
slavery was voted up or down. Horace Greeley's

preference for Douglas was well known, and was doubtless founded, as Lincoln himself said it was, on the belief that to elect so powerful a convert would be the best aid to the anti-slavery cause, — the consideration which probably also weighed most with the other Eastern leaders who showed signs of hostility or lukewarmness to the Republican candidate. To demonstrate not only to his party but also to the anti-slavery Democrats that Douglas was not a real convert, was to be Lincoln's chief object in the campaign. " They remind us," he said, in one of his many passages on this point, " that he is a great man, and that the largest of us are very small ones. Let this be granted, but 'a living dog is better than a dead lion.' Judge Douglas, if not a dead lion for this work, is at least a caged and toothless one. How can he oppose the advances of slavery? He doesn't care anything about it." If he could show to the North that his opponent was not willing to take strong ground against the spread of slavery, and to the South, already angered by the refusal of Douglas to consent to gross fraud, that he was not a champion of their cause, Lincoln doubtless believed that his position would be promising even for the present election, in the doubtful state of public opinion in Illinois, and much more promising a little later when the issues should be more sharply drawn. During the progress of this campaign he urged Douglas to answer this question : " Can the people of the United States territory, in any lawful way, against the wish of any citizen of the United States, exclude slavery from its limits, prior to the formation of a state constitution ? " When his friends objected to having this point pressed, Lincoln replied that, whatever might be the effect in the Senatorial fight, Douglas could not answer the question and win the presidency in 1860. " I am killing larger game," Lincoln is reported as saying. " The battle of 1860 is worth a hundred of this." That he said practically this is reasonably certain. That he thought of the presidency for himself, as all American politicians do, is a matter of course. That he referred then to his own chances is extremely doubtful. Douglas was the leader of one great party. Lincoln was an ardent Republican. In all probability he meant that he was killing big game for his party and his principles in 1860, not for his own personal gain. To suppose that he was " taking the wind out of Seward's sails " is fanciful.

To race prejudice Douglas appealed with constant energy. Lincoln answered patiently, repeating his distinction about the slave and the wife, making other telling illustrations, sometimes solemnly, sometimes wittily. " The judge," he said in Chicago, July 10, 1858, " regales us with the terrible enormities that take place by the mixture of races, that the inferior race bears the superior down. Why, Judge, if we don't let them get together in the territories they won't mix there." In earnest vein he pressed the analogy between slavery and despotism, between kings and slave-owners, one living on the toil of another. In his style the impassioned and the elevated were mixed with the racy and the colloquial, and nothing was more characteristic of him or of Illinois than a demonstrated truth followed by such a remark as, " This is as plain as the weight of three small hogs."

Comparing his standing with his opponent's, on July 17, Lincoln remarked that all the anxious politicians of the Democratic party expected Douglas at no very distant day to be President of the United States. In his " round, jolly, fruitful " face, they saw possibilities of every kind of office, " bursting and sprouting out in wonderful exuberance." " On the contrary, nobody has expected me to be President. In my poor, lean, lank face, nobody has ever seen that any cabbages were sprouting out." Douglas referred to his antagonist with a sort of genial condescension, and this relation of superior and inferior was seized upon and given half ironic emphasis by the adroit Lincoln, who used his own humbleness as a contrast to the superiority of his principles,

He argued that the anti-slavery cause belonged in no sense to Douglas, but wholly to the Republican party; and that although the judge and the Republicans were at one on the anti-Nebraska fight, there was no reason for his taking so much credit to himself because on one detail he agreed with Lincoln's party. He had no right to the standing of a returning sinner. "If the judge claims the benefit of that parable, let him repent."

The reader of this speech of July 17 will see in it a large part of the points clung to by Lincoln in the subsequent joint debates, with the same arts and policy of the orator. If Douglas could appeal loudly to race prejudice, Lincoln could drop a passing reference to the assault of Brooks on Sumner and the praise with which the unprovoked and cowardly deed was greeted at the South. In attack and defence Lincoln shows that he is equally at home, as far as clear demonstration is concerned, but he makes a much better impression when he is dealing blows at the inconsistency of his opponent and the immorality of his cause, than when he is explaining away the charges of abolitionism constantly urged by Douglas. Lincoln replies that he has no ambition to force people to freeze ice in Florida, no desire to interfere with the cranberry laws of Indiana because cranberries did not grow in Illinois, but the fact that whatever he might say about non-interference he believed and wished that the policy of the Republican party would, in some way or other, end in the extinction of slavery, South as well as North, had to be met, and it was kept before the people with unremitting diligence by the wily judge.

Lincoln, on July 24, 1858, took one of the wisest steps of his life by challenging Douglas to a series of joint debates. The judge accepted for seven meetings, which were held in the presence of immense crowds, drawn together by profound excitement over the slavery question and by the fact that it was being discussed by the two ablest speakers in Illinois. Two champions could scarcely be in clearer contrast. Douglas was the most brilliant leader in his party, bold, adroit, subtle, charming, a master both in steady flow of sounding language and in all the tricks of misinterpretation, ambiguity, and plausible fallacy necessary to confuse an opponent. James G. Blaine, who writes that Douglas was without either wit or humor, adds that as an orator and debater he was exactly the kind for the almost physical fight demanded by such a stump contest. This same astute observer not only said, after the fact, that Douglas failed to look ahead, as Lincoln did, but Lamon tells us that he saw in Lincoln's possession, shortly before his death, a letter written by Blaine during the campaign of 1858 and widely circulated, in which he ventured the remarkable prophecy that Douglas would beat Lincoln for the senatorship but would be beaten by him in 1860 for the presidency.

Lincoln, inferior to Douglas in nimble fencing, although no mean hand at that game himself, relied mainly on his power to hit straight blows. His manner as well as his mind accomplished much when it was earnest. It was when his shrill voice grew warm with conviction, and his dark yellow face lighted up with intensity, that he struck the listeners with a kind of confidence never given by his opponent. Horace Greeley, certainly not too favorable, said that Lincoln became the foremost *convincer* of his time, the one who could do his cause more good and less harm than any other living man. In this campaign canvassing, in these stump battles before all sorts of men, the speaker, if his statement of the case does not produce conviction, "justifies, varies, reenforces it," and while he educates his hearers he educates himself. In this kind of struggle, where the subject was thrashed out between the orators and the audience, Lincoln's native love of truth made him grow more strong and clear with every speech, both in his comprehension of the various aspects of the great issue, and in that understanding of the average American mind which lay at the foundation of his greatness as a war president.

The first of the joint debates was held at Ottawa, on August 21. Douglas, in accepting the challenge, had chosen to open and close four times to his rival's three, but Lincoln was too eager for the fray to be stopped by such an advantage. Douglas in this first joint debate charged that in 1854 " Lincoln went to work to abolitionize the old Whig party all over the state." He showered the term " Black Republican " on him and his associates. He accused him of hostility to the Mexican War, and even went off into side-tracks of misrepresentation to amuse his audience and waste his opponent's time in reply. He told with mock admiration how nobly Lincoln presided at fist-fights and horse-races, and how he " could ruin more liquor than all the boys of the town together."

The audience at such an encounter was not overburdened with awe or etiquette, but both speakers knew how to manage it. While Lincoln was trying to explain the speech which he had made in the contest of 1854, a voice in the crowd cried, " Put on your specs." " Yes, sir," replied Lincoln, " I am obliged to; I am no longer a young man." Not only disrespectful jests but searching questions were likely to be shouted out of the throng at any moment, and each combatant had to be either fertile in resources or certain of his ground. Douglas was one. Lincoln was both. It is not difficult, in reading the speeches now, in cold blood, with a knowledge of the issue, to see the superiority of Lincoln's, nor is it difficult to see the brilliant skill with which Douglas kept the contest on the points most dangerous to his adversary. One of the lighter replies in this first battle has a particular flavor of Lincoln's character. Douglas had spoken of him, in his superior way, as a " kind, amiable, and intelligent gentleman." Lincoln pretended to be overjoyed with such praise from such a source, and likened himself to the hoozier who said he reckoned he loved gingerbread better than any other man, and got less of it.

The second meeting took place August 27, at Freeport. The state of public feeling in Illinois is indicated by the stress that the judge thought it wise to put on the fact that the negro Fred Douglass had been seen driving with a white woman. It was apparently one of the most excited of the meetings, with interruptions which led Douglas to charge one element of the crowd with vulgarity and blackguardism. Lincoln replied that he should not receive any vulgarity and blackguardism himself because he would not inflict any. Personalities were pretty severe in this debate, and also in the next, September 15, at Janesboro, containing an elaborately disputed question of veracity. In the fourth debate at Charlestown, September 18, Lincoln explained clearly that he was not in favor of giving the negroes votes, the right to sit on juries, or any sort of social equality; but just as clearly in the sixth, October 13, at Quincy, he insisted on the moral foundation of the whole political question. Throughout Lincoln's whole career, two points of view must be kept in mind, and then his attitude will be seen to be surprisingly consistent. One aspect is what he wished for in the end, and that was universal freedom, but only such political and social equality as progress by the negroes should invite. The other aspect is what he would advise doing under the immediate circumstances, and in treating that side he went so far as to say he would not have all fugitive slave laws done away with, and, of course, he would not interfere with slavery in slave states. The hardest question Douglas pressed in the whole debate was one that Lincoln long hesitated to answer, finally acknowledging that he would vote to admit to the Union, under slave constitution, territory owned by the United States, provided the inhabitants desired to have slavery. Douglas also gave Lincoln trouble over the Dred Scott decision, for while it was easy, consistent, and reasonable to hold that the law must be recognized as long as it existed, but that it would probably

L

some time cease to be law, this was not an easy distinction to force through all the intricacies of debate. Douglas, on the other hand, was troubled by Lincoln's questions about the right of the people in a territory to exclude slavery prior to the formation of a state constitution, and about the right of slaveholders in territories to have their property protected by Congress. Over the first question he wriggled furiously and created the " Freeport Doctrine " of popular sovereignty, which ultimately destroyed him. When the second was put he exclaimed, " Repeat that; I want to answer that question." But he never did. It should be remembered that the combatants chose their points not solely for the crowd in front of them, but for leisurely readers of the newspapers, and in the end it was by them that the answers of Douglas were weighed and found wanting.

The last debate was at Alton, on October 15. The election followed soon, and Douglas won. In popular vote the Republicans had a small plurality, but the legislature, which elected the senator was slightly Democratic in both branches. On November 15, Lincoln wrote: " Douglas had the ingenuity to be supported in the late contest both as the best means to break down and to uphold the slave interest. No ingenuity can keep these antagonistic elements in har-

mony long. Another explosion will soon come."
Horace Greeley says that on the real issue fought
out between Lincoln and Douglas, Illinois was
about equally divided, and that in the autumn
Douglas was elected after borrowing and disbursing in the canvass $80,000, a debt which weighed
him down to the grave, while Lincoln, who had
spent less than $1000, came out stronger politi-
cally than he went in. Herndon tells us about
George B. McClellan's taking Douglas around in
a special train, while Lincoln sometimes found it
hard to secure a seat when he was exhausted.
Whatever details counted in the result, there
seems to be little doubt that the fight was carried
on with such ability that each combatant gained
admiration from his party and the country, although it is probably also true that the thorough
airing given to the views of Douglas did much to
deprive him in 1860 of Southern support on the
one hand and Northern support on the other.

After this campaign Lincoln found himself hard
pressed for money. His income from the law,
according to his partner, was not over $3000,
and there were current political expenses. He
tried lecturing, one address on " Inventions "
being delivered in several towns, but his failure
was so evident that he soon abandoned the experiment. While he did some law work, he kept
very actively in politics. He had tried to get the

Springfield publishers to print his speeches and those of Douglas in a book, but they had refused. In 1859 the Republican State Committee asked for their publication, and the next year they were printed at Columbus and used as campaign documents.

He followed Douglas to Ohio in a gubernatorial contest in September, 1859, and made some speeches. In one of these speeches he said: " Now, what is Judge Douglas's popular sovereignty? It is as a principle no other than that, if one man chooses to make a slave of another man, neither that other man nor anybody else has a right to object." Again, of Douglas: " I suppose the institution of slavery really looks small to him. He is so put up by nature that a lash upon his back would hurt him, but a lash upon anybody else's back does not hurt him." The following month he received an invitation to speak during the winter in New York. Herndon had some time previously made a trip East for the purpose of conciliating the Republican leaders, but nothing did so much to strengthen Lincoln in this part of the country as a speech which he delivered at Cooper Union on February 27. Horace Greeley says that from the point of view of the canvasser, by which he means the persuader of all sorts of men, it is the very best address to which he ever listened, "and I have heard some of Webster's grandest." The opportunity to make this great speech, like the invitations of the preceding year to speak all over the Northwest, grew directly out of the Douglas debates, which not only left him known throughout the country at once, but contained such a complete and able statement of Republican doctrine that the more they were read by the leaders the more highly was Lincoln regarded. As Blaine has said, Lincoln "did not seek to say merely the thing that was for the day's debate, but the thing which would stand the test of time and square itself with eternal justice." He was now rapidly reaping his reward.

Of this Cooper Institute gathering the *New York Tribune*, Greeley's paper, said, "Since the days of Clay and Webster no man has spoken to a larger assemblage of the intellect and mental culture of our city." The speech was serious. It contained none of the raciness intended for Western stumps, but put the whole question in all its branches in the solidest form to confirm or convince the minds of educated men whose interest was keenly centred. Lincoln was always a man who understood opportunity. Stories and jests were laid aside, and he grasped the occasion to paint the situation more accurately than anybody else. In spite of its thoroughness, its treatment of all sides of the central controversy, it had such unity that one idea dominated the whole: "All they ask we could readily grant, if we thought slavery right; all we ask they could as readily grant, if they thought it wrong." To support duty was the straight road; "then let us stand by our duty, fearlessly and effectively."

"Mr. Lincoln," said Greeley's paper the next day, "is one of nature's orators." The *Evening Post* and most of the other leading papers were almost equally enthusiastic. He spoke elsewhere in the East, holding fast to the main issue, and to the principles on which he believed it should be decided, and when he returned to the West he was in the best of form to try for the great prize to be awarded the succeeding year.

CHAPTER VIII

NOMINATION AND ELECTION

WITH this native wisdom, the shrewdness of a trained politician, and the aid of the men in Illinois most adroit in such manipulation, Lincoln went to work to secure one of the prizes, the highest if possible. In America a presidential candidate usually gains by remaining in the background, and Lincoln found reason to declare himself unworthy of the chief office and unentitled to the vice-presidency, which was sought by other Illinois statesmen whom he did not wish to antagonize. All the time he was strengthening himself as much as he could, and watching events, to see just what steps should be taken as opportunity opened before him. He wrote letters, mostly short ones, to politicians in all parts of the country. The party leaders in the East had their own candidates for the presidency, but they thought much of Lincoln for second place, which would naturally go to the West. Under the adroit management of the Republican State Committee, who were preparing the ground all through 1859, the Illinois papers came out one at a time, at considerable intervals, for Lincoln, as if by a natural growth of public opinion, culminating February 16, 1860, in the *Chicago Tribune*, whose editor was one of the leading workers of this scheme. The public opinion really existed, but it was gathered together and intensified by party tactics. Lincoln himself wrote to a Western politician: —

"As to your kind wishes for myself, allow me to say I cannot enter the ring on the money basis — first, because in the main it is wrong; and secondly, I have not and cannot get the money. I say in the main the use of money is wrong; but for certain objects in a political contest the use of same is both right and indispensable. With me, as with yourself, this long struggle has been one of great pecuniary loss. I now distinctly say this: If you shall be appointed a delegate to Chicago, I will furnish one hundred dollars to bear the expenses of the trip." Herndon tells a number of stories about Lincoln's methods of conciliating newspaper men, which shows he was not squeamish in trifles.

The selection of Chicago by the Republicans was the first victory for the Illinois managers. Norman B. Judd, who led in the effort to bring the convention to Chicago, also saw to it that reduced railway fares were initiated, and that there were other inducements to lure the citizens of Illinois to the seat of war. Lincoln had taken this position, expressed in a letter to Judd: "I am not in a position where it would hurt much for me not to be nominated on the national ticket; but I am where it would hurt some for me not to get the Illinois delegates." The first point was to fix Illinois, and the future would show what could be done when the various states exchanged their views. Mr. Whitney, who was in Chicago for several days in March and April preceding the nomination, when Lincoln was trying the sand-bar case, went with him to a minstrel show at Metropolitan Hall, Chicago, where it was then thought the convention might be held.

"Possibly," said Whitney, "in a few weeks you will be nominated for the presidency right here."

"It is enough honor," said Lincoln, "for me to be talked about for it."

The Republican State Convention met at Decatur, May 9 and 10. The result had already been prepared, but it was to be called out in a manner that struck one of the most effective chords in the succeeding battle. The "wigwam" was crowded, and Lincoln was seated on his heels in an aisle among the onlookers. Governor Oglesby, the presiding officer, suggested that a distinguished citizen of Illinois who was present, and whom his fellow-citizens always delighted to honor, should have a seat on the platform. The crowd was so dense that Lincoln could not make his way, and he was seized and lifted over the spectators to the stand, with loud applause. Later, Oglesby mysteriously hinted that an old Democrat outside had something which he wished to present to the convention. It was voted that this something should be received. The door was opened, to admit John Hanks, the rustic cousin of Lincoln, who had been chosen and coached for this particular demonstration. He marched into the assembly, bearing two small triangular rails and a banner, on which were these words, which were associated not remotely with victory in the fall: —

"ABRAHAM LINCOLN

THE RAIL CANDIDATE

FOR PRESIDENT IN 1860

Two rails from a lot of 3000 made in 1830 by Thos. Hanks and Abe Lincoln — whose father was the first pioneer of Macon County."

Lincoln, after the immense tumult had subsided, in his half embarrassed and half easy way, stood up on the platform and responded: " I suppose I am expected to reply to that. I cannot say whether

I made those rails or not, but I am quite sure I have made a great many just as good."

The convention resolved that Lincoln was its first choice, and instructed delegates to give the vote of the state as a unit. They were really almost unanimous by this time, and a little more work by the leaders made them so. About the National Convention Lincoln said, "I am a little too much of a candidate to go, and not quite enough of a candidate to stay away; but upon the whole I believe I will not go."

When the Republicans met in Chicago just a week later, May 16, they found a complicated situation. It was their second national convention. Fremont, who was nominated by them at Philadelphia in 1856, had been defeated by the slave states, except Maryland, aided by Illinois, Indiana, Pennsylvania, New Jersey, and California. Illinois had always been Democratic. In 1836 Ohio and Indiana went for Harrison, but Illinois did not enter the Whig ranks. In 1840 Illinois was the only free state except New Hampshire to go Democratic. In 1844 she increased her majority. "She never," says Horace Greeley, "cast an electoral vote for any other than the Democratic nominee till she cast all she had for her own Lincoln." Now it was Lincoln who had shown in the Senatorial fight with Douglas that Illinois might be rescued for the Republicans. The other Northern Democratic states might also be changed, as indicated by the elections of 1858. The first four on the list were the most impor-tant, and among them Pennsylvania and New Jer-sey were first, because they, voting in October, would have an immense influence on the others. The leaders were to decide practically on these facts alone.

Had it not been for the split of the Democrats the Republicans would have had less confidence. After a long fight the Democrats had adjourned, on May 3, their convention held at Charleston, fifty-seven ballots having shown that, while Doug-las was far in the lead, he was bitterly opposed by the extreme slavery element. The extent of the split became evident only after the Republicans had made their choice, but it was clearly evident that the Democrats were sufficiently divided to offer a good opportunity. On May 6 a peace party calling itself the Constitutional Union Party, having an avoidance of the slavery issue as its only principle, had nominated John Bell of Tennessee and Edward Everett of Massachusetts, but it was a minor element in the problem.

The leading candidate, when the Republicans assembled in Chicago, was William H. Seward of New York. What the Lincoln men most feared was a Seward victory on the first ballot. That once passed they felt their chances good, for

Seward was too offensive to various elements in the party to be the centre of any compromise. Although the address in which he spoke of an "irrepressible conflict" between slavery and freedom was four months later than Lincoln's "house divided against itself," Seward, partly because of his greater prominence, partly because of other expressions made eight years earlier, was looked upon as much more of an abolitionist. One of his delegates sent a despatch to the supporters of Edward Bates, a Missouri candidate representing moderation, saying that Lincoln was as radical as Seward. Lincoln, although he was trusting his fortunes in the hands of David Davis, Judd, and a few others, wrote from Springfield to Davis, when he saw this despatch: " Lincoln agrees with Seward in his irrepressible conflict idea, and in negro equality; but he is opposed to Seward's Higher Law. *Make no contracts that will bind me.*" The last sentence was underlined. The Higher Law sentence referred to the contention of Seward, made in 1850, that the moral law stood above the Constitution; and Lincoln had always made it clear that, with all his hatred of slavery, his loyalty to the Constitution was first. The belief, therefore, that Seward was the more radical, was justly founded, for he had, to balance an equal hostility to slavery, a smaller ballast of respect for established institutions. Moreover, he had the misfortune to have gained unpopularity in the two states on which all eyes were fixed, Pennsylvania and Indiana, by his attitude on a school question. His managers were able, and better known than those of his principal rival, but in this affair they were less shrewd. Thurlow Weed, the notorious New York politician, was at the head, with Governor Morgan and Henry Raymond, of the *New York Times*, as assistants, and William M. Evarts to make the nomination. Colonel McClure divides Lincoln's managers as follows: David Davis for counsel, Leonard Swett for sagacity, Norman B. Judd for tireless hustling. They had filled Chicago with a multitude of Illinois men wild for Lincoln, and while the Seward advocates were making a great noise and display in the streets, the Lincoln leaders, far ahead of the time for balloting, packed the whole wigwam, the great temporary building in which the convention was finally held, so full of their supporters that when the Seward celebrators got there they found room for few more than their delegates and lost the advantages of the enthusiastic cheering of a multitude. If Seward was outgeneralled, however, the more important fact is that he had aroused more hostility and that he did not come from a doubtful state.

Lincoln's friends, not overawed by the under-scored passage forbidding bargains, made wise ones. To gain the support of Indiana, it was agreed that if Lincoln should be elected, William P. Dole, a clever politician of that state, should be Commissioner of Indian Affairs, and Caleb B. Smith, of the same state, Secretary of the Treasury. The Indiana delegation was thus prepared to tell the wavering delegates that only Lincoln could carry their state and Illinois, and this work was industriously executed.

Pennsylvania had a "favorite son" in Simon Cameron. Of this notoriously corrupt individual Lincoln had written to Judd, December 9, 1859, perhaps in response to a suggestion that Cameron and Lincoln might be the ticket: "If the Republicans of the great state of Pennsylvania shall present Mr. Cameron as their candidate for the presidency, such an indorsement of his fitness for the place could scarcely be deemed insufficient." The Pennsylvania politicians had nothing against Lincoln and little hope of nominating Cameron, so all they wished was a fair price. With the two October states in line the outlook would be cheerful. According to the best authority there is on this subject, the Pennsylvania delegation was secured in the small hours of the day on which the balloting was held. The negotiations were carried on by several political friends of Cameron, on the one side, and by Davis, Swett, Logan, Judd, and Dole on

the other, Indiana and Illinois being already con·
solidated.   The agreement as finally reached was
this : —

1. These negotiations shall be forever secret
and confidential.

2. Lincoln's friends have no actual authority
— none but a moral right.

3. If Lincoln shall be President, Cameron shall
have a place in his cabinet.

4. And he shall procure the indorsement of
the Republican State Committee.

The second clause made trouble, especially as
Lincoln's message was known, but this difficulty
finally succumbed to the argument that he could
hardly go back on Davis, Logan, and Swett.

There was further stumbling over the choice
of the cabinet position.   Cameron thought it
would be particularly satisfactory to get his teeth
into the treasury department, but as the Illinois
men, remembering the wrecking of the treasury
under Buchanan and the record of Cameron,
were obstinate against that, the exact place was
left undecided.

The real work having been done, the balloting
began.   In the presence of possibly ten thousand
people William M. Evarts said, " I take the liberty to name as a candidate to be nominated by
this convention for the office of President of the
United States, William H. Seward."

Norman B. Judd arose and said, " I desire,
on behalf of the delegation from Illinois, to
put in nomination as a candidate for President of the United States, Abraham Lincoln,
of Illinois."

Others were nominated, but the applause
showed that these were the only real candidates.
The first ballot stood: —

Whole number	465
Necessary for choice	233
William H. Seward, of New York,	$173\frac{1}{2}$
Abraham Lincoln, of Illinois,	102
Simon Cameron, of Pennsylvania,	$50\frac{1}{2}$
Salmon P. Chase, of Ohio,	49
Edward Bates, of Missouri,	48
William L. Dayton, of New Jersey,	14
John McLean, of Ohio,	12
Jacob Collamer, of Vermont,	10
Scattering	6

On the second ballot most of Cameron's votes
went to Lincoln, and there were smaller driftings
toward him.   The result was: —

Seward	$184\frac{1}{2}$
Lincoln	181
Cameron	2
Chase	$42\frac{1}{2}$
Bates	35
Dayton	10
McLean	8
Scattering	2

M

The third ballot saw Lincoln's gain coming from all directions.   It stood : —

Seward	180
Lincoln	231½
Chase	24½
Bates	22
Dayton	1
McLean	5
Scattering	1

Before it was announced, votes were changed until Lincoln's total was 354.   The nomination was then made unanimous.   Hannibal Hamlin, of Maine, was the nominee for Vice-President. When Douglas heard the news of Lincoln's nomination he said to a group of Republican senators that they had nominated a very honest and a very able man.   After discussing the various theories of what really led to this nomination, Horace Greeley says that Lincoln was nominated in 1860 because he could obtain more electoral votes than anybody else, — the same reason that nominated Harrison in 1839, Polk in 1844, Taylor in 1848, Pierce in 1852, and Buchanan in 1856.

Lincoln, who heard the returns in Springfield, passed in his usual manner from cheerfulness to gloom and back again, but from this time to the end of his life heavy responsibility added one more weight to his spirits and probably some-

what increased his habitual melancholy. He was
sensitive, too, and the campaign soon furnished
him with personal abuse more bitter than any he
had yet endured. The first important news, however, which he received after his nomination was
encouraging. The Democrats met again in convention on June 18, and made the division in their
ranks more nearly hopeless than ever. Douglas
was nominated, and on June 28, at Baltimore
also, the Southern wing of the Democracy met in
convention and nominated John C. Breckenridge
of Kentucky. The Republicans, already ardent
with the inspiration of clear conviction, were
spurred to greater efforts by the confidence of
victory given by the disturbed condition of their
opponents. The famous Wide-Awake Clubs began the system, now grown tame and perfunctory,
of torch-light processions, and they marched every
night all over the North. The appeal to the
average voter was made partly on the origin of
the candidate. As General Harrison had been
carried to victory on a wave of enthusiasm created
not only by his military record but by his log-
cabin origin, the rails, which had done such flam-
boyant work at Springfield, continued to be one
of the favorite symbols of the campaign, and
Honest Abe and the Rail Splitter became common appellations.

It was easier to make the idea of Lincoln

appeal to the public than to recommend it to the cultivated leaders of the East. In spite of his Douglas debates, his Cooper Union speeches, his term in Congress, his long leadership in Illinois, beginning by the time he was thirty years old, his reputation was not sufficiently national and tested to satisfy the men who had wanted some candidate with the prominence of Seward. Charles Francis Adams, Lincoln's minister to England, said, after the President's death: " I must then affirm, without hesitation, that in the history of our government, down to this hour, no experiment so rash has ever been made as that of elevating to the head of affairs a man with so little previous preparation for his task as Mr. Lincoln."   False to absurdity as this affirmation is, it was made by many at the time. " When Lincoln was nominated," said Emerson in 1865, " we heard the result coldly and sadly. It seemed too rash, on a purely local reputation, to build so great a trust in such anxious times; " but Emerson is wise enough to see that the result was not disconnected with the profound good opinion of Lincoln which was held by the people of Illinois and the neighboring states. Wendell Phillips wished to know, " Who is this huckster in politics? Who is this country court advocate? " This was the same man, who, fairly representing the extreme and cultivated abolitionists, published an article called "Abraham Lincoln, the Slave-Hound of Illinois," because Lincoln had not been in favor of wholly abolishing the fugitive slave laws.

Most violent of all his opponents, naturally enough, were the Southerners, who were taught to look upon him as the incarnation of the abolition spirit. After the election they were fiercest, but they were sufficiently harsh before. Negro-lover was one of their milder epithets. He was described as a "nigger," and some of the papers said his father was an imported gorilla from Mozambique. The campaign picture reproduced here is typical of many portraits which helped to furnish the idea of his appearance to the voting masses. Lincoln read the papers more or less, and, especially after the election until his inauguration, the Richmond and Charleston journals. It was always his habit to know the objections to what he was doing, and all through his presidential career he read the discontented papers, like the *New York Tribune* and the *Cincinnati Commercial*, more than he did those which agreed with his own policy.

He did not take the stump during the campaign, as Douglas did, undoubtedly because he believed that the cause was so likely to win if it was not tinkered with that the safest course was silence. His friend, Swett, is quoted as saying:

" He employed tactics wholly different from any other politician we ever had. He believed in the results to which certain great causes tend, and did not believe those results could be hastened, changed, or impeded by personal interference. Hence he was no political manipulator." This statement is inaccurate, but it is true that there were times when he thought interference would be dangerous, and this was one of them. Swett also says that after Lincoln was nominated, and on account of the signs of lukewarmness in the East friends proposed sending delegates there to induce union and partisan activity, he alone opposed it. Late in the summer he consented that Judge Davis should go, purely on his own behalf, on a tour of inspection, but even this consent was reluctant.

He stayed quietly in Springfield and watched the signs. He gave up his law practice, although not his partnership with Herndon, and spent his time in the Governor's room in the State House, which was set aside for his use. There he talked with everybody, important visitors and intruders alike, but consulted almost nobody. Judge Davis, who was supposed to have influence with him, said that Lincoln never asked his advice on any subject, except occasionally on money. Swett says that in his eleven years with him at the bar the only time he knew him to come anywhere near asking advice about anything was when he read to a few friends the questions he proposed to put in the Senatorial contest and asked them to answer from the point of view of Douglas. He heard everybody, asked questions, told stories, and kept his own counsel. No more did he answer any of the accusations made against him. He was again charged with Know-Nothingism, purely for campaign purposes, but he refused to reply. Of course nothing could be farther than that party's principles from all Lincoln's convictions. He was, indeed, so much in favor of extending rather than restricting the suffrage that Herndon tells of Lincoln's refusing to argue a law case because it involved the restrictive view of that question.

As the campaign progressed the chances all pointed to Lincoln's election, and the only danger was that by a fusion of the two Democratic parties in some states the election might be thrown into the House of Representatives. The fall state election increased Republican confidence. When the election was held November 6, 1860, the result was as follows:—

States	Popular Vote				Electoral Vote			
	Abraham Lincoln, Illinois	Stephen A. Douglas, Illinois	John C. Breckenridge, Kentucky	John Bell, Tennessee	Lincoln	Douglas	Breckenridge	Bell
Maine	62,811	26,693	6,368	2,046	8	—	—	—
New Hampshire	37,519	25,881	2,112	441	5	—	—	—
Vermont	33,808	6,849	218	1,969	5	—	—	—
Massachusetts	106,533	34,372	5,939	22,231	13	—	—	—
Rhode Island	12,244	7,707 [2]	—	—	4	—	—	—
Connecticut	43,792	15,522	14,641	3,291	6	—	—	—
New York	362,646	312,510 [2]	—	—	35	—	—	—
New Jersey	58,324	62,801 [2]	—	—	4	3	—	—
Pennsylvania	268,030	16,765	178,781 [2]	12,776	27	—	—	—
Delaware	3,815	1,023	7,337	3,864	—	—	3	—
Maryland	2,294	5,966	42,482	41,760	—	—	8	—
Virginia	1,929	16,290	74,323	74,681	—	—	—	15
North Carolina	—	2,701	48,539	44,990	—	—	10	—
South Carolina [1]	—	—	—	—	—	—	8	—
Georgia	—	11,590	51,889	42,886	—	—	10	—
Florida	—	367	8,543	5,437	—	—	3	—
Alabama	—	13,651	48,831	27,875	—	—	9	—
Mississippi	—	3,283	40,797	25,040	—	—	7	—
Louisiana	—	7,625	22,861	20,204	—	—	6	—
Texas	—	—	47,548	15,438 [2]	—	—	4	—
Arkansas	—	5,227	28,732	20,094	—	—	4	—
Missouri	17,028	58,801	31,317	58,372	—	9	—	—
Tennessee	—	11,350	64,709	69,274	—	—	—	12
Kentucky	1,364	25,651	53,143	66,058	—	—	—	12
Ohio	231,610	187,232	11,405	12,194	23	—	—	—
Michigan	88,480	65,057	805	405	6	—	—	—
Indiana	139,033	115,509	12,295	5,306	13	—	—	—
Illinois	172,161	160,215	2,404	4,913	11	—	—	—
Wisconsin	86,110	65,021	888	161	5	—	—	—
Minnesota	22,069	11,920	748	62	4	—	—	—
Iowa	70,409	55,111	1,048	1,763	4	—	—	—
California	39,173	38,516	34,334	6,817	4	—	—	—
Oregon	5,270	3,951	5,006	183	3	—	—	—
Totals	1,866,452	1,375,157	847,953	590,631	180	12	72	39

[1] By legislature.   [2] Fusion electoral tickets.

Shortly after the election Lincoln had a vision, which was thus related by him to Noah Brooks:

"It was just after my election in 1860, when the news had been coming in thick and fast all day, and there had been a great 'Hurrah boys!' so that I was well tired out, and went home to rest, throwing myself down on a lounge in my chamber. Opposite where I lay was a bureau, with a swinging glass upon it " — (and here he got up and placed furniture to illustrate the position), — "and, looking in that glass, I saw myself reflected, nearly at full length; but my face, I noticed, had two separate and distinct images, the tip of the nose of one being about three inches from the tip of the other. I was a little bothered, perhaps startled, and got up and looked in the glass, but the illusion vanished. On lying down again I saw it a second time — plainer, if possible, than before; and I noticed that one of the faces was a little paler, say five shades, than the other. I got up and the thing melted away, and I went off, and, in the excitement of the hour, forgot all about it — nearly, but not quite, for the thing would once in a while come up, and give me a little pang, as though something uncomfortable had happened. Later in the day, I told my wife about it, and a few days after I tried the experiment again, when (with a laugh), sure enough, the thing came again; but I never succeeded in bringing the ghost back after that, though I once tried very industriously to show it to my wife, who was worried about it somewhat. She thought it was 'a sign' that I was to be elected to a second term of office, and that the paleness of one of the faces was an omen that I should not see life through the last term."

We shall find this side of Lincoln's strange character reappearing later, but it may now be mentioned that among his favorite lines were the following from Byron's dream: —

> "Sleep hath its own world,
> A boundary between the things misnamed
> Death and existence : Sleep hath its own world
> And a wild realm of wild reality.
> And dreams in their development hath breath,
> And tears and tortures, and the touch of joy ;
> They leave a weight upon our waking thoughts,
> They take a weight from off our waking toils,
> They do divide our being."

CHAPTER IX

FACING THE STORM

FROM his election to his inauguration Lincoln was compelled to watch the end of Buchanan's government proceed on a course the
opposite of the one he deemed wise. His election was the signal for a secession movement
throughout the South. Never before had the
territory of the country been so open to slavery;
but the leaders knew that an election which
meant no further yielding struck also the final
doom of their institution, and they were determined to found a slave empire while they could,
peaceably if possible, forcibly if necessary. It
was the only time in the history of the Republic that a President had been chosen by one
of the two hostile sections alone. Lincoln and
Douglas had divided almost the entire vote of
the North, Breckenridge and Bell almost the
whole of the South, and for the first time since
the nation was founded the President had received no electoral vote from a slave state. In
this situation the secession leaders saw that the
hour had come. The mass of the slave-owners

were not ready for war, probably not even for secession, as shown later by the manner in which the Southern states withdrew; but a few influential men were able to make the conflict inevitable. As Blaine explains, slavery as an economic institution and slavery as a political force were distinct, and the war was brought on by those who wished to use the question as a political engine for the consolidation of power.

Lincoln characteristically remained quiet on all subordinate issues, and, having as yet no power to act on the main question, did nothing to inflame it, but none the less told his spokesmen where he stood. Not for a moment did he encourage the talk about peaceable secession which was so widespread throughout the North. Buchanan's cabinet was partly composed of Southern conspirators, Washington was full of them, they were in every Northern city, and the President, although loyal, was so weak that he took in a confused and frightened way the position that if the South wished to go he saw no way to prevent it. That was bad enough, but when Lincoln beheld the abolitionists themselves arguing for the right of secession, he required all of his own convictions to maintain the stand which he never lost. Not only did Greeley argue in his influential paper that the Southern right to secede was as good as that of the Colonists in 1776, a statement put in more exaggerated form by the *New York Herald* and many other papers, both Democratic and Republican, but the mass of the Northern people seemed as weak-kneed as their leaders. This was true not only in the Middle States, but even in New England, for in Boston itself, Wendell Phillips needed the protection of the police, and so sudden was the change in sentiment that George William Curtis had to abandon a lecture in Philadelphia, for fear of a riot, five weeks after that city had given Lincoln an immense majority. To vote for a conviction was one thing; to fight for it was another.

Lincoln, living quietly in his Springfield home, watched the sentiment at the North, knowing that when the lapse of a few months called him to action, he should stand for the straight course, however raging the storm. A fortnight after the election, when Springfield was holding a jubilee, he spoke a few simple words, among them these: " I rejoice with you in the success which has thus far attended that cause. Yet in all our rejoicings, let us neither express nor cherish any hard feelings toward any citizen, who by his vote has differed with us. Let us at all times remember that all American citizens are brothers of a common country, and should dwell together in the bonds of fraternal feeling." But kindness was no clearer in his attitude than determination. While he was for conciliation he was opposed to the only possible compromise, which was concession either of more territory for slavery or of the right to secede. He granted the enforcement of the Fugitive Slave Law and nothing more. "My opinion," he wrote to Thurlow Weed, December 17, 1860, "is, that no state can in any way lawfully get out of the Union without the consent of the others; and that it is the duty of the President and other government functionaries to run the machine as it is." To W. Kellogg, representative from Illinois on December 11, he wrote: "Entertain no proposition for a compromise in regard to the extension of slavery. The tug has got to come, and better now than later." Two days later he wrote to Mr. Washburne: "Your long letter received: Prevent as far as possible any of our friends from demoralizing themselves and their cause by entertaining propositions for compromise of any sort on slavery extension. There is no possible compromise upon it but what puts us under again, and all our work to do over again. Whether it be a Missouri line or Eli Thayer's popular sovereignty, it is all the same. Let either be done, and immediately filibustering and extending slavery recommences. On that point hold firm as a chain of steel."

This stand he held with calmness in the face of those who clamored for aggressive talk and of those who were for conciliation. Some even went so far as to propose that, now that the principle of freedom had been vindicated at the polls, the way to peace should be prepared by Lincoln's retirement and the choice of some one more acceptable to the South. To the wild suggestions with which he was so plentifully supplied he said nothing. " In this country," says Lowell, " where the rough-and-ready understanding of the people is sure at last to be the controlling power, a profound common sense is the best genius for statesmanship." It was part of Lincoln's common sense, when, as Emerson puts it, " the new pilot was hurried to the helm in a tornado," to say as little as was necessary, and to speak only on the points which were at once crucial and certain. Salmon P. Chase, so soon to be a member of the cabinet, wrote on January 9, 1861, to Thaddeus Stevens, " *He is a man to be depended on.* He may, as all men may, make mistakes; but the cause will be want of sufficient information, not of soundness of judgment or of devotedness to principle." This confidence was not, however, so widespread but that the President-elect needed his power of thinking calmly in the midst of timidity, distrust, and considerable hysteria. Against his will he invited Thurlow Weed to Springfield, to talk over the situation, but this was for party harmony, and was almost an only instance.

While the South was rapidly being forced into secession by her leaders, and part of the North believed war inevitable, while the rest thought the idea inconceivable, nobody will ever know what Lincoln's opinion was. The signs as we look back on them seem indubitable enough. South Carolina sent circulars to the governors of other states in October and got mainly replies unfavorable to secession, but the little hotbed of rebellion framed a government for herself in November, modelled on our national form, her United States senators resigned, and Governor Pickens appointed a cabinet. Before the newly organized government sent commissioners to Washington, however, Buchanan's cabinet, thinned by various quarrels, had been filled with stronger men, and the President's own weakness was thus diminished. Driven by Judge Black, Secretary of State, and Edwin M. Stanton, Attorney-General, he gave the commissioners such a response to their demand for recognition as the representative of a foreign power that on January 2, a few days after they reached Washington, they went home in disgust. A few days later the cabinet was still further strengthened by the appointment as Secretary of the Interior of John A. Dix, who on January 29 sent the telegram ending in these words, " If any one attempts to haul down the American flag, shoot him on the spot."

On January 5, the senators from Georgia, Alabama, Louisiana, Arkansas, Texas, Mississippi, and Florida, held a meeting and sent out statements to the leading politicians and officials in their states that all must secede in time for a convention at Montgomery, if possible not later than February 15, certainly before the Federal inauguration, the object being to confront Lincoln on his accession with a confederacy in actual existence. In some states the resolution of secession was submitted to the people, and in some it was not; in part it was carried easily and in part by a close vote; but all except Arkansas of these seven states seceded, making with South Carolina the original group. They proceeded with such vigor and boldness that in the time preceding Lincoln's inauguration they took possession of every fort, arsenal, dockyard, mint, custom-house, and court-house in their territory, except three, the United States army holding Fort Sumter, Fort Pickens, and Key West. The Southerners thus took from the government in time of peace all the arms, ammunition, and supplies needed for

N

the first months of war. In the danger threatening the forts which still flew the American flag,
Lincoln wrote to Washburne, who had seen
General Scott: "Please present my respects to
the general, and tell him, confidentially, I shall
be obliged to him to be as well prepared as he
can to either hold or retake the forts, as the case
may require, at and after the inauguration." He
also, with some hesitation, consented to publish
a letter declaring the right of each state to control its own domestic institutions necessary to the
balance of powers on which the endurance of the
political fabric depended, on condition that six of
the twelve United States Senators from the seceding states should sign a request to the people of
their states to suspend all action for dismember-
ment of the Union, at least until some act in
violation of their rights was done by the incom-
ing administration. Out of this reluctant proposal of compromise nothing ever came.

On February 4, the delegates from the six
seceding states met at Montgomery, and on the
9th, Jefferson Davis was elected president. Steps
to organize an army and navy were taken immediately, and the leaders were liberal in statements that any Federal interference would mean
war. There was some talk about preventing the
official count of the electoral vote, but a prompt
stand, by General Scott, removed whatever prob-

ability of resistance there may have been, and Lincoln and Hamlin were officially declared elected.

On February 11, Lincoln left Springfield for Washington, after borrowing money to pay the expenses of his early months at the White House, which he repaid out of his salary for the first quarter. Before leaving, he visited his stepmother and the grave of his father, for which he ordered a stone. He took leave of his law partner with the request that the old sign be allowed to remain, as in four years they would go on practising as if nothing had happened. To the neighbors who gathered in the station at Springfield to see him off, he said:—

" My friends: no one, not in my situation, can appreciate my feeling of sadness at this parting. To this place, and the kindness of these people, I owe everything. Here I have lived a quarter of a century, and have passed from a young to an old man. Here my children have been born, and one is buried. I now leave, not knowing when or whether ever I may return, with a task before me greater than that which rested upon Washington. Without the assistance of that Divine Being who ever attended him, I cannot succeed. With that assistance, I cannot fail. Trusting in Him, who can go with me, and remain with you, and be everywhere for good, let us confidently hope that all will yet be well. To His care commending you, as I hope in your prayers you will commend me, I bid you an affectionate farewell."

The next two weeks he spent in visiting part of the towns on his route to which he had been invited. In the first address which he made, at Indianapolis, he characteristically reminded the people that the preservation of the Union was their business more than his. The same day, addressing the legislature, he said that, in the view of the secessionists, the Union was not a marriage, but a sort of free love arrangement; and he asked some brisk questions about state rights, especially about "that assumed primary right of a state to rule all which is less than itself and ruin all which is larger than itself." At Cincinnati the next day he said that he deemed it his duty to wait for the last moment for a development of the national difficulties before saying what his course would be. The little addresses are all solemn, — some of them kept from being commonplace by a pervading tone of the responsibility of the situation, — brief, usually without a touch of lightness. On the 14th he assured his hearers that during his administration the majority should control. He spoke of the crisis as artificial and needless, but such efforts at inspiring confidences seemed darkened by an overhanging gloom. To the Assembly of New Jersey he said: "The man does not live who is more devoted to peace than I am, none who would do more to preserve it, but it may be necessary to put the foot down firmly." In Independence Hall, Philadelphia, he said that the great principle or idea which had kept the Union together so long was "that which gave promise that in due time the weights should be lifted from the shoulders of all men, and that all should have an equal chance. . . . If this country cannot be saved without giving up that principle, I was about to say I would rather be assassinated on this spot than surrender it." Frequently he assured his hearers that his heart was right, and that the future must decide whether his head was equal to the task. The speeches seem to have been rather disappointing at the time, as the people longed for less cautious declarations.

Lincoln's trip was cut short by evidence of a plot to assassinate him in Baltimore. The evidence does not amount to proof, and was not taken by him at the time as conclusive; but he accepted the position of those friends who believed it was strong enough to warrant a secret and sudden trip to Washington and the abandonment of the rest of the intended stops. Lincoln and his advisers weighed the probability of public ridicule and made up their minds to brave that rather than run what still seems to have been a real risk. After a special train back to Philadelphia from Harrisburg and the detention of the

Baltimore sleeper had been arranged for, and the telegraph officials had agreed to make the transmission of information about his movements impossible, Lincoln left Harrisburg, escorted only by Ward H. Lamon, was taken in a carriage across Philadelphia from one station to another, supervised by Pinkerton, passed through Baltimore unrecognized, and reached Washington on the morning of February 23.

During the few days before the inauguration, he was largely occupied with the official routine of paying and receiving visits, and the most important things he did were taking the final steps about his cabinet and putting the finishing touches on his inaugural. When he began the preparation of this document in Springfield he told Herndon to bring him Henry Clay's famous speech of 1850, Jackson's proclamation against nullification, and Webster's reply to Hayne, which last he deemed the grandest piece of oratory in American literature. In a room over the store he composed most of his inaugural. From time to time he showed it to friends and made various changes, mainly in the direction of softness. The firm tone was originally his, the gentleness and occasional vagueness he introduced partly on advice. The day after his arrival in Washington a long letter from Seward, with many slight changes, suggested the excision of a declaration that the property of the government would be reclaimed and the insertion instead of something more ambiguous and forbearing. A similar change was suggested and made, substituting an intention to hold the forts in possession of the government for the determination to recapture those already seized by the Confederates. He labored to the end over this paper, with regard both to substance and to style, making all the changes in the direction of mildness, one which he suggested himself being a declaration of readiness to submit to the people the question of revising the Constitution. Before he reached Washington he gave in a comical spirit a description of this address, which he feared had been hopelessly mislaid: " Lamon, I guess I have lost my certificate of moral character, written by myself. Bob has lost my gripsack, containing my inaugural address. I want you to help me find it. I feel a good deal as the old member of the Methodist Church did when he lost his wife at the camp-meeting, and went up to an old elder of the church and asked him if he could tell him whereabouts in hell his wife was. In fact I am in a worse fix than my Methodist friend, for if it were nothing but a wife that was missing mine would be sure to pop up serenely." The inaugural also popped up, and it may be mentioned incidentally that practically all the clergy in Springfield voted against Lincoln.

The cabinet measures also taken in these few days in Washington were of course only the finishing touches to a series of negotiations which had begun before the nomination and had never ceased. Lincoln's idea from the beginning was to make his cabinet include the most prominent leaders in his own party, Republicans who had been Democrats as well as those who had been Whigs, and also leading citizens of the South. William H. Seward he had chosen as Secretary of State, although after deliberation yet almost as a matter of course, as his strongest rival for the presidency and a recognized leader of the Republicans. A conflict among the Illinois factions served Lincoln with an excuse for giving no cabinet position to his own state. Judge Davis says that Alexander H. Stephens would have been offered a cabinet office but for the fear that Georgia might secede. Guthrie of Kentucky, one of the leaders at the Charleston convention, was offered the Treasury Department, which he declined. Lincoln considered the names of several other men from the border states with pro-slavery antecedents, and he commissioned Thurlow Weed to offer a place to Gilmore of North Carolina, who declined because his state seemed likely to secede. His rivals for the presidency, Chase and Bates, the latter from the slave state of Missouri, were chosen Secretary of the Treasury and Attorney-

General, as part of the general policy of consolidating the strength of the party. Caleb B. Smith of Indiana was named Secretary of the Interior in pursuance of the Chicago bargain, which Lincoln decided to carry out after many misgivings, leading to such changes of attitude as he seldom indulged in. Cameron was the worst nightmare that confronted the President-elect during the whole interregnum. He and his friends went to Springfield to exact the pound of flesh. Pennsylvania politicians opposed to Cameron, as well as men of position all over the country, pleaded his total unfitness. Lincoln was so troubled that he first promised Cameron the position, then withdrew it, and finally granted it. Montgomery Blair, of Maryland, who with his brother Frank had led the Bates forces in Chicago, was made Postmaster-General, and Gideon Welles of Connecticut Secretary of the Navy. The slate finally stood:—

For Secretary of State, William H. Seward, of New York.

For Secretary of the Treasury, Salmon P. Chase, of Ohio.

For Secretary of War, Simon Cameron, of Pennsylvania.

For Secretary of the Navy, Gideon Welles, of Connecticut.

For Secretary of the Interior, Caleb B. Smith, of Indiana.

For Attorney-General, Edward Bates, of Missouri.

For Postmaster-General, Montgomery Blair, of Maryland.

There was considerable trouble up to the very day of inauguration, especially through Seward and his partisans, who objected to the eclectic nature of the cabinet. Lincoln did something to quiet their outcries when, commenting on rumors that Blair was to be dropped, he said: " No, if that slate is to be broken again it will be at the top." Seward withdrew his name March 2. Lincoln wrote to him inauguration day, saying to a friend that he " could not afford to let Seward take the first trick," and the Secretary of State withdrew his declination March 6 after a long talk with the President. A Republican described Lincoln's cabinet as " an assortment of rivals whom he had appointed out of courtesy (Seward, Chase, and Cameron), one stump speaker from Indiana (Caleb Smith), and two representatives of the Blair family," this last meaning that Frank Blair had procured the appointment of Bates.

When his presidential term began, Lincoln weighed about 180 pounds. He had few, if any gray hairs; marked rings under his hollow eyes; a sallow face, with deep lines, worn and full of care; ears which stood at right angles to his head ; a thick and hanging lower lip. He was slightly pigeon-toed. His dress was almost as careless, his tastes as simple, as ever. Besides his house and lot, his whole fortune, after years of successful law practice and politics, consisted of a little wild land in Iowa, entered for him under warrants received for his services in the Black Hawk War. His habits of distracted walks and long reveries continued. The general close opinion of him was that he was "at once miserable and kind." The first impression he made in Washington was partly of confidence and partly of distrust, but no one asserted that he was great. He had never held a ministerial or executive office, and he was generally deemed inexperienced. He himself felt now despondent over the magnitude of his task, now equal to it. He had no reverence for great men, no belief in their existence as a race apart, and he despised the biographies which painted them in the conventional way. He once refused to read a life of Burke on the ground that books about famous men could just as well be written in blank, names to be filled in as they were needed. Years before, when he first began to meet well-known statesmen in Illinois, he had remarked that they were much like ordinary men. Now in Washington he was about to face his advisers, his generals, his enemies, with the same level look of intelligence and suavity.

CHAPTER X

In spite of some fears the inauguration passed off without disturbance. In the presence of an enormous open-air crowd, Lincoln took the oath, administered by Chief Justice Taney, and delivered his first inaugural address from a platform on which sat James Buchanan and Stephen A. Douglas. One of the most picturesque minor incidents of the day grew out of the presence of the Little Giant. He who had done so much, in opposing Lincoln, to make him, had been among the first to come to his support as President, and now, when he saw his successful rival standing before a great audience of the people who had elected him, holding his new silk hat awkwardly and not quite knowing what to do with it, Senator Douglas quietly relieved him of the incumbrance.

Lincoln's practised voice carried the words of the inaugural to the multitude before him. That document, one of the most important in the history of the country, sounded a note of gentle firmness on the one great issue to which it was mostly confined, — Union against Secession. It was intended to breathe at once confidence to the

North and friendliness to the South. It succeeded, especially as it was read at leisure, in stiffening the courage of the loyal states; but soft words could no longer affect the trend toward secession, and what the Southern people saw was not that the President wished them well, but that he refused them their most important demand. "I hold," he said, "that, in contemplation of universal law and of the Constitution, the union of these states is perpetual." He declared that no state, upon its own mere motion, could lawfully get out of the Union, and that acts of violence against the United States were insurrectionary or revolutionary. One of his most definite statements was: "To the extent of my ability I shall take care, as the Constitution itself expressly enjoins upon me, that the laws of the Union be faithfully executed in all the states." Although he gave the greatest amount of time and emphasis to the question of Union, he touched upon slavery, summing it up in his favorite way: "One section of our country believes slavery is *right*, and ought to be extended, while the other believes it is *wrong*, and ought not to be extended. This is the only substantial dispute." To the Southerners, he said: "In *your* hands, my dissatisfied fellow-countrymen, and not in *mine*, is the momentous issue of civil war. The government will not assail *you*. You can have no conflict, without being yourselves the aggressors. *You* have no oath registered in Heaven to destroy the government, while I shall have the most solemn one to 'preserve, protect, and defend it.'" The famous end of this inaugural shows in its origin a quality which was one of Lincoln's strongest, an instinct for assimilating and impressing the thoughts of others. Mr. Seward made two suggestions for an ending, thinking that argument ought not, as in the President's first draft, to be the final word. His first suggestion was long and dull. His second was this: "I close. We are not, we must not be, aliens or enemies, but fellow-countrymen and brethren. Although passion has strained our bonds of affection too hardly, they must not, I am sure they will not, be broken. The mystic chords which, proceeding from so many battlefields and so many patriot graves, pass through all the hearts and all the hearths in this broad continent of ours will yet again harmonize in their ancient music when breathed upon by the guardian angel of the nation."

Lincoln took the central hint and wrote this: "I am loath to close. We are not enemies, but friends. We must not be enemies. Though passion may have strained, it must not break our bonds of affection. The mystic chords of memory, stretching from every battlefield and patriot grave, to every living heart and hearthstone, all over this broad land, will yet swell the chorus of the Union, when again touched, as surely they will be, by the better angels of our nature."

On the morning after inauguration, the new President received the news that Fort Sumter must be reënforced within a few weeks or abandoned. The military situation which he saw before him was discouraging. The South was thoroughly prepared and aggressive. The Northern army and navy were small and scattered. General Scott was old, and although thoroughly determined, did not inspire the greatest confidence. The day before the inauguration he proposed in a private letter to Seward to "let the wayward sisters go in peace." Added to this, the lack of unanimity in the North and in the government had to be reckoned with by the President. Republican leaders distrusted Lincoln, and gave him little support, although younger men were more actively favorable; and the Democratic Douglas, in spite of some charlatanism in the Senate, gave sincere help. The cabinet was hardly an aggregation to quiet the nerves of the President. Seward wrote to C. F. Adams, minister to England, on April 10: "Only an imperial and despotic government could subjugate thoroughly disaffected and insurrectionary members of the state. This Federal, republican country of ours is, of all forms of government, the very one which is the most unfitted for such a labor." Chase thought possible dissolution was better than a conflict. Welles was a rather watery character, Smith and Bates were old, Cameron and Blair were ordinary politicians. The Senate that met in executive session on the day of inauguration counted twenty-nine Republicans, some disaffected, thirty-two Democrats, one American hostile to the administration, with five vacancies from Southern states that were not filled during the war. It was only the later retirement of senators from seceding states that gave the administration a majority in both branches of Congress. More important, however, than soldiers or politicians, were the mass of the people, and what they felt it was Lincoln's intention to learn by experience. "Step by step he walked before them, slow with their slowness, quickening his march by theirs." He felt that he could master all the rest, however big in name, if he could only keep the resources of the Northern people just behind him. Wendell Phillips declared in New Bedford, on April 9, that the Southern states had a right to secede, and added, "You cannot go through Massachusetts and recruit men to bombard Charleston or New Orleans." If the leading abolition orator was right, then the new President was going to be in a hopeless position when the tocsin sounded; but it was the President and not the orator who understood the people.

General Scott after full deliberation advocated the evacuation of Fort Sumter. Lincoln refused to accept his decision, for reasons which he himself stated in his message to Congress on the following 4th of July: " It was believed, however, that to so abandon that position, under the circumstances, would be utterly ruinous; that the necessity under which it was to be done would not be fully understood; that by many it would be construed as a part of a voluntary policy; that at home it would discourage the friends of the Union, embolden its adversaries, and go far to insure to the latter a recognition abroad; that in fact it would be our national destruction consummated. This could not be allowed." When Lincoln consulted his cabinet, March 15, he found only Blair really in favor of provisioning Fort Sumter, all the rest being squarely against it, except Chase, who said he would oppose it if it meant war, but he thought it need not mean that. By March 28, Scott had advised the evacuation of Fort Pickens as well as of Fort Sumter. Soon after this Seward expressed to Judge Campbell, who was helping the Confederate commissioners in Washington in their persistent attempt to win recognition and concession, the belief that

Sumter would be abandoned within five days. By this time, however, Seward and Smith stood alone in favor of evacuation, the rest of the cabinet having moved toward what was the President's position also, although he kept quiet about it in order to make preparations as advantageously as possible. On March 29, after a cabinet meeting, he ordered the Secretary of War and the Secretary of the Navy to be ready for an expedition by sea not later than April 6. An order for the reënforcement of Fort Pickens had been sent two weeks before.

On April 1, Lincoln received from his Secretary of State a paper which perhaps gives better than any other document on record an idea of the sea of troubles which met the untried President. Here was his principal adviser not only suggesting the virtual abdication of the President and the dictatorship of the Secretary of State, but coupling this arrogant superiority with some of the most insane propositions which emerged from any brain during the war. In this insinuation that he should be the head of affairs, Seward but acted on the ideas which he shared with such men as Adams, Scott, and the other officials who felt that the raw Westerner must, by a process of natural selection, step aside for the experienced party leader and polished statesman. This marvellous document was as follows : —

SOME THOUGHTS FOR THE PRESIDENT'S CONSIDERATION.

April 1, 1861.

"FIRST. We are at the end of a month's administration, and yet without a policy, either domestic or foreign.

"SECOND. This, however, is not culpable, and it has even been unavoidable. The presence of the Senate, with the need to meet applications for patronage, have prevented attention to other and more grave matters.

"THIRD. But further delay to adopt and prosecute our policy for both domestic and foreign affairs would not only bring scandal on the administration, but danger upon the country.

"FOURTH. To do this we must dismiss the applicant for office. But how? I suggest that we make a local appointment forthwith leaving foreign or general ones for ulterior and occasional action.

"FIFTH. The policy at home. I am aware that my views are singular, and perhaps not sufficiently explained. My system is built upon this *idea* as a ruling one, namely, that we must

"CHANGE THE QUESTION BEFORE THE PUBLIC FROM ONE UPON SLAVERY, OR ABOUT SLAVERY, FOR A QUESTION UPON UNION OR DISUNION.

"In other words, from what would be regarded as a party question, to one of *Patriotism or Union*.

"The occupation or evacuation of Fort Sumter, although not in fact a slavery or a party question, is so *regarded*. Witness the temper manifested by the Republicans in the free states and even by the Union men in the South.

" I would, therefore, terminate it as a safe means for changing the issue. I deem it fortunate that the last administration created the necessity.

" For the rest I would simultaneously defend and re-enforce all the forts in the Gulf, and have the navy recalled from foreign stations to be prepared for a blockade. Put the island of Key West under martial law. This will raise distinctly the question of *Union or Disunion*. I would maintain every fort and possession in the South.

FOR FOREIGN NATIONS.

" I would demand explanations from Spain and France, categorically, at once.

" I would seek explanations from Great Britain and Russia, and send agents into Canada, Mexico, and Central America, to rouse a vigorous continental spirit of independence on this continent against European intervention.

" And, if satisfactory explanations are not received from Spain and France,

" Would convene Congress and declare war against them.

" But whatever policy we adopt, there must be an energetic prosecution of it.

" For this purpose it must be somebody's business to pursue and direct it incessantly.

" Either the President must do it himself, and be all the while active in it, or

" Devolve it on some member of his cabinet. Once adopted, debates on it must end, and all agree and abide.

"It is not in my especial province.

"But I neither seek to evade or assume responsibility."

With a combination of meekness and firmness of which history probably does not offer another equally striking example in any powerful ruler, Lincoln replied on the same day in one of his masterpieces. To Seward's first proposition he said: —

"At the beginning of that month, in the inaugural, I said, 'The power confided to me will be used to hold, occupy, and possess the property and places belonging to the government, and to collect the duties and imposts!' This had your distinct approval at the time; and, taken in connection with the order I immediately gave General Scott, directing him to employ every means in his power to strengthen and hold the forts, comprises the exact domestic policy you now urge, with the single exception that it does not propose to abandon Fort Sumter.

"Again, I do not perceive how the reënforcement of Fort Sumter would be done on a slavery or party issue, while that of Fort Pickens would be on a more national and patriotic one.

"The news received yesterday in regard to St. Domingo certainly brings a new item within the range of our foreign policy; but up to that time we have been preparing circulars and instructions to ministers and the like, all in perfect harmony, without even a suggestion that we had no foreign policy."

To the later and more insulting propositions, Lincoln replied merely, after repeating Seward's language : —

"I remark that if this must be done, I must do it. When a general line of policy is adopted, I apprehend there is no danger of its being changed without good reason or continuing to be a subject of unnecessary debate; still, upon points arising in its progress I wish, and suppose I am entitled to have, the advice of all the cabinet."

To Seward's credit, it should be admitted that when a few such experiences as this taught him who was master, he nobly obeyed. When Henry Clay said, "Mr. Seward is a man of no convictions," he certainly wronged an erratic but generous and enthusiastic nature. The very ardor with which Seward lent himself to the work in hand, guided by his superior, led to the later attempt to assassinate him also. He and his friends had been disappointed that Lincoln would not give them a Seward cabinet; they were disappointed that he would not delegate his responsibilities; but, while some of them sulked on, the Secretary of State turned in for work.

A cartoon published on March 23 by *Vanity Fair*, called "Professor Lincoln in his Great Feat of Balancing," represents a feeling that was growing. Although there was more stolidity than the retrospective observer might expect, there was also grumbling. The Confederates thought Jefferson Davis ought to take sharper measures, and public opinion was now less divided in the South than it was in the North, where any estimate of the respective numbers really favoring aggressive action, concession, and balancing was impossible. The pressure of public sentiment at the South, however, combined with action by the administration, was soon to bring on the crisis before which both sides showed some hesitation. The expedition for the relief of Fort Pickens sailed April 6, that for Sumter April 9, both having been prepared with the greatest possible secrecy. The Southern spies in Washington were unable to tell the Confederates the destination of the expedition. The President's first bad mistake was made in these preparations. The frigate *Powhatan* had been assigned by Secretary Welles for the Sumter expedition. On the advice of Seward, Lincoln signed a paper ordering it to Fort Pickens, which was done so secretly that when the conflict was discovered at the last moment it was too late. When the President's attention was called to the fact that he had ordered away from the Sumter expedition a ship vitally essential to it, he said he had confused the names of *Pocahontas* and *Pow-*

hatan. Seward had intended just what had been done, and he now tried to persuade Lincoln that the *Powhatan* ought to go to Fort Pickens. The President, however, definitely ordered Seward to telegraph an order giving up the *Powhatan* to the Sumter expedition. This despatch was received at the Brooklyn navy-yard a few hours after the ship had sailed, and was sent off in a tug which overtook the *Powhatan*. The commander, however, seeing it signed only "Seward" sailed on under the former order signed by Lincoln.

On April 11 the Confederate General Beauregard, having been notified by President Lincoln that provisions were to be put if possible into Fort Sumter, sent to the commander, Major Anderson, a request for surrender. Anderson refused, and said incidentally that his provisions would last but a few days. The next day the Confederates opened fire, and after a slight defence by the small Federal force, the fort became so injured that it had to be surrendered by the unprovisioned garrison on the evening of the 13th. The relief expedition, meantime, was lying outside the bar, waiting for the *Powhatan*, as nothing was known about the change of plan. Thus the strongest fortress on the South Atlantic coast was lost to the Union through one of the few blunders

universally admitted as having been made by
the President. Of course Seward and others
shared the error, and it is remarkable enough
that, furnished so liberally with bad advice,
Lincoln's course should have been so clear
that this is one of few examples of undoubted
errors.

The capture of Sumter began actual war, and
filled both divisions of the country with excitement and determination. North and South
alike were consolidated by actual combat, the
minority growing smaller and quieter, so that
only the voice of the secessionists was heard
in their states and the voice of loyalty throughout most of the North. Most of the hesitating
Southern states seceded rapidly, and the blaze
of fury that passed over the North made it
seem a different country from the one in which
but a few weeks before even New York had
seemed in danger of secession. Lincoln knew
his people. Had he not been content to wait
for Southern aggression, at whatever military
cost, the people would not have stood so
stanchly. He had to deal with a peaceable
populace, of industrial habits, while the Southerners had the warlike spirit of a sporting
aristocracy. The regular Federal army was
much less than 20,000 men badly scattered,
and there was not enough of a navy to make

one large squadron.   The revenues were not
yielding over $30,000,000 a year, and Secretary
Chase's hesitation about risking war by reliev-
ing Sumter was largely caused by the poor
credit of the government, which had been
forced to pay one per cent a month before
the end of Buchanan's administration.   The resources of the North, on the other hand, were
vastly beyond those of the South, and Lincoln, with the eye of a statesman, never lost
sight of the fact that what he needed was the
tactful patience to keep his course so conservative that any deep division would be avoided.
The military problem was second to the political one.   It was by a slowness which required
fortitude in the face of criticism that he had
held the Northern Democrats and forced Douglas to drop hostile comment on the administration for enthusiastic defence of his country.
"They," Lincoln had already said, referring to
the Democrats, "are just where we Whigs were
in 1848 about the Mexican War. We had
to take the Locofoco preamble when Taylor
wanted help, or else vote against helping Taylor, and the Democrats must vote to hold the
Union now, without bothering whether we or
the Southern men got things where they are.
And we must make it easy for them to do this,
for we cannot live through the case without

them." He then told about the Illinois man who was chased by a fierce bull in a pasture, and, dodging around a tree, caught the tail of the pursuing beast. After pawing the earth for a time the bull broke away on a run, blowing at every jump, while the man clinging to its tail cried on, " Darn you, who commenced this fuss ? " This knowledge of plain, essential human nature had led the President to wait every possible minute for the other side to begin the fuss. In the same connection in which he had illustrated by the bull story the difficulties of satisfying all the critics in the North, he had shown by another tale his belief in the impossibility of any real alliance between secession and Northern Democrats. Some pious member of the church wished to build a bridge over a dangerous river, but found great difficulty in securing an engineer competent for the work. Brother Jones suggested one Myers who announced that he could build one to hell, if necessary. Jones, to quiet his friends, and at the same time support his engineer, remarked that he believed Myers so honest a man and so able an architect that he could accomplish this task if he said he could; but that he himself felt bound to express some doubt about the abutment on the infernal side. Lincoln explained that, in hearing any talk of accommodation between the two branches of the Democracy, he had always had his doubts about the abutment on the other side.

Even after Sumter was fired upon his step was as cautious as it was firm. To a committee from the Virginia convention, which waited upon him April 11, while the news of the firing on the fort was coming in, he explained again that invasion was no part of his policy at present. "My policy is to have no policy," he often said. He was ruling a Democracy, and he could learn nothing from the history of other lands. But with patience went decision, and to this same delegation he said: "If, as now appears to be true, in pursuit of a purpose to drive the United States authority from these places, an unprovoked assault has been made upon Fort Sumter, I shall hold myself at liberty to repossess, if I can, like places which had been seized before the government was devolved upon me. And in every event I shall, to the extent of my ability, repel force by force. In case it proves true that Fort Sumter has been assaulted, as is reported, I shall perhaps cause the United States mails to be withdrawn from all the states which claim to have seceded, believing that the commencement of actual war against the government justifies and possibly demands this."

When the next morning brought the news

of Sumter's fall, he made his first test of Northern feeling by a proclamation, drawn by him that day and published Monday, in the papers that gave the first full story of the fight, calling for 75,000 militia to serve three months. Nobody had any idea how many troops would be needed to put down the rebellion, but all through the war Lincoln's insistent desire to accept every regiment that offered showed not only his willingness to conciliate the particular officers and men, as part of public sentiment, but his feeling of the size of his task. To an adviser, who, in discussing this first call for troops, spoke slightingly of the South, the President replied: "We must not forget that the people of the seceded states, like those of the loyal ones, are American citizens, with essentially the same characteristics and powers. Exceptional advantages on one side are counterbalanced by exceptional advantages on the other. We must make up our minds that, man for man, the soldier from the South will be a match for the soldier from the North and vice versa."

To all who had doubted the fighting spirit of the North, the response to Lincoln's proclamation was a surprise. The free states answered with enthusiasm. The governors found themselves in a position where it was difficult not to give more troops than were wanted. Camps

sprung up everywhere. "Ten days ago," came
the reply from Iowa, "we had two parties in this
state; to-day we have but one, and that one is
for the Constitution and Union unconditionally."
Ohio offered as many militia as the government
would accept, Indiana replied that she was ready
with more than twice her quota. One day after
the Governor's call forty companies had been
tendered in Illinois. A regiment marched fully
equipped from Massachusetts within forty-eight
hours. Michigan offered 50,000 men if they were
needed. Factories began to work on ammunition at once; money, credit, and the use of railroads were offered. The War Department, with
all its wish to keep down the number of troops,
was obliged to accept nearly 16,000 more than
the President had required.

The South prepared for the battle with no
less decision. The Secretary of War asked for
32,000 more troops. Virginia seceded on the
17th and on the same day Jefferson Davis issued a proclamation inviting privateers to prey
on United States commerce. To this last move
President Lincoln replied two days later with a
blockade of the Southern ports and a declaration
that privateers would be treated as pirates. The
governors of Kentucky, North Carolina, Arkansas, Tennessee, and Missouri sent sharp refusals
to the call for troops. All the border states in-

cluding Maryland, which held the national capital, showed a division of feeling which proved them one of the most important stakes to play for in the opening moves of the game. Delaware alone of the slave states sent an acceptance to the President's call, and it was in guarded language. Some of the best officers in the army and navy were deserting, and doing it in a secret way that made the government hardly know whom it could trust. The command of the Virginia troops was offered to General Scott, who replied: " I have served my country under the flag of the Union for more than fifty years, and as long as God permits me to live, I will defend that flag with my sword, even if my own native state assails it." The man, however, whom General Scott had selected as the ablest officer in the Northern army to take command of the forces in the field, had helped Virginia to rebellion by saying, even while he was in the Federal army, that he would follow her right or wrong; and April 23, three days after his resignation, Robert E. Lee was in command of her troops. Nearly one-third of the commissioned officers resigned. In the navy treachery destroyed or delivered to the South several of the most efficient vessels, among them the famous *Merrimac*. Singularly enough the common soldiers and sailors did not follow their officers. Over a fifth of the muskets and over a fourth of the rifles in the country had been sent to the South, which had also been buying in Europe while the North lay waiting.

While the attitude of the North on the whole was encouraging, the position of Washington, in its Southern location, was disquieting. On April 18 a rumor reached the city, which had not over 2500 armed troops, that a large Confederate force was on the way to attack it, and the immediate capture of the capital was a constant Southern boast. The South was as clamorous for aggressive action as the North, and it is probable that only Lee's advice now kept the Virginia troops from marching against Washington. There was but one railroad running north from the city, and within a day or two Maryland authorities and mobs had destroyed many bridges, telegraph wires, and rails. The regiments on their way to the defence of the capital from Massachusetts, Pennsylvania, New York, and Rhode Island had not arrived. The Sixth Massachusetts, attacked by a mob in Baltimore on the 19th, reached Washington demoralized, bearing the wounded, the dead having been left behind. The next day a delegation of Baltimore men came to the President at the White House to ask that no more troops be marched through their city. On the advice of General Scott, Lincoln made this concession, adding, what turned out to be true, that they would come back the next day demanding that no troops march around the city. When committees did come with this new demand, that soldiers should not march across Maryland against her sister states, Lincoln replied: "We must have troops; and as they can neither crawl under Maryland nor fly over it, they must come across it." To one committee, whose spokesman was a clergyman, he said: "The rebels attack Fort Sumter, and your citizens attack troops sent to the defence of the government, and the lives and property in Washington, and yet you would have me break my oath and surrender the government without a blow. There is no Washington in that — no Jackson in that — there is no manhood or honor in that. I have no desire to invade the South; but I must have troops to defend this capital. Geographically it lies surrounded by the soil of Maryland; and mathematically the necessity exists that they should come over her territory. Our men are not moles, and can't dig under the earth; they are not birds, and can't fly through the air. There is no way but to march across, and that they must do. But in doing this, there is no need of collision. Keep your rowdies in Baltimore, and there will be no bloodshed. Go home and tell your people that if they will not attack us, we will not attack them;

P.

but if they do attack us, we will return it, and that severely."

On the 21st the telegraph to the North was stopped entirely and the news from the South was all about expeditions against the capital. Many women and children had been sent out of the city. The President himself began to show signs of intense nervousness. As the troops failed to arrive he said one day to some Massachusetts soldiers, "I begin to believe that there is no North. The Seventh Regiment is a myth. Rhode Island is another." At another time, believing himself alone, pacing the floor and straining his eyes in the direction of the expected aid, he was heard to cry, "Why don't they come! Why don't they come!" On the 25th the Seventh New York finally reached the alarmed city and was rapturously welcomed.

One little incident of the troubles in Washington during these early days throws light on the President's method of dealing with men and growing more popular the more widely he was known. An officer who had broken up a riot in the capital woke the President at two in the morning to consult him about it. Lincoln assured him that as he had merely done his duty he had nothing to fear. The intrusive officer replied that he was aware of that fact but just wanted to talk with him about the matter. The President told him to go to bed and sleep, and added: "Let me give you this piece of advice. Hereafter when you have occasion to strike a man, don't hit him with your fist. Strike him with a club, a crowbar, or with something that won't kill him." In such flattering humor as this lay part of Lincoln's uncommon skill as a politician.

Not only did Washington feel more at ease as the troops began to pour in, but her immediate surroundings became quieter. Both the legislature and the populace in Maryland began to subside. General Benjamin F. Butler, with a few men, without orders, daringly and suddenly took possession of Baltimore, and held it, probably without losing sleep over the reprimand he received from General Scott. Lincoln gave Scott power to suspend the writ of habeas corpus whenever it was necessary, and when Chief Justice Taney, of Dred Scott fame, said the act was illegal, the President held his ground, and the verdict of history has been in his favor.

How Lincoln felt about the general situation at this time, in its larger aspects, is well expressed in one of his remarks recorded in Mr. Hay's diary: "For my own part, I consider the first necessity that is upon us, is of proving that popular government is not an absurdity. We must settle this question now, — whether in a free government the minority have the right to break it up whenever they choose. If we fail, it will go far to prove the incapability of the people to govern themselves. There may be one consideration used in stay of such final judgment, but that is not for us to use in advance. That is, that there exists in our case an instance of a vast and far-reaching disturbing element which the history of no other free nation will probably ever present. That, however, is not for us to say at present. Taking the government as we found it, we will see if the majority can preserve it." Thus, his central ideas remained always before him. Two years before he had said to Herndon that the advocates of state sovereignty reminded him of the fellow who contended that the proper place for the big kettle was inside the little one. For the edification of the same friend he filled a sieve with gravel and shook it until only the biggest pebbles were left, to point the moral that upheavals bring the best men to the front. He was now well launched on a commotion big enough to test everybody. Sometimes his heart seemed to quail, and he even said he wished he was back in Springfield, but more often his sad face was calm and resolute, as if he felt able to decide each question as fate put it before him.

Although military matters held the foreground, the President's activity was of many kinds. In response to mere requests for autographs he

signed his name twenty or thirty times a day.
His correspondence is studded with notes to the
cabinet officers asking for places with which he
wished to conciliate various politicians. In the
campaign of 1860 he had said to a friend: " They
won't give up the offices. Were it believed that
vacant places could be had at the North Pole,
the road there would be lined with dead Vir-
ginians." To another friend he said, referring to
Daniel Webster: " I was greatly pleased with a
speech which I heard him deliver in which he
said, ' Politicians are not sunflowers; they don't
. . . turn to their God when he sets the same
look which they turned when he rose." When
he stood on the verge of war and his office was
besieged with office-seekers, he wished he could
get time to attend to the Southern question. " I
am like a man so busy in letting rooms at one
end of his house that he cannot stop to put out
the fire that is burning in the other." He is
quoted as going even so far as to exclaim: " If
our American Society and the United States
government are demoralized and overthrown, it
will come from the voracious desire for office,
this wriggle to live without toil, work, and labor,
from which I am not free myself."

However, although he doubtless had moods in
which he bitterly resented the politicians, he had
said, more than once, " I must run the machine

as I find it," and he saw that war in the United States was inevitably in large part a game of politics. Seward said that in dealing with office-seekers, Lincoln showed a cunning that amounted to genius. In his relations to the soldiers his motives were more mixed, a very warm and soft heart acting in conjunction, doubtless, with a shrewd knowledge of the value of a reputation for sympathy with the common soldier. When a general once reproached him for pardoning everybody and destroying discipline, a complaint often made during the war, saying: "Why do you interfere? Congress has taken from you all the responsibility," Lincoln replied, "Yes, Congress has taken the responsibility and left the women to howl about me." He used to say it was a fortunate thing he wasn't born a woman. One paper which he sent to James B. Fry, who was in charge of the appointment branch of the adjutant general's office, had on it: " On this day Mrs. —— called upon me. She is the wife of Major ——, of the regular army. She wants her husband made a brigadier general. She is a saucy little woman, and I think she will torment me until I have to do it. A. L." And she did.

While his kindness and his sense of the value of personal popularity made him yielding, his readiness in repartee frequently got him out of difficult situations. Early in the war a temperance committee came to him to say that the reason we did not win was because our army drank so much whiskey as to bring the curse of the Lord upon it. Lincoln replied that this was rather unfair upon the part of the aforesaid curse, as the other side drank more and worse whiskey than ours. Sometimes, but very seldom, he was sharp-tongued with some obtrusive caller, but never in any way did he have the appearance or manner of superiority. He did what his petitioners wanted him to, or made them think he would if he could, or dexterously turned them off with a story, or convinced them of the impossibility by strong and racy logic.

To a young officer reprimanded for a quarrel with an associate he said, according to Nicolay and Hay: " The advice of a father to his son, ' Beware of entrance to a quarrel, but being in, bear it that the opposed may beware of thee!' is good, but not the best. Quarrel not at all. No man, resolved to make the most of himself, can spare time for personal contention. Still less can he afford to take the consequences, including the vitiation of his temper and the loss of self-control. Yield larger things to which you show no more than equal right; and yield lesser ones though clearly your own. Better give your path to a dog than be bitten by him in contesting for the right. Even killing the dog would not cure the bite."

To a delegation of ministers full of advice he said: "Gentlemen, suppose all the property you possess were in gold, and you had placed it in the hands of Blondin to carry across the Niagara River on a rope. With slow, cautious, steady step he walks the rope, bearing your all. Would you shake the cable, and keep shouting to him, 'Blondin! stand up a little straighter! Blondin! stoop a little more; go a little faster; lean more to the south! Now lean a little more to the north!'— would that be your behavior in such an emergency? No; you would hold your breath, every one of you, as well as your tongues. You would keep your hands off until he was safe on the other side. This government, gentlemen, is carrying an immense weight; untold treasures are in its hands. The persons managing the ship of state in this storm are doing the best they can. Don't worry them with needless warnings and complaints. Keep silence, be patient and we will get you safe across. Good day, gentlemen. I have other duties pressing upon me that must be attended to."

Adroitness in all the daily routine of life went hand in hand with shrewdness in what are usually deemed the higher problems of statesmanship. Under date of May 21, is a despatch to Charles Francis Adams, minister to England, written by Secretary Seward, and corrected by President Lincoln, as shown by the following facsimile:—

Charles Francis Adams, Esqre.
No. 10.

Department of State,
Washington, 20th May, 1862.

Sir.

This Government considers that our own relations in Europe have reached a crisis in which it is necessary for it to take a decided stand on which so not only its free, immediate measures, but its ultimate and enduring permanent policy can be determined and depend. At the same time, it neither means to menace Great Britain nor to wound the susceptibilities of this or any other

... nature that policy is ~~developed~~ ... ~~for you are ...~~ in this picture ... not to be read or shown to the British Secretary of State, nor any ... ~~...~~ ... indirectly ... made known to them ... I will see you ... you will take care, however, as you go along, ... saying, or doing anything that will be ~~...~~ incur ... or encounter with the views herein ... to the end that there may be in ~~the ...~~ the future no ... of ... by the British ... that ... ... policy and no less than into error

This Government

The paper itself is not to be seen or shown to the Prussian Secretary of State nor any of its portions to be prematurely unnecessarily or undesiredly made known. But its spirit will be your guide. You will keep back nothing, where the true occasion of its being said with proximity and effect, and you will all the while be careful. to say nothing that will be incorrect, or uncandid, with the views which it contains.

Department of State,
Washington May 21st 1861

Mr. Dallas in a brief dispatch
of May. 2d (No 333) tells us that Lord
John Russell recently requested an interview with him on account of the solici-
tude which His Lordship felt concerning
the effect of certain measures represented
as likely to be adopted by the President.
In that conversation the British Secretary
told Mr. Dallas that the three Representatives
of the Southern Confederacy were then in
London, that Lord John Russell had not
yet seen them, but that he was not unwilling to see them unofficially. He farther
informs Mr. Dallas that an understanding
exists between the British and French
Governments which would lead both to
take one and the same course as to recognition. His Lordship then referred to

C. F. Adams Esqr

the rumor of a meditated blockade by
us of Southern ports and a discontinuance
of them as ports, of entry   Mr Dallas
answered that he knew nothing on those
topics and therefore could say nothing.
He added that you were expected to
arrive in two weeks. Upon this statement
Lord John Russell acquiesced in the
expediency of waiting for the full
knowledge you were expected to bring.

Mr Dallas transmitted to us
some newspaper reports of Ministerial
explanations made in Parliament.

You will base no proceedings
on parliamentary debates farther than
to seek explanations when necessary
and communicate them to this Department. [We intend to have a clear
and simple account of whatever issue
may arise between us and Great
Britain]

The President regrets [is surprised and
grieved]

~~proved~~ that Mr. Dallas did not protest against the proposed un-official intercourse between the British Government and the missionaries of the insurgents, ~~as well perhaps as against the demand for explanation made by the British Government.~~ It is due however to Mr. Dallas to say that our instructions had been given only to you and not to him, and that his loyalty and fidelity too rare in these times ~~[crossed out]~~ are appreciated.

Intercourse of any kind with the so-called Commissioners is liable to be construed as a recognition of the authority which appointed them. Such intercourse would be none the less hurtful to us, for being called unofficial, and it might be even more injurious, because we should have no means of knowing what point might be resolved by it. Moreover, unofficial

unofficial intercourse is useless
and meaningless, if it is not expected
to ripen into official intercourse
and direct recognition. It is left
doubtful here whether the proposed
unofficial intercourse has yet
actually begun. Your ~~existing~~
present instructions are deemed
explicit enough, and it is hoped
that you have not misunderstood
them. You will in any event
desist from all intercourse
whatever, unofficial as well as
official with the British Government, so long as it shall continue
intercourse of either kind with
the domestic enemies of this country;
~~confining yourself simply to
a delivery of a copy of this
paper to the Secretary of State.~~
~~* After doing this you will~~
communicate with this
Department and receive
further directions.

Lord John Russell has informed us of an understanding between the British and French Governments that they will act together in regard to our affairs. This communication however loses something of its value from the circumstance that the communication was withheld until after the Knowledge of the fact had been acquired by us from other sources. We know also another fact that has not yet been officially communicated to us namely that other European States are apprized by France and England of their agreement and are expected to concur with or follow them in whatever measures they adopt on the subject of recognition. The United States have been impartial and just in all their conduct towards the several nations of Europe. They will not complain however of the combination now announced by the two leading powers, although they think they had a right to expect a more independent if not a more

friendly course from each of them.
You will take no notice of that or
any other alliance Whenever the
European governments shall see
fit to communicate directly with
us we shall be as heretofore
frank and explicit in our reply,
    As to the blockade, you will
say that by the laws of nature
and of nations this government has
a clear right to suppress insurrection.
An exclusion of commerce from national
ports which have been seized by the
insurgents, in the equitable form of
blockade, is a proper means to that
end You will not insist that our
blockade is not to be respected
if it be not maintained by a
competent force — but you will
add that it is now and it will
continue to be so maintained,
and therefore we expect it to
be respected by Great Britain.
You will add that we have

That question as not
now a practice or
or at least on
might or

225

already revoked the exequatur of a Russian
Consul who had enlisted in the Military
service of the insurgents and we shall dis
miss or demand the recall of every foreign
agent; Consular or Diplomatic who shall
either disobey the Federal laws or disown
the Federal authority

As to the recognition of the so called
Southern Confederacy it is not to be made
a subject of technical definition. It is of cou
~~and that~~ recognition to publish an acknowledgment
of the sovereignty and independence of
a new power. It is ~~quite simply~~ recognition to receive
its ambassadors Ministers agents or
commissioners officially, A concession
of belligerent rights is liable to be con
strued as a recognition of them. No one of
these proceedings will ~~be borne~~ by the
United States in this case

Hitherto recognition has been
moved only on the assumption that the so
called Confederate States are de facto a
self sustaining power. Now after long
forbearance, designed to soothe discontent and avert the need of civil war,

the land and naval forces of the
United States have been put
in motion to repress the insurrection
The true character of the pretended
new State is at once revealed
It is seen to be a Power existing
in pronunciamentos only. It has
never won a field. It has obtained
no forts that were not virtually
betrayed into its hands or seized
in breach of trust. It commands
not a single port on the coast
nor any highway out from its
pretended Capital by land. Under
these circumstances Great Britain
is called upon to intervene and give
it body and independence resting by nothing
our measures of suppression.
British recognition would be British intervention

vention to create within our own
territory a hostile State by overthrow
ing this Republic itself. When this
act of intervention is distinctly
performed, we from that hour
shall cease to be friends and (become once more, as we have
twice before been) forced to become enemies of Great Britain

As to the treatment of privateers in the insurgent service
you will say that this is a
question exclusively our own.
We treat them as pirates. They
are our own citizens or persons
employed by our citizens, prey-
ing on the commerce of our coun
try: If Great Britain shall
choose to recognise them as
lawful belligerents, and give
them shelter from our pursuit
and punishment the laws
of nations afford an ade-
quate and proper remedy.
(And we shall avail ourselves
of it — And now while you need not to
say this in advance be sure that you
say nothing inconsistent with it.)

Happily, however the Britannic Majesty's Government can avoid all these difficulties. It invited us in 1856 to accede to the declaration of the Congress of Paris, of which body Great Britain was herself a member, abolishing privateering everywhere in all cases and for ever. You always have our authority to propose to her our accession to that declaration. If she refuse to receive it it can only be because she is willing to become the patron of privateering when aimed at our devastation.

These positions are not elaborately defended now, because to vindicate them would imply a possibility of our waiving them.

We are not insensible of the grave importance of this occasion. We see how upon the result of the debate in which we are engaged, a war may

This paper is for your own guidance only, and not to be read, or shown to any one—

ensue, between the United States and
one, two, or even more European nations
War in any case is as exceptionable from
the habits as it is revolting ~~to~~ from the sentiments
of the American people. But if it come it
will be fully seen that it results from
the action of Great Britain, not our own,
that Great Britain will have decided ~~to~~
fraternize with our domestic enemy either
without waiting to hear from you our re-
monstrances and our ~~wrongs~~ warning or after ~~having~~
heard them. War in defence of national life
is not immoral, and war in defence of
independence is an inevitable part of the
discipline of nations.

The dispute will be between the
European and the American branches of the
British race. All who belong to that race
will especially deprecate it as they ought.
It may well be believed that men of ~~any~~ every
race and kindred will deplore it. A
war not unlike it ~~occurred~~ between the
same parties occurred at the close of the
last century Europe atoned by forty years
of suffering for the ~~same~~ error that Great Britain
committed in provoking that contest

If that nation will three now repeat the same
great error the social calamities consequences which will
follow may not be so long but they will be
more general. When they shall have ceased,
it will, we think, be seen, whatever may
have been the fortunes of other nations that
it will not be is not the United States that will
have come out of them with its precious constitution altered or its honestly obtained
dominion in any degree abridged. Great
Britain has but to wait a few months
and all her present inconveniences will
cease with all our own troubles. If she
take a different course she will calculate
for herself the ultimate as well as the
immediate consequences, and will consider
what position she will hold when she
shall have forever lost the sympathies and
the affections of the only nation on whose
sympathies and affections she has a natural
claim. In making that calculation she will
do well to remember that in the controversy she proposes
to open we shall be actuated by neither pride, nor
passion, nor cupidity, nor ambition; but we shall
stand simply on the principle of self preservation
and that our cause will involve the independence
of nations and the rights of human nature
        I am, Sir, respectfully your obedient servant
            W. H. S.

This despatch is chiefly famous for the changes made in it by President Lincoln. It conveyed the first full instructions sent to Adams after the outbreak of the rebellion. What is most noticeable in the changes are the added accuracy and caution made by the President. Every change is either to avoid asperity, strengthen a position, or give more exact expression to a principle. Instance may be seen in his change of "wrongful" to "hurtful," to describe any intercourse of the British government with the Confederate commissioners; the softening of "no one of these proceedings will be borne" by substituting "will pass unquestioned"; the omission of an open threat of war if Great Britain recognized the Confederacy. These and other similar alterations, made at a critical period, so early in the administration that the President was practically without diplomatic experience, have been steadily admired from that day to this as a proof of the natural diplomacy of shrewd common sense. By this time it had become tolerably clear who was to run the government. Seward, who so short time ago thought he ought to be dictator, had now learned enough to write, with the generosity that kept pace with his eccentric egotism, "there is but one vote in the cabinet and that is cast by the President." He soon after wrote to his wife, "The President is the best of us all."

Northern impatience made it impossible, politically, to give in to General Scott's desire for further preparation and methodical and broad lines of attack, and Lincoln decided that, to satisfy the country, an advance must be made, even if, as the General in Chief anticipated, any victory gained in this superficial way should prove indecisive. On the night of May 23, the heights from Arlington to Alexandria, where the President had been able to see, from the White House, the Confederate flag flying, were occupied by the Federal troops. Again, after this little advance, he allowed his generals as much time for getting the army into shape as the popular voice permitted. Before a real battle came Congress had met. Lincoln, on assuming the office, had put the call for the next meeting of Congress as late as July 4, so that the members might approach their work with a knowledge of what the spirit of the North really was, and also, as Blaine and others say, doubtless correctly, because the President wished every possible moment for the canvass of Kentucky. An observer, Dr. Furness, seeing how much stress Lincoln put on the border states, once remarked, " The President *would like* to have God on his side, but he *must* have Kentucky." The result showed him justified. Of the ten representatives chosen, nine were for the Union, an outcome which did much to influence

Virginia, Missouri, and Maryland. This favor able sign was needed. New states had seceded, so that the number was now eleven, and Congress itself sat in a fortified city fearing assault. The few skirmishes that had occurred meant nothing. The first pitched battle was soon to come. Meantime all was excitement and preparation. So distinctly were the lines now drawn that Andrew Johnson was the only Senator who appeared from the eleven seceding states.

The President's message spoke even more firmly than his inaugural, and showed such fixed intentions that Congress followed its requests almost without exception. He first narrated what had thus far been done, again showing how the South had forced the issue. "And this issue embraces more than the fate of these United States. It presents to the whole family of man the question whether a constitutional republic or democracy — a government of the people, by the same people — can or cannot retain its territorial integrity against its own domestic foes." He spoke with satisfaction of the response of the country to the call to arms, described the present sentiment in the border states, and sharply answered the doctrine of "armed neutrality" prevailing in those states, which included the intention to prevent either side from sending forces across them. "This," said the President, "would be disunion completed. Figuratively speaking, it would be the building of an impassable wall along the line of separation — and yet not quite an impassable one, for under the guise of neutrality it would tie the hands of Union men and freely pass supplies from among them to the insurrectionists, which it could not do as an open enemy. . . . It recognizes no fidelity to the Constitution, no obligation to maintain the Union; and while very many who have favored it are doubtless loyal citizens, it is, nevertheless, very injurious in effect." He explained shortly his reasons on *habeas corpus*, rejoiced in the more favorable attitude of foreign powers, and requested at least 400,000 men and $400,000,000. "A right result at this time will be worth more to the world than ten times the money."

He then went again fully into the principle of secession, adding nothing new, but putting his firmness unmistakably before the country. One incident connected with this passage is too characteristic of the President to omit. Speaking of the "sophism" of peaceable withdrawal from the Union, he said, "With rebellion thus sugar-coated they have been drugging the public mind of their section for more than thirty years." When, according to Lamon, the document was put in the hands of the public printer, who happened to be a friend of Lincoln, he hurried to the President and told him that "sugar-coated," which might do before a mass-meeting in Illinois, would not be good taste in a message to the Congress of the United States, a message which would become part of the public history of the country. Lincoln laughed and replied: " That term expresses precisely my idea, and I am not going to change it. 'Sugar-coated' must stand. The time will never come in this country when the people will not understand exactly what 'sugar-coated' means."

Toward the end of the message appeared this significant statement. " This is essentially a people's contest. On the side of the Union it is a struggle for maintaining in the world that form and substance of government whose leading object is to elevate the condition of men — to lift artificial weights from all shoulders. . . . I am most happy to believe that the plain people understand and appreciate this. It is worthy of note that while in this, the government's time of trial, large numbers of those in the army and navy who had been favored with the offices have resigned and proved false to the hand which had pampered them, not one common soldier or common sailor is known to have deserted his flag."

CHAPTER XI

FOR a time the President was allowed to go
through the ordinary course of his duties with no
great shock of either success or disaster, although
the cry " On to Richmond ! " ringing in his ears
taught him that a forward movement before long
was a political necessity.   He found Congress
giving him 500,000 men where he had asked
for 400,000 and $500,000,000 where he asked for
$400,000,000.   He felt the North strongly behind
him, but to keep it so, and to win the doubtful
states, it was imperative that he keep in touch
with the politicians and the people.   Much of his
time went to this, but he found hours to go out
and test new guns himself, to examine balloons for
war purposes, to listen to inventors of every sort.
He met every problem, every emergency, that
offered itself, and he remained the simple Westerner.   He was forced occasionally to change
his appearance slightly for official occasions, but
throughout his term the utterly popular nature of
his life and manners never lessened.   He spoke
of the White House as " this place."   He often

went to see his cabinet officials where another would have called them to him. Joke books stood piled up on his miscellaneous work-table with papers of State. While a long line of people were waiting to shake hands with him at a public reception, he stopped one man for several minutes while he extracted in whispers the point of a story which he imperfectly remembered. He read much in "Recollections of A. Ward, Showman," "Flush Time in Alabama," "Petroleum V. Nasby's Letters." While his head was full of military plans and political details, he talked about Shakespeare and recited the King's Speech in Hamlet, "Oh my offence is rank," from memory, or anon went about saying in a sing-song: —

> "Mortal man, with face of clay,
> Here to-morrow, gone to-day."

Life was responsibility, tragedy, burlesque, to him. He took the machine as he found it. He found great problems of State, foreign complications, questions of warlike strategy, politicians and their tricks, widows and their sorrows, old friends and Illinois jokes; and he mixed them all in his daily life, and responded to all, smelling of the Western prairie's soil, hard sense and no "frills."

At one time John Ganson of Buffalo, who was perfectly bald, called on Lincoln and said: "We are voting and acting in the dark in Congress, and I demand to know what is the present situation; what are the prospects and conditions of the several campaigns and armies. "Ganson," said the President, gazing at the top of his head, "how clean you shave."

A member of Congress from Ohio came into his presence inebriate, and, knowing Lincoln's fondness for a certain poem, sank into a chair and exclaimed: "Oh, why should (hic) er spirit of mortal be proud?"

"My dear sir," replied the President, "I see no reason whatever."

A New Jersey congressman introduced two friends to him, saying "they are among the weightiest men in southern New Jersey." When they had gone Lincoln said, "I wonder that end of the state didn't tip up when they got off of it."

Lord Lyons, the British minister, presented to him an autograph letter from Queen Victoria, announcing, in the usual royal manner, a marriage in her family, and added that whatever response the President would make he would immediately transmit to his royal mistress. Shaking the document at the bachelor minister, Lincoln exclaimed: "Go, thou, and do likewise."

The Austrian minister introduced a Count who wished a position in the Federal army. Although after such an introduction no further recommendation was called for, the nobleman rather elaborately described his title and his family. Tapping him on the shoulder the President remarked, " Never mind, you shall be treated with just as much consideration, for all that. I will see to it that your bearing a title shall not hurt you."

This was the man whom the South had been taught to believe half tiger and half ape. As he sat at his table biting his pen, or squatted onto the White House steps to finish a chat, or went with the strength of perfect lucidity to the heart of matters in his messages to Congress or his advice to generals, or bore insults from his inferiors and yet ruled then inexorably, his was a kind of greatness with which the world was for the first time to become familiar. Perhaps if anybody had pointed the way, it was Benjamin Franklin. John Stuart Mill said: " Abraham Lincoln was the kind of man Carlyle in his better days taught us to worship as a hero," and some one else has remarked that his was a character in which Plutarch would have rejoiced.

The next great event which we are to see him undergo was the first pitched battle of the war. On July 21, 1861, General McDowell, unwillingly, forced by the President, who voiced the imperious will of the North, with 35,000 men attacked the Confederate army at Bull Run. At first victory seemed certain for the Federal troops, but through the incompetency of General Patterson, who failed to do what he had been told to do, and the promptness of General Johnson in coming to the assistance of Beauregard, the Union army was surprised, defeated, and hurled back panic-stricken to the Potomac. The North was in despair, the South reached the very madness of confidence and joy. A little later the Southern Congress warned all persons not in sympathy with the Confederacy to get out within forty days.

For the President, who had forced General Scott and General McDowell into taking a step which was probably not a misfortune, since the beginning had sometime to be made, it now remained to take immediate action for recuperation. On the day after the battle he called to Washington General George B. McClellan, a young man of thirty-four, highly educated in military matters, who had been doing good work in small battles in West Virginia. It was the general opinion that he was the best officer in the North to get the army into shape. He arrived in Washington on July 26, and the next day he wrote privately: " I find myself in a new and strange position here: President, Cabinet, General Scott, and all deferring to me. By some strange operation of magic, I seem to have become the power of the land." Deference immediately went to his head, but he knew one part of his business thoroughly, and the raw troops rapidly became a

R

well-drilled army. General Meade, referring to this power of organization, once said, " Had there been no McClellan there could have been no Grant, for the army made no essential improvement under any of his successors."

The estimation in which this new young Napoleon was held, at the time he was so ably teaching the army the primary routine, is indicated with sufficient truth in one of the general's letters to his wife, dated August 9, 1861: " I receive letter after letter, have conversation after conversation, calling on me to save the nation, alluding to the presidency, dictatorship, etc. As I hope one day to be united with you forever in heaven, I have no such aspiration. I would cheerfully take the dictatorship and agree to lay down my life when the country is saved. I am not spoiled by my unexpected new position. I feel sure that God will give me strength and wisdom to preserve this great nation." It was about this wide-spread dictatorship talk that Lincoln told the story of the man in the thunder-shower who prayed for a little less noise and a little more light. He may possibly have remembered an earlier expression of his, praising some one for being able to compress more words into fewer ideas than anybody he had ever met. " The President is honest and means well," said the patronizing McClellan. "My relations with Mr. Lincoln," he says in another place, "were generally very pleasant, and I seldom had trouble with him when we could meet face to face. The difficulty always arose behind my back. I believe that he liked me personally, and certainly he was always much influenced by me when we were together." It was part of the President's nature to seem influenced by everybody, even when his will was fixed beyond recall, but there is no doubt that at this time he and the country both believed that McClellan was incomparably the best accessible reliance.

While McClellan was drilling the army Lincoln was steadily keeping up his fight for the political solidarity of the North and the conciliation of the border states. When Congress adjourned August 6, and Congressman McClernand, who had represented lower Illinois for many years, came to say good-by to the President, Lincoln handed him a brigadier general's commission and told him to "keep Egypt right side up." About this time General Fremont was making trouble in Missouri by his arbitrary and meddlesome behavior, among his exploits being a proclamation confiscating property and liberating slaves. Nothing shows more intimately what Lincoln's policy was at this time than a letter to his old friend Browning, dated September 22, 1861, and marked "private and confidential." Fremont was liked by the abolitionists, naturally, and a tap at them will easily be found in the President's letter. What he says about the impropriety of emancipation without legislation is also important, but the most significant of all is what bears on his persistent border policy. "He *must* have Kentucky." The principal part of the letter is:

"General Fremont's proclamation as to confiscation of property and the liberation of slaves is purely political and not within the range of military law or necessity. If a commanding general finds a necessity to seize the farm of a private owner for a pasture, an encampment, or a fortification, he has the right to do so, and to so hold it as long as the necessity lasts; and this is within military law, because within military necessity. But to say the farm shall no longer belong to the owner, or his heirs forever, and this as well when the farm is not needed for military purposes as when it is, is purely political, without the savor of military law about it. And the same is true of slaves. If the general needs them, he can seize them and use them; but when the need is past, it is not for him to fix their permanent future condition. That must be settled according to laws made by law-makers, and not by military proclamations. The proclamation in the point in question is simply 'dictatorship.' It assumes that the general may do anything he pleases — confiscate the lands and free the slaves of loyal people, as well as of disloyal ones. And going the whole figure, I have no doubt, would be more popular with some thoughtless people than that which has been done. But I cannot assume this reckless position, nor allow others to assume it on my responsibility.

"You speak of it as being the only means of saving the government. On the contrary, it is itself the surrender of the government. Can it be pretended that it is any longer the government of the United States — any government of the constitution and laws — wherein a general or a President may make permanent rules of property by proclamation? I do not say Congress might not with propriety pass a law on the point, just such as General Fremont proclaimed. I do not say I might not, as a member of Congress, vote for it. What I object to is, that I, as President, shall expressly or impliedly seize and exercise the permanent legislative functions of the government.

"So much as to principle. Now as to policy. No doubt the thing was popular in some quarters, and would have been more so if it had been a general declaration of emancipation. The Kentucky legislature would not budge till that proclamation was modified; and General Anderson telegraphed me that on the news of General Fremont having actually issued deeds of manumission, a whole company of our volunteers threw down their arms and disbanded. I was so assured as to think it probable that the very arms we had furnished Kentucky would be turned against us. I think to lose Kentucky is nearly the same as to lose the whole game. Kentucky gone, we cannot hold Missouri, nor, as I think, Maryland. These all against us, and the job on our hands is too large for us. We would as well consent to separation at once, including the surrender of this capital. On the contrary, if you will give up your restlessness for new positions, and back me manfully on the grounds upon which you and other kind friends gave me the election and have approved in my public documents, we shall go through triumphantly."

On the question of emancipation Secretary Cameron agreed with Fremont, and did what he could to help him, besides making other moves in the same direction; but the President was firm. The amount which he would permit in the present state of public opinion was limited by the Act of Congress, passed in August, freeing slaves employed by the Confederates in military service, which had already been done practically by General Butler's ingenious doctrine that they were "contraband of war."

The North was again growing impatient for a fight, but McClellan had more resisting power than the preceding generals, and he remained firm. A small battle with which he had nothing to do was fought, disastrously to the Federals, at Ball's Bluff on October 21, and cost the life of Colonel Baker, Senator from Oregon, and a friend of Lincoln. When the President left McClellan's office after learning this news he was seen to totter, as if about to fall, and the tears were streaming down his cheeks. Ten days later General

Scott resigned, and General McClellan was put at the head of the army. His confidence in his own opinion was unlimited; he felt that his troops were not ready; and he cared nothing for political considerations. Therefore, he began to exasperate the North beyond endurance, but the President, sensitive as he was to popular feeling, did not finally force his general into action until many months later.

Meanwhile he did quietly one of the most useful deeds of wisdom in his whole career. Just as he had checked Seward's pertness to England in the instructions to Adams he now reined in the fury of the North at British hostility, when the capture of Mason and Slidell brought the bitter feelings on both sides to the front. These two men were the Confederate envoys to England and France, respectively. They ran the blockade at Charleston, went to Havana, and sailed from that city November 7, by the British mail steamship *Trent*. Captain Wilkes, of the United States war sloop *San Jacinto*, on November 8, took the delegates off the *Trent*, after firing a shot across her bows and receiving a protest. Mason and Slidell were confined in Fort Warren, Boston Harbor, and the whole North broke out in enthusiastic approval of the deed, and Secretary Welles sent Wilkes the official approval of the Navy Department. Not so

Lincoln. He knew the difference between popular clamor and immovable popular will. He saw that the act was unwise and wrong, and he lost no time in saying so. On the day the news was received, he said in private: " I fear the traitors will prove to be white elephants. We must stick to American principles concerning the rights of neutrals. We fought Great Britain for insisting, by theory and practice, on the right to do precisely what Captain Wilkes has done. If Great Britain shall now protest against the act, and demand their release, we must give them up, apologize for the act as a violation of our doctrines, and thus forever bind her over to keep the peace in relation to neutrals, and so acknowledge that she has been wrong for sixty years."

England was not slow in showing her resentment. The British government ordered immediate preparations for war and demanded reparation within seven days. Lincoln wished arbitration, but the British demand was for immediate yielding. The Federal government yielded, and the President dropped a most astute phrase to help public opinion reconcile itself to the submission. " One war at a time," said he, thus allowing anybody who was hungry for an international fight to live in hope, although the President himself had never lost sight of the fact that British insolence did not change the truth that the United

States was in the wrong. He, supported by Seward, acted in defiance both of the mass of the people and of the leaders, and thus avoided giving the South the active aid of Great Britain and probably of France. John Stuart Mill wrote of this deed: " If reparation were made at all, of which few of us felt more than a hope, we thought that it would be made obviously as a concession to prudence, not to principle. We thought that there would have been truckling to the newspaper editors and supposed fire-eaters who were crying out for retaining the prisoners at all hazards. . . . We expected everything, in short, which would have been weak, and timid, and paltry. The only thing which no one seemed to expect is what has actually happened. Mr. Lincoln's government have done none of these things. Like honest men they have said in direct terms that our demand was right; that they yielded to it because it was just; that if they themselves had received the same treatment, they would have demanded the same reparation; and if what seemed to be the American side of the question was not the just side, they would be on the side of justice, happy as they were to find after their resolution had been taken, that it was also the side which America had formerly defended. Is there any one capable of a moral judgment or feeling, who will say that his opinion of America and American statesmen is not raised by such an act, done on such grounds?"

When Congress met in December Lincoln in his message said: "In considering the policy to be adopted for suppressing the insurrection, I have been anxious and careful that the inevitable conflict for the purpose shall not degenerate into a violent and remorseless revolutionary struggle. I have, therefore, in every case thought it proper to keep the integrity of the Union prominent as the primary object of the contest on our part; leaving all questions which are not of vital military importance to the more deliberate action of the legislature." The Secretary of War did not agree in this policy, however, and his differences with the President speedily made his place too hot for him. As Cameron was an ordinary machine politician, whom Lincoln had appointed purely to satisfy certain party leaders, he naturally in such a crisis caused no end of trouble by his inefficiency and lack of business integrity. His meddling with emancipation was the final step which led to a change of the greatest moment in the history of the rebellion and in the life of Lincoln, bringing into his cabinet one of the big figures of the war. In his first annual report Cameron, without the knowledge of the President, recommended the arming of the slaves and sent the report in printed form to the postmasters all over the country for delivery to the newspapers, before it had been delivered to Congress. Lincoln, as soon as he heard of this, ordered the copies recalled by telegraph, had the report revised, and a new edition printed. In its final form the recommendation stood thus:—

"It is as clearly a right of the government to arm slaves when it may become necessary, as it is to use gunpowder taken from the enemy. What to do with that species of property is a question that time and circumstance will solve, and need not be anticipated further than to repeat that they cannot be held by the government as slaves. It would be useless to keep them as prisoners of war; and self-preservation, the highest duty of a government or of individuals, demands that they should be disposed of or employed in the most effective manner that will tend most speedily to suppress the insurrection and restore the authority of the government. If it shall be found that the men who have been held by the rebels as slaves are capable of bearing arms and performing efficient military service, it is the right, and may become the duty, of the government to arm and equip them, and employ their services against the rebels under proper military regulation, discipline, and command.

"It is already a grave question what shall be done with those slaves who were abandoned by their owners on the advance of our troops into southern territory, as at Beaufort district in South Carolina. The number left within our control at that point is very considerable, and similar cases will probably occur. What shall be done with them? Can we afford to send them forward to their masters, to be by them armed against us or used in producing supplies to sustain the rebellion? Their labor may be useful to us; withheld from the enemy, it lessens his military resources, and withholding them has no tendency to induce the horrors of insurrection, even in the rebel communities. They constitute a military resource, and, being such, that they should not be turned over to the enemy is too plain to discuss. Why deprive him of supplies by a blockade, and voluntarily give him men to produce them?"

It has been said that Lincoln did not remove Cameron immediately for this act merely because he did not wish to antagonize the abolitionists, and knew that the financial pressure would soon force his removal, as the business men of the country were angry over the disgraceful way in which the War Department contracts were handled. In January, Lincoln took final action. Nicolay and Hay quote under date of January 11, the following: —

"My dear Sir: As you have more than once expressed a desire for a change of position, I can now gratify you consistently with my view of the public interest. I therefore propose nominating you to the Senate, next Monday, as minister to Russia.

"Very sincerely your friend,

"A. LINCOLN."

Colonel McClure says, probably accurately, that that is not the letter which Cameron received. According to the account of Colonel McClure, who on many points has given facts where the official biographers indulge in friendly embellishment, which in this case was certainly needless, Lincoln sent the letter by Chase, who delivered it in entire ignorance of its contents. McClure saw Cameron that night and found him agitated, weeping, and saying that the President's act meant his personal degradation. The letter, which McClure saw, he says he remembers almost literally. It was as follows: "I have this day nominated Hon. Edwin M. Stanton to be Secretary of War, and you to be minister to Russia." On the following day Lincoln was requested to withdraw this dismissal and allow Cameron to antedate a letter of resignation. The President was willing, a new correspondence was prepared, and a month later it was given to the public.

No member of the cabinet, according to the best evidence, knew of Lincoln's intention to appoint Stanton. The President acted alone, and it was one of the most striking things he

ever did. Years before Stanton had bitterly in-
sulted him. Some references to his appearance
Lincoln enjoyed. He used to tell himself about
the man who offered him a knife on a railway
train, saying it had been given him to keep
until he met some one uglier than himself. But
Stanton's scorching contempt had been a different matter and had stung him sharply. Since the
new administration the comments made on the
President by Stanton were frequent and violent.
He had spoken of " venality and corruption," by
which he meant a use of the patronage that he
never countenanced for a second after he accepted
the President's offer. One of his phrases was
the " painful imbecility of Lincoln." Above all
things he hated wire-pulling and office-seekers,
and he speedily modified the state of things in
which, according to a newspaper, " a boy threw a
stone at a dog on Pennsylvania Avenue and hit
three brigadier generals." For Lincoln to select
such a man, when he had such cause for personal
sensitiveness, but more particularly when his own
strength lay in submitting to all sorts of minor
abuses, and even committing them, in order to
gain in exchange some more fundamental good,
while Stanton rode roughshod, harsh, and un-
compromising straight for his goal, was certainly
a proof of brilliant magnanimity, instinct, and
wisdom.

McClellan had been satisfied with Cameron, because the Secretary had never interfered with him, but the general in his book makes the significant exception that he could not always dispose of arms and supplies as he thought the good of the service demanded. Several weeks before the removal McClellan heard that a committee of New York bankers had called on Chase to demand Cameron's retirement. It often happened, McClellan says, that when a shipment of unusually good arms arrived from Europe and he wished them for the Army of the Potomac, he found that Cameron had promised them to some political friend for future use in some remote state. Nevertheless, so fond of his own way was the general, that he did his best to keep this Secretary in office, fearing (what happened) that the next Minister of War might mix in military matters. It was casually that McClellan heard one day of the change, and immediately after Stanton called, to say that his nomination had been sent to the Senate. Lincoln called to mollify the general by telling him he knew Stanton was a friend of his, and he would have consulted him except that he feared it would be said that McClellan dragooned him into it. McClellan thus proceeds with his narrative.

"From the light that has since been thrown on Stanton's character, I am satisfied that from an early date he was in this treasonable conspiracy, and that his course in ingratiating himself with me, and pretending to be my friend before he was in office, was only a part of his long system of treachery. . . .

" I had never seen Mr. Stanton, and probably had not even heard of him, before reaching Washington in 1861. Not many weeks after arriving I was introduced to him as a safe adviser on legal points. From that moment he did his best to ingratiate himself with me, and professed the warmest friendship and devotion. I had no reason to suspect his sincerity, and therefore believed him to be what he professed. The most disagreeable thing about him was the extreme virulence with which he abused the President, the administration, and the Republican party. He carried this to such an extent that I was often shocked by it.

" He never spoke of the President in any other way than as the 'original gorilla,' and often said that Du Chaillu was a fool to wander all the way to Africa in search of what he could so easily have found at Springfield, Illinois. Nothing could be more bitter than his words and manner always were when speaking of the administration and the Republican party. He never gave them credit for honesty or patriotism, and very seldom for any ability.

" At some time during the autumn of 1861, Secretary Cameron made quite an abolition speech to some newly arrived regiment. Next day Stanton urged me to arrest him for inciting to insubordination. He often advocated the propriety of my seizing the government and taking affairs into my own hands."

Such was the character whom the President recognized as the best possible man to undertake the enormous duties of the War Department. " Lincoln was a supreme politician," says Charles A. Dana. " He understood politics because he understood human nature." Such a move as this shows that he understood its large and strange aspects as well as he did its details and weaknesses. He trusted nobody absolutely, and he saw what was useful in anybody. It is reported plausibly that he once said there was but one man in Congress of whose personal and political friendship he was entirely sure; and yet it would be impossible to call him distrustful. He merely had the trait of seeing some very important matters with an almost inhuman lack of prejudice.

As the war progressed, Lincoln spent much of his time in the War Department, reading his file of copies of the department telegrams. When he got to the end of the new ones and began on those he had seen before, he frequently remarked, " Well, I guess I have got down to the raisins,' which observation he explained by the story of a little girl who began by eating a lot of raisins, followed them with sweets, became sick, and at a certain point in her proceedings made the above remark.   Apparently one change was made in regard to this file of telegrams in the President's room at the War Department.   Albert E. H. Johnson, Stanton's confidential clerk, says in the *Washington Post*, July 14, 1891: "Mr. Stanton's theory was that everything concerned his own department.   It was he who was carrying on the war. It was he who would be held responsible for the secret machinations of the enemy in the rear as well as the unwarranted success of the enemy in front.   Hence he established a system of military censorship which has never, for vastness of scope or completeness of detail, been equalled in any war before or since, or in any other country under the sun.   The whole telegraphic system of the United States, with its infinite ramifications, centred in his office.   There, adjoining his own personal rooms sat General Eckert, David H. Bates, Albert B. Chandler, and Charles A. Tinker, — all of them young men of brilliant promise and now shining lights in the electrical world.   Every hour in the day and night, under all circumstances, in all seasons, there sat at their instruments sundry members of this little group.   The passage between their room and the Secretary's was unobstructed.   It was an interior communication — they did not have even to go through the corridor to reach him — and every despatch relating to the war or party politics that passed over the Western Union wires, north or south, they read. Cipher telegrams were considered especially suspicious, so every one of those was reported. The young men I have mentioned were masters of cipher-translation. Every message to or from the President or any member of his household passed under the eye of the Secretary. If one cabinet minister communicated with another over the wire by a secret code, Mr. Stanton had the message deciphered and read to him. If General McClellan telegraphed to his wife from the front, Mr. Stanton knew the contents of every despatch. Hence, as far as the conduct of the war was concerned, Mr. Stanton knew a thousand secrets where Lincoln knew one; for the Secretary's instructions were that telegrams indiscriminately should not be shown to the President."

At the time this change was made certain Republicans wished a general reconstruction of the cabinet. Welles was objected to and characterized in a cartoon as the Old Man of the Sea on the neck of Sinbad Lincoln. Seward had one set of enemies, and nearly every member of the cabinet another. The President, in answer to one of their demands for a general upheaval, told of the man who lay behind his woodpile to watch for a skunk. In place of the expected one, seven appeared. He fired, and killed one, but it " raised such a stink he decided to let the other six go."

As the winter wore on the dissatisfaction with McClellan increased. The President tried in vain to get him to move. He had all sorts of excuses. He saw always the Confederate advantages and his own disadvantages, never the reverse. R. E. Fenton tells how he and Schuyler Colfax called on the President, December 18, and Lincoln said that sky and earth seemed to beckon the army on, but that he supposed General McClellan knew his business and had his reasons for disregarding these hints of Providence. He advised Congress to take a recess for a few weeks, and then if McClellan had not moved, Providence would have stepped in and said it was impossible. That was true. Bad weather came and offered another excuse, for, as Lincoln said, McClellan believed the rain fell only on the just. The general also, like nearly everybody else, had a notion of finishing the war in one battle, for which he wished to get elaborately ready. That the real nature of the task was in no way understood so early is hinted by General Burnside's answer to a question by Colonel McClure, who asked why McClellan didn't move on Richmond. General Burnside said that it would not be a difficult task for McClellan's army to capture Manassas, march upon Richmond, and enter that capital, "but," he added, emphatically, as if naming a conclusive objection, "it would cost ten thousand men to do it." McClellan's fear, however, was not of the great loss, but of defeat. He had the most exaggerated idea of the strength of the armies opposed to him. Lincoln bitterly said that if the commander had no use for his army, he would like to "borrow" it. "If Mc-Clellan can't fish," he observed, "he ought to cut bait at a time like this." Finally, he positively ordered a forward movement not later than February 22, which was to be made on a plan approved by him and some of his generals, and opposed by McClellan, who had one of his own; and the result was that McClellan had his way. The general opinion is that Lincoln showed remarkable intelligence in grasping the art of war on short notice, and that in his differences with some of his generals he was usually right on purely strategic matters, and always right on political grounds. There are some who think he interfered in too much detail, but they are few. His differences with McClellan on the purely military advantages of opposite plans are of interest mainly to military men. Some conclusions they reach about the President's character are: that he put an immense value on the safety of his capital; that he was able to see very clearly all kinds of military arguments; and that he felt the one absolutely certain thing was that indefinite delay wearied the North and gained nothing. McClellan would not move, however, and on March 9 came the news that the Confederates had retired from their position on the Potomac, feeling unable to hold it. This proof of the needlessness of McClellan's caution enraged the North. Lincoln removed him from the command of the armies of the United States March 11, after the general had personally taken the field on hearing of the Confederate retreat. He retained command of the Army of the Potomac. For a time Stanton was practically the Commander-in-Chief, and a very bad one he is agreed to have been. Just as Mc-Clellan was about finally to meet the enemy, he heard that Lincoln, believing that Washington was unsafe, had retained for the defence of the capital a corps under McDowell which had been promised to McClellan for a particular purpose in the campaign. The excuse for the President's action is that McClellan had failed to carry out his agreement to leave Washington properly protected, and opinion is divided on the question of whether the President's act was justifiable. McClellan continued his tactics. May 3 the Confederates again withdrew just before he was ready to attack, and then the Northern army continued its advance. Lincoln's next interference was unfortunate. He forbade McDowell, who had finally been allowed to act under McClellan, to advance on the day he thought wisest, because, as one of McDowell's staff officers told Mr. Morse, it was Sunday, the day on which Bull Run had been fought, and he dreaded the omen.

Immediately after, he, perhaps influenced by Stanton's panic, withdrew McDowell from McClellan altogether, frightened by Stonewall Jackson's feint at the capital. McDowell protested in vain against being duped by Jackson's trick, but Lincoln was firm, and Jackson, having accomplished his purpose, withdrew. The one thing that seemed able to make the President lose his head was a possible attack on Washington. It is also true, as Mr. Morse says, that although almost infallible in judgment, given time, he was slow, and this decision, like the one with which he spoiled the Sumter expedition, had to be made in haste. With this excuse of needless weakening, McClellan remained almost quiet until the Confederates forced him south to the James River. Some battles were fought, but not enough to count for anything, and the North, although not the army, was as indignant at McClellan as he was at the administration. The general's language of reproach was such that Lincoln's keeping him in command so long and answering him only with mild reason is another proof of rare patience.

Meantime no political step of immediate effect followed for some time after the appointment of Stanton. In March the President sent to Congress a resolution that the United States ought to give pecuniary aid to any state which might adopt gradual abolishment of slavery. In his December message he had already suggested colonization of negroes freed under the act of August 6 in some "climate congenial to them." He had always feared the race problems which would result from emancipation, and it was part of his slight grasp of certain mathematical truths that he believed colonization possible. Slavery was abolished in the District of Columbia, the President signing the bill April 16. In March, Representative Arnold, of Illinois, introduced a bill prohibiting slavery wherever Congress could prohibit it, in the territories and on all national property, such as forts and vessels; the bill passed, and Lincoln signed it, as he did another bill going far in the direction of freeing slaves whose owners had rebelled. In many ways, however, he held back. In May he revoked an order of emancipation issued in the South by General Hunter, as he had already revoked that of General

Fremont in Missouri. About the arming of negroes he was also cautious, for while there was a strong feeling for it in certain parts of the North there was equal hostility to it nearer the border. In the late fall General Butler had informed Lincoln that he thought there was too much politics in the war, and asked permission to raise volunteers and select their officers. In ninety days he enlisted in New England 6000 men, appointed officers who were all Democrats, and then called on the President before sailing for Ship Island, toward the end of February. Lincoln asked him not to interfere with the slavery question, as Fremont had done, "and as your man Phelps has been doing on Ship Island."

"May I not arm the negroes?"

"Not yet. Not yet."

"Jackson did."

"But not to fight against their masters, but with them."

By spring, however, General Hunter had organized a negro regiment, and by July Lincoln was ready to sign a bill permitting the enlistment of slaves of rebel owners; although to lessen the rage in the border states he delayed action under it for some time. He worked hard with members of Congress from the border states, to try to win them to his pet doctrines of compensation and colonization, but with little or no result.

This was one of the gloomiest periods of the war, and the President hardly dared tell the country what was needed. On June 28 he wrote to Seward: —

"MY DEAR SIR: My view of the present condition of the war is about as follows: —

"The evacuation of Corinth and our delay by the flood in the Chickahominy have enabled the enemy to concentrate too much force in Richmond for McClellan to successfully attack. In fact there soon will be no substantial rebel force anywhere else. But if we send all the force from here to McClellan, the enemy will, before we can know of it, send a force from Richmond and take Washington. Or if a large part of the Western army be brought here to McClellan they will let us have Richmond, and retake Tennessee, Kentucky, Missouri, etc. What should be done is to hold what we have in the West, open the Mississippi, and take Chattanooga and East Tennessee without more. A reasonable force should in every event be kept about Washington for its protection. Then let the country give us a hundred thousand new troops in the shortest possible time, which, added to McClellan directly or indirectly, will take Richmond without endangering any other place which we now hold, and will substantially end the war. I expect to maintain this contest until successful, or till I die, or am conquered, or my term expires, or Congress or the country forsake me; and I would publicly appeal to the country for this new force were it not that I fear a general panic and stampede would follow, so hard it is to have a thing understood as it really is."

Under date of July 1, 300,000 volunteers were called for, and on July 3 Lincoln wrote a "confidential and private" letter to the governors, saying, among other things, "If I had 50,000 additional troops here now, I believe I could substantially close the war in two weeks."

CHAPTER XII

THIS summer of 1862 marks the beginning of the gloomiest year which the President had to meet. From a military and from a political point of view the outlook was almost equally dark, and in his family life Lincoln had been suffering from the loss of a little son, who died in the winter. More than one observer felt that his face grew suddenly older. Foreign affairs were still threatening. Volunteering had so nearly stopped that compulsory military service was a necessity. McClellan, after considerable fighting, had intrenched himself on the James River, where he seemed likely to accomplish nothing, complaining that he had but 50,000 men left with their colors, and that he needed 100,000 more. Lincoln went down himself to Harrison's Landing to see where the army of 160,000 men had gone. He concluded that sending troops to McClellan was about as effective as shovelling fleas across a barn, so few of them arrived. He also decided that the military efforts had been futile enough to make an experiment in emancipation wise as a war measure, and it is said that he drew up the first draft of a proclamation on his return. Still, he hated to relinquish his idea of compensated emancipation, and kept trying to get it started in spite of the lack of interest shown by the border states in his scheme. They were either hostile or indifferent. Bates and Blair, the border members of the cabinet, were friendly, but lukewarm and sceptical. Meantime, the abolitionists were howling constantly for universal emancipation. Shrewd politicians were warning the President that such a step would lose many Northern states to the Republican party. To a committee of clergymen who called to argue in favor of a proclamation Lincoln said it would be about as effective as the Pope's bull against the comet. He knew that it could mean nothing unless it was followed by Union victory, and he feared that it might lose support in the border states and cause desertions in the army. At the same time the omens were so dark that he was less settled against a step which so many thought meant salvation. This was one of the problems which led him half in earnest to suggest his resignation, a proposition which he made more than once in these hopeless days. To some senators who wished to muster slaves into the army he

said : "Gentlemen, I have put two hundred thou
sand muskets into the hands of loyal citizens of
Tennessee, Kentucky, and western North Carolina. They have said they could defend themselves, if they had guns. I have given them the
guns. Now, these men do not believe in mustering in the negro. If I do it, these two hundred thousand muskets will be turned against us.
We should lose more than we should gain."

At a meeting July 22, however, he told his
cabinet that he had called them merely for advice about a step on which he was already determined, which was emancipation by proclamation.
The principal suggestion came from Seward, who
said that if the step was taken after such reverses
and in so depressed a time, the public would look
upon it as the last measure of an exhausted government. "His idea," Lincoln is quoted as saying, "was that it would be considered our last
shriek, on the retreat." Lincoln, who had already had the same idea, at least at times, therefore put his draft aside, touching it up now and
then, adding or changing a line, and waiting.

His tone in these dismal weeks is firm and
gloomy. To a preacher who objected to the
presence of the Union army in Louisiana, Lincoln wrote : —

"I distrust the wisdom if not the sincerity of friends
who would hold my hands while my enemies stab me.

This appeal of professed friends has paralyzed me more in this struggle than any other one thing. You remember telling me, the day after the Baltimore mob in April, 1861, that it would crush all Union feeling in Maryland for me to attempt bringing troops over Maryland soil to Washington. I brought the troops notwithstanding, and yet there was Union feeling enough left to elect a legislature the next autumn, which in turn elected a very excellent Union United States senator! I am a patient man — always willing to forgive on the Christian terms of repentance, and also to give ample time for repentance. Still, I must save this government, if possible. What I cannot do, of course, I will not do; but it may as well be understood, once for all, that I shall not surrender this game leaving any available card unplayed."

In another letter to Louisiana he says: —

"He even thinks it injurious to the Union cause that they should be restrained in trade and passage without taking sides. They are to touch neither a sail nor a pump, but to be merely passengers — deadheads at that — to be carried snug and dry throughout the storm, and safely landed right side up. Nay, more: even a mutineer is to go untouched, lest these sacred passengers receive an accidental wound. Of course the rebellion will never be suppressed in Louisiana if the professed Union men there will neither help to do it nor permit the government to do it without their help."

He then suggests that the Union men in Louisiana restore the national authority, and adds: —

"If they will not do this — if they prefer to hazard all for the sake of destroying the government, it is for them to consider whether it is probable I will surrender the government to save them from losing all. If they decline what I suggest, you scarcely need to ask what I will do. What would you do in my position? Would you drop the war where it is? Or would you prosecute it in future with elder-stalk squirts charged with rose-water? Would you deal lighter blows rather than heavier ones? Would you give up the contest, leaving any available means unapplied? I am in no boastful mood. I shall not do more than I can, and I shall do all I can, to save the government, which is my sworn duty as well as my personal inclination. I shall do nothing in malice. What I deal with is too vast for malicious dealing."

To Augustus Belmont he wrote: —

"Broken eggs cannot be mended; but Louisiana has nothing to do now but to take her place in the Union as it was, barring the already broken eggs. The sooner she does so, the smaller will be the amount of that which will be past mending. This government cannot much longer play a game in which it stakes all, and its enemies stake nothing. Those enemies must understand that they cannot experiment for ten years trying to destroy the government, and if they fail still come back into the Union unhurt."

The next dramatic incident came August 20, when military reverses left the President seemingly further away than ever from issuing the Emancipation Proclamation. Horace Greeley printed a signed editorial in his paper, with the modest title of " The Prayer of 20,000,000," giving harsh expressions to the abolitionist point of view. Lincoln was probably glad of the opportunity to state his views, which he did in an answer that undoubtedly strengthened him with the country. He did not confide to Mr. Greeley that the document was already drawn. He simply gave the strongest possible expression to his policy. The central passage is:

" I would save the Union. I would save it the shortest way under the Constitution. The sooner the national authority can be restored the nearer the Union will be the Union as it was. If there be those who would not save the Union unless they could at the same time save slavery, I do not agree with them. If there be those who would not save the Union unless they could at the same time destroy slavery, I do not agree with them. My paramount object in this struggle is to save the Union, and is not either to save or to destroy slavery. If I could save the Union without freeing any slaves, I would do it; and if I could save it by freeing all the slaves, I would do it; and if I could save it by freeing some and leaving others alone, I would also do that. What I do about slavery and the colored race, I do because I believe it helps to save the Union; and what I forbear, I forbear because I do not believe it would help to save the Union. I shall **do less when-**

ever I shall believe what I am doing hurts the cause, and I shall do more whenever I shall believe doing more will help the cause. I shall try to correct errors when shown to be errors, and I shall adopt new views so fast as they shall appear to be true views."

Horace Greeley is reported by a friend to have said, after reading his reply, that Lincoln had prepared it in advance and merely took that opportunity to get his views before the public. "Sub rosa, I can't trust your 'honest old Abe,'" said the unsatisfied Greeley, "he is too smart for me. He thinks me a d——d fool; but I am never fooled twice by the same individual." So the *Tribune* continued to growl, while Lincoln kept on waiting for a victory.

Just after his trip of inspection to Harrison's Landing, the President, on July 11, had appointed General Halleck General-in-Chief, and General Pope, who had won some success in the West, had already been put at the head of the new "Army of Virginia," made by uniting the corps of Fremont, McDowell, and Banks, although a little while before the President had refused him promotion on the ground that "major-generalships in the regular army are not as plenty as blackberries." On the advice of these two generals, Lincoln recalled McClellan from the Peninsula, where he was talking about another advance on Richmond. Pope and Banks were badly outgeneralled by Lee and Jackson, and the Union army suffered several defeats, culminating in the second Bull Run. Washington and the North were terrified. Halleck telegraphed to the man who had been deposed in his favor, " I beg of you to assist me in this crisis, with your ability and experience." Pope had been proved incompetent. Lincoln saw but one thing to do, and without consulting a single soul he did it. Although the public was hostile to McClellan, although the Secretary of War detested him, his organizing skill was again needed, and the President decided to use it.

When the cabinet met on September 2, Stanton came in and said in great excitement he had just learned from General Halleck that McClellan had been placed by the President in command of the forces in Washington. Lincoln soon entered. Chase asked if the story was true. The President said it was. Several members showed regret, and Stanton remarked that no such order had issued from the War Department. The President remarked that the order was his. He then explained. The army and the whole country were demoralized, and something must be done. Who else could so well reorganize the shattered army? If the Secretary of War or any other member could name a general as fit for this task he would appoint him. As a fighting general he admitted McClellan was a failure. He had the "slows." He had never been ready for battle, and probably never would be. Now, however, organization and defence were needed, and he was the best man in the country for that. After a long and patient talk most of the members were reconciled, but Chase said he feared the reinstatement would prove a national calamity.

After a few days spent in organization, McClellan was sent off to meet Lee, who suddenly threatened an invasion of Maryland. By slowness, the Northern general allowed his opponent to concentrate his forces, and then, when the battle of Antietam was finally fought September 17, McClellan, with almost twice as many men, allowed Lee to go away without pursuit. Lincoln had been telegraphing McClellan several days before not to let Lee get off without being hurt, and to destroy his army if possible, but it was in vain. McClellan thought his well-fed troops in no condition to follow the ragged Southerners. Still, Antietam was technically a victory, discouragingly indecisive as it was, and the President decided to use it as an excuse for the great step of emancipation. The memorable cabinet meeting is best described in the entry in Secretary Chase's diary : —

"Monday, September 22, 1862.

"To department about 9. State Department messenger came with notice to heads of departments to meet at 12. Received sundry callers. Went to White House. All the members of the cabinet were in attendance. There was a general talk; and the President mentioned that Artemus Ward had sent him his book. Proposed to read a chapter which he thought very funny. Read it, and seemed to enjoy it very much; the heads also (except Stanton), of course. The chapter was 'High-Handed Outrage at Utica.'

"The President then took a graver tone and said:—

"'Gentlemen: I have, as you are aware, thought a great deal about the relation of this war to slavery; and you all remember that, several weeks ago, I read to you an order I had prepared on this subject, which, on account of objections made by some of you, was not issued. Ever since then my mind has been much occupied with this subject, and I have thought, all along, that the time for acting on it might probably come. I think the time has come now. I wish it was a better time. I wish that we were in a better condition. The action of the army against the rebels has not been quite what I should have best liked. But they have been driven out of Maryland, and Pennsylvania is no longer in danger of invasion. When the rebel army was at Frederick I determined, as soon as it should be driven out of Maryland, to issue a proclamation of emancipation, such as I thought most likely to be useful. I said nothing to any one; but I made the promise to myself and (hesitating a little) to my Maker. The rebel army is now driven out, and I am going to fulfil that promise. I have got you together to hear what I have written down. I do not wish your advice about the main matter; for that I have determined for myself. This I say without intending anything but respect for any of you. But I already know the views of each on this question. They have been heretofore expressed, and I have considered them as thoroughly and carefully as I can. What I have written is that which my reflections have determined me to say. If there is anything in the expressions I use, or in any minor matter, which any one of you thinks had best be changed, I shall be glad to receive the suggestions. One other observation I will make. I know very well that many others might, in this matter as in others, do better than I can; and if I was satisfied that the public confidence was more fully possessed by any one of them than by me, and knew of any constitutional way in which he could be put in my place, he should have it. I would gladly yield it to him. But, though I believe that I have not so much of the confidence of the people as I had, some time since, I do not know that, all things considered, any other person has more; and however this may be, there is no way in which I can have any other man put where I am. I am here. I must do the best I can, and bear the responsibility of taking the course which I feel I ought to take.' "

It was only a few days before this meeting that Lincoln had told the ministers he did " not want to issue a document that the whole world will see must necessarily be inoperative, like the Pope's bull against the comet." To the same men he had said :—

"I admit that slavery is the root of the rebellion, or at least its *sine qua non*. The ambition of politicians may have instigated them to act, but they would have been impotent without slavery as their instrument. I will also concede that emancipation would help us in Europe, and convince them that we are incited by something more than ambition. I grant, further, that it would help somewhat at the North, though not so much, I fear, as you and those you represent imagine. Still, some additional strength would be added in that way to the war, and then, unquestionably, it would weaken the rebels by drawing off their laborers, which is of great importance; but I am not so sure we could do much with the blacks. If we were to arm them, I fear that in a few weeks the arms would be in the hands of the rebels; and, indeed, thus far we have not had arms enough to equip our white troops. I will mention another thing, though it meet only your scorn and contempt. There are fifty thousand bayonets in the Union armies from the border slave states. It would be a serious matter if, in consequence of a proclamation such as you desire, they should go over to the rebels. I do not think they all would — not so many, indeed, as a year ago, or as six months ago — not so many to-day as yesterday. Every day increases their Union feeling. They are also getting their pride enlisted, and want to beat the rebels. Let me say one thing more; I think you should admit that we already have an important principle to rally and unite the people, in the fact that constitutional government is at stake. This is a fundamental idea going down about as deep as anything.

"Do not misunderstand me because I have mentioned these objections. They indicate the difficulties that have thus far prevented my action in some such way as you desire. I have not decided against a proclamation of liberty to the slaves, but hold the matter under advisement; and I can assure you that the subject is on my mind, by day and night, more than any other. Whatever shall appear to be God's will, I will do."

To Hannibal Hamlin he wrote a few days after the publication in the newspapers: —

"It is known to some that while I hope something from the proclamation, my expectations are not as sanguine as are those of some friends. The time for its effect southward has not come; but northward the effect should be instantaneous.

"It is six days old, and while commendation in newspapers and by distinguished individuals is all that a vain man could wish, the stocks have declined, and troops come forward more slowly than ever. This, looked soberly in the face, is not very satisfactory. We have fewer troops in the field at the end of the six days than we had at the beginning — the attrition among the old outnumbering the addition by the new. The North responds to the proclamation sufficiently in breath; but breath alone kills no rebels."

The immediate political consequences of this step were unpromising. The emancipation was not to be made until January 1, but this preliminary proclamation declared that all persons held as slaves in states in rebellion on that day should be declared free. Military failure counted for much in the ensuing fall elections, but it is generally believed that the proclamation also helped the Democrats. Never had the President suffered more distrust. Talk about the need of a Cromwell continued. Influential politicians thought the country was on the verge of destruction. The October elections showed that even the people, Lincoln's strongest support, were not wholly with the administration. The Democrats won heavily in New York, Pennsylvania, Indiana, and Illinois; and in other states, where the Republicans won, it was with reduced majorities. By November, however, the results were better, and when the border states came to vote the outcome was decidedly satisfactory.

A trip which the President made to the battlefield of Antietam served to bring out some of the intense hostility to him through the malicious stories circulated and believed in the North about his levity in the terrible place. Lamon, who accompanied Lincoln, urged him later to deny some of these tales. "No," said the philosophic chief, "in politics every man must skin his own skunk. These fellows are welcome to the hide of this one." Still, although Lamon denies singing any frivolous songs on the battlefield, he says the President always laughed immoderately when he sang this parody on "Life on the Ocean Wave."

> "Oh, a life on the ocean wave,
>   And a home on the rolling deep !
>   With ratlins fried three times a day
>   And a leaky old berth for to sleep ;
>   Where the gray-beard cockroach roams,
>   On thoughts of kind intent . . ."

and so on.

The rest of the song grows coarser, but Lamon was one of those Westerners, — full of health, spirits, and a humor quite without squeamishness, — that Lincoln rejoiced in.   Another bit with which he used to rejoice the President was " The Blue-Tailed Fly," of which these lines are given by Lamon as samples : —

> "When I was young I used to wait
>   At massa's table, 'n' hand de plate,
>   An' pass de bottle when he was dry,
>   An' brush away de blue-tailed fly.

> "Ole massa's dead ; oh, let him rest !
>   Dey say all things am for de best ;
>   But I can't forget until I die
>   Ole massa an' de blue-tailed fly."

In these days, when his burden was hardest, Lincoln kept himself sane with humor, from the coarsest fun to the subtlest irony, as he always did; and the attempts constantly made to turn this into a proof of callousness are but one indication of the vindictive hatred which was showered upon him.   Lamon thinks he was even

fonder of the patriotic airs and songs of senti-
mental nature, as " Ben Bolt," " The Sword of
Bunker Hill," and " The Lament of the Irish
Emigrant." From the last come these lines: —

> " I'm very lonely now, Mary,
>   For the poor make no new friends;
> But, oh, they love the better still
>   The few our Father sends !
> And you were all I had, Mary,
>   My blessing and my pride;
> There's nothing left to care for now,
>   Since my poor Mary died."

He was particularly fond of this: —

" I've wandered to the village, Tom; I've sat beneath the tree
Upon the schoolhouse playground, that sheltered you and me :
But none were left to greet me, Tom, and few were left to know
Who played with us upon the green, some twenty years ago.

" Near by the spring, upon the elm you know I cut your name, —
Your sweetheart's just beneath it, Tom; and you did mine the
        same.
Some heartless wretch has peeled the bark, — 'twas dying sure
        but slow,
Just as *she* died whose name you cut, some twenty years ago.

" My lids have long been dry, Tom, but tears came to my eyes;
I thought of her I loved so well, those early broken ties;
I visited the old churchyard, and took some flowers to strew
Upon the graves of those we loved, some twenty years ago."

The figure of this great man of the people would
surely lose much of its unique grandeur if white-

washing biographers and moralists were able to smooth away these striking contrasts.

After Antietam there was no light in any direction. While the elections were going against the administration in the most important Northern states, McClellan was again exhibiting his total inability to carry on an offensive campaign. Lincoln urged him forward with the clearest, firmest, and kindest arguments. "If we never try, we shall never succeed," he said. "As we must beat him somewhere, or fail finally, we can do it, if at all, easier near to us than far away." He therefore urged McClellan with all earnestness to break Lee's communications with Richmond and attack him, but in vain, although it is almost impossible to understand the general's dread of motion. Finally, on November 7th, the command of the army was, by Lincoln's order, turned over to General Burnside, whom he is said to have preferred to Hooker because he was "a good housekeeper."

This was the end of McClellan. Lincoln, who had stood by him so long, would stand by him no longer. He was getting hungrier and hungrier for the death-grapple between the armies, and he now plunged into the series of experiments in generals which continued until a quiet Westerner gave him what he wanted. McClellan's own impression of the President is less hostile than it is to several other members of the administration, Stanton being his special abhorrence. Of Lincoln's stories, concerning which he remarks that they "were seldom refined, but were always to the point," he relates one from which he ought to have been able to draw some useful conclusions for his own use. In a telegram to McClellan an officer commanding a regiment on the Upper Potomac told about desperate fighting and ended with a small list of killed and wounded. Lincoln was reminded of a man who instructed his servant to touch him in some way if his stories became too large. He was telling some friends about a building in Europe a mile and a half long and half a mile high when the servant's foot descended on his toe. "How broad was the building?" asked one of the listeners. "About a foot," replied the narrator. McClellan's mind was given to hopelessly magnifying difficulties, and nothing which any human being could do had any effect in making him see how small were his lacks compared with those of his antagonist.

Petty annoyances were not wanting as a variation on the great ones. Congress had a Committee on the Conduct of the War which investigated everything and accomplished nothing. Lincoln said of it that its only purpose was to put an additional clog on his freedom and efficiency of action. There were so many people crying for peace, that

Emerson said, " It is wonderful to behold the unseasonable senility of what is called the Peace Party." Others wanted a coup d'état. Opponents of the war abroad said that the armies of England, France, and Austria, could not coerce 8,000,000 of free people to come under the government. The cabinet bickered. Every politician or soldier or citizen who was turned off gruffly by Stanton came to the President. Sometimes he tried to soften the decrees of his War Minister, " Mars," as he sometimes called him. At other times he escaped as adroitly as he could, alleging once, when some one had appealed from Stanton, that he had very little influence with this administration but expected to have more with the next. One of the Secretary's acts, a press censorship, brought the newspaper men about the President's ears. Once when two of them in a passion were explaining the annoyances of the censorship, Lincoln, who had listened in a dreamy way, finally said : —

" I don't know much about this censorship, but come downstairs and I will show you the origin of one of the pet phrases of you newspaper fellows."

Leading the way down into the basement, he opened the door of a larder, and solemnly pointed to the hanging carcass of a gigantic sheep.

" There," said he, " now you know what *Reve·*

nons à nos moutons means. It was raised by Deacon Buffum at Manchester, up in New Hampshire. Who can say, after looking at it, that New Hampshire's only product is granite?'

Lincoln was once asked how it was that one caller who went to him in a rage came away smiling. The President told about the farmer who had been troubled by a big log in the middle of his field but announced one day that he had got rid of it. "How did you do it?" a neighbor asked. "It was too big to haul, too knotty to split, too wet and soggy to burn." The farmer replied that if his questioner would promise to keep the secret he would divulge it. "I ploughed around it." "I," continued Lincoln, "ploughed around Governor ———, but it took me three mortal hours to do it, and I was afraid every minute he would see what I was at."

Thus in almost every month of Lincoln's history as President we find the great tragedies and the little comedies, or the great comedies and the little tragedies, keeping along side by side. During this particular part of 1862 the next event of deep significance was the first battle of the new reliance. General Burnside decided upon a new plan, an advance upon Richmond by way of Fredericksburg. Lincoln said that this plan could succeed only if it was rapidly executed. Burnside was so slow that he found Lee strongly intrenched, and was frightfully defeated at Fredericksburg on December 13. Thus one more experiment failed. Lincoln's fear that after getting rid of McClellan he should not readily do better was justified. To the Democratic Colonel W. R. Morrison Lincoln had written in November, "In considering military merit, the world has abundant evidence that I disregard politics." To Carl Schurz he was compelled to write a little later: —

"If I must discard my own judgment and take yours, I must also take that of others; and by the time I should reject all I should be advised to reject, I should have none left, Republicans or others — not even yourself. For be assured, my dear sir, there are men who have 'heart in it' that think you are performing your part as poorly as you think I am performing mine. I certainly have been dissatisfied with the slowness of Buell and McClellan; but before I relieved them I had great fears I should not find successors to them who would do better; and I am sorry to add that I have seen little since to relieve those fears.

"I do not clearly see the prospect of any more rapid movements. I fear we shall at last find out that the difficulty is in our case rather than in particular generals. I wish to disparage no one — certainly not those who sympathize with me; but I must say I need success more than I need sympathy, and that I have not seen the so much greater evidence of getting success from my sympathizers than from those who are denounced as the contrary. It does seem to me that in the field the two classes have been very much alike in what they have done and what they have failed to do. In sealing their faith with their blood, Baker and Lyon and Bohlen and Richardson, Republicans, did all that men could do; but did they any more than Kearny and Stevens and Reno and Mansfield, none of whom were Republicans, and some at least of whom have been bitterly and repeatedly denounced to me as secession sympathizers? I will not perform the ungrateful task of comparing cases of failure."

Nobody could have been moved more solely by the desire to select the best men, and yet the President seemed for a long time unable to find any one competent to meet the Confederate leaders in the East. Burnside was soon dropped, immediately through differences with his subordinates, and "Fighting Joe" Hooker took his place.

Toward the end of 1862 matters in the cabinet reached their greatest tension. Seward, through his conservatism, was making enemies, but the President knew his Secretary's value too well to be shaken. Chase was also doing excellent service in his department, but he was vain, dissatisfied, extremely radical about slavery, fond of making trouble, disdainful and hostile toward Lincoln and Seward. The Senate was so hostile to Seward that a caucus voted to demand his

U

dismissal. This decision was so far modified that instead a committee was instructed to present to the President resolutions requesting him to reconstruct the cabinet. Reporting this interview, Lincoln afterward said, " While they seemed to believe in my honesty, they also appeared to think that when I had in me any good purpose or intention Seward contrived to suck it out of me unperceived." At the time, he merely asked the committee to meet him in the evening. Meantime, he laid the whole matter frankly before his cabinet, explaining that he did not mean to intimate a desire for the resignation of any of them, and requested them to meet again in the evening. Seward stayed away. Having brought the cabinet and the committee together, Lincoln required a frank statement of the views of both sides. The final result of the complaints was that both Seward and Chase resigned. This outcome delighted Lincoln, who valued Seward highly. He knew of Chase's wire-pulling against the Secretary of State, and yet felt the difficulty of resisting the immense opposition to Seward. The President was now able, by declining to accept either resignation, to seem impartial between the two elements in his party, whereas had he not succeeded in getting Chase's resignation at the same time, a refusal to accept Seward's would have identified him with one wing. After it was all over, and the two Secretaries were back in the cabinet, Lincoln said to a friend, " Now I can ride ; I have got a pumpkin in each bag." Later he said, as recorded in Mr. Hay's diary: "If I had yielded to that storm and dismissed Seward, the thing would all have slumped over one way, and we should have been left with a scanty handful of supporters. When Chase gave in his resignation, I saw that the game was in my hands, and I put it through."

A few days after this Lincoln took his great final step of emancipation, not without fears. To a visitor a little while before he said: " As for the negroes, Doctor, and what is going to become of them: I told Ben Wade the other day, that it made me think of a story I read in one of my first books, Æsop's Fables. It was an old edition, and had curious rough woodcuts, one of which showed four white men scrubbing a negro in a potash kettle filled with cold water. The text explained that the men thought that by scrubbing the negro they might make him white. Just about the time they thought they were succeeding, he took cold and died. Now, I am afraid that by the time we get through this war the negro will catch cold and die."

On the afternoon of January 1, with some half jocose remarks about the trembling of his hand, he signed the document which formally declared

all slaves in the rebellious states forever free and
added that they would be received into the armed
service of the United States. At the suggestion of Secretary Chase, the President invoked
" the gracious favor of the Almighty God."

CHAPTER XIII

Two good effects of the Emancipation Proclamation were immediately seen, — a slightly more favorable European attitude and a greater use of negro troops, which was found to have comparatively little effect on the soldiers from the border states. Never, on the other hand, had " Copperheadism," or lukewarmness approaching Southern sympathy, been so bad in the North. In dealing with Copperheads the President showed tact equal to his skilful manipulation of the border states. The army, too, required all his gentle but clear-cut insight. Compulsory service had now to be resorted to, and the result was a lowering of the average character of the soldiers and a great bickering among the states, each trying to avoid its quota, with many charges of partisanship against the administration. Moreover, there were defeats and no great victories, the struggle was long and dreary, and the President looked upon the increasing desertions from the army with the leniency of sympathetic comprehension. His story from January 1 to July 4,

1863, is one of patience, tact, kindness, and steady although hardly visible progress.   At no time in his whole life does he show in complete fulness more sides of a great nature.

To Major General Dix on January 14 he wrote, marked "private and confidential," the following : —

" The proclamation has been issued.   We were not succeeding — at best were progressing too slowly — without it.   Now that we have it, and bear all the disadvantages of it (as we do bear some in certain quarters), we must also take some benefit from it, if practicable.   I, therefore, will thank you for your well-considered opinion, whether Fortress Monroe and Yorktown, one or both, could not, in whole or in part, be garrisoned by colored troops, leaving the white forces now necessary at those places to be employed elsewhere."

Even before the proclamation had been issued the President's feelings about the policy of returning slaves had progressed so far that he wrote a private letter, which on reflection he did not send, thus : —

" Your despatch of yesterday is just received.   I believe you are acquainted with the American classics (if there be such), and probably remember a speech of Patrick Henry in which he represented a certain character in the Revolutionary times as totally disregarding all questions of country, and ' hoarsely bawling, " Beef ! beef !! beef !!! " '

"Do you not know that I may as well surrender the contest directly as to make any order the obvious purpose of which would be to return fugitive slaves?"

By March we find him writing to Andrew Johnson, military governor of Tennessee and afterward Vice-President and President of the United States:—

"I am told you have at least thought of raising a negro military force. In my opinion the country now needs no specific thing so much as some man of your ability and position to go to this work. When I speak of your position, I mean that of an eminent citizen of a slave state and himself a slaveholder. The colored population is the great available and yet unavailed of force for restoring the Union. The bare sight of fifty thousand armed and drilled black soldiers upon the banks of the Mississippi would end the rebellion at once; and who doubts that we can present that sight if we but take hold in earnest? If you have been thinking of it, please do not dismiss the thought."

To General Banks a few days later he says that to raise colored troops is "very important, if not indispensable." To General Hunter he writes privately on April 1:—

"I am glad to see the accounts of your colored force at Jacksonville, Florida. I see the enemy are driving at them fiercely, as is to be expected. It is important to the enemy that such a force shall not take shape and grow and thrive in the South, and in precisely the same proportion it is important to us that it shall. Hence the utmost caution and vigilance is necessary on our part. The enemy will make extra efforts to destroy them, and we should do the same to preserve and increase them."

Rage at the South over the use of negro troops was unbounded. In 1862 Jefferson Davis had declared Generals Hunter and Butler, and their commissioned officers, outlaws, robbers, and criminals, who, if captured, were not to be treated as prisoners of war but to be held for execution. When the proclamation was issued he extended this principle to all commissioned officers captured in the territory covered. The Confederate Secretary of War wrote to General Kirby Smith the suggestion that white men leading negro troops "be dealt with red-handed on the field of war or immediately after." Such amenities naturally raised at the North a demand for reciprocity. In the summer the well-known negro Frederick Douglass, who was recruiting colored soldiers, called on the President and said that if these troops were to be a success four things were necessary: —

1. Colored soldiers must have the same pay as white soldiers.

2. The government must compel the Confederates to treat captured negro soldiers as prisoners of war.

3. Brave and meritorious service should lead to promotion precisely as with white soldiers.

4. If any negro soldiers were murdered in cold blood, the North should retaliate in kind.

Lincoln, in reply, Douglass tells us, described the opposition to employing black soldiers at all, and the advantage to the colored race that would result from employment in defence of their country. He regarded it as an experiment. He had with difficulty got them into United States uniforms, against the opposition of those who proposed a different dress, and that was something gained. In the matter of pay, also, he felt that some concession must be made to prejudice; and besides it was not proved that the negro could make as good a soldier as the white man. " I assure you," the President added, however, "that in the end they shall have the same pay as white soldiers." He admitted the justice of the demand for promotion, and said that he would insist on their being entitled to all the privileges of prisoners of war; but in regard to retaliation he said, with a quiver in his voice, "once begun, I do not know where such a measure would stop," and added that, although if he could get hold of the actual perpetrators of the crime the case might be different, he could not kill the innocent for the guilty. He did, however, after the summer victories, order that "for every soldier of the

United States killed in violation of the laws of the war a rebel soldier shall be executed." As it turned out, practically nothing came of the threats on either side.

Toward the white soldiers, with whom he purposely came in contact as much as possible, his feelings seemed to become if possible kinder as their own stability diminished. He pardoned to an extent which drove his generals and the Secretary of War into despair. "If," he once said, "a man had more than one life, I think a little hanging would not hurt this one, but after he is once dead we cannot bring him back, no matter how sorry we may be, so the boy should be pardoned." General Butler says that the President promised to let him execute whomever he chose, but did not keep his word, frequently giving orders to have some convicted person sent to the Dry Tortugas. The same general reminded him that the bounties given for enlistment led to desertions, so that the men could go home and enlist in other regiments, — and this practice of " bounty-jumping " soon became frequent.

" How can it be stopped ? " asked Lincoln.

" Shoot every deserter," said Butler.

" You may be right," replied the President, "probably are: but Lord help me, how can I have a butcher's day every Friday in the Army of the Potomac ? "

In a case of cowardice he said that a man could not always control his legs; or that he never felt sure he might not run away himself if he were in battle. This was mainly jocose, for there is little doubt of his personal bravery. General Butler tells us that when Lincoln visited his department he rode six miles within three hundred yards of the enemy, where officers inspected him through their glasses, and he refused to make his position more safe.

Schuyler Colfax[1] gives a scene from the early days of the war. When Judge Holt, the judge-advocate-general of the army, laid the first case before the President and explained it, he replied that he would wait a few days until he had more time to read the testimony.

When the judge read the next case Lincoln said, " I must put this by until I can settle in my mind whether this soldier can better serve the country dead than living."

To the third he remarked that as the general commanding the brigade would be in Washington in a few days he would wait and talk it over with him.

Finally there came a very flagrant case. A soldier in the crisis of a battle demoralized his regiment by throwing down his gun and hiding

[1] A number of interesting anecdotes by men who knew Lincoln are to be found in a volume of reminiscences edited by A. T. Rice.

behind a stump. The court-martial found that he had no dependents and that he was a thief, stealing continually from his comrades. Judge Holt remarked that this man might meet the President's requirement of serving his country better dead than living. The excuses were all gone, but Lincoln said that any way he thought he would put it with his "leg cases." Pointing to some pigeon-holes, he proceeded: " They are cases that you call by that long title, 'Cowardice in the face of the enemy,' but I call them, for short, my leg cases. If Almighty God has given a man a cowardly pair of legs, how can he help running away with them?"

Some escaped because he knew their fathers, others because he liked their frankness, many for their youth. It may have done something to destroy discipline, but it probably did more good than harm. The President had in mind the kind of citizens who went into the army, and no one knew better how to manage them. "With us every soldier is a man of character," he wrote to a French nobleman, "and must be treated with more consideration than is customary in Europe." His humor, as always, served him well. Meeting a soldier who considerably surpassed in height his own six feet four, Lincoln examined him with wondering admiration, and finally asked, " Hello, comrade, how do you know when your feet get cold?"

In handling the troubles which grew out of compulsory military service the President showed the importance of politics in a democracy at war. The very idea of forcing men to fight was widely denounced as despotic and contrary to American institutions, and to make it as little offensive as possible called into play all of Lincoln's adroitness. Stanton was always an obstacle to any sacrifice of what he deemed principle to what is now ironically called "harmony," but Lincoln was able to use this obstacle as an excuse when he wished, and to overcome it when he chose. General Fry, who was at the head of this department, gives an instance. The states and districts tried to fill their quotas, and save their citizens from being drafted, by voting bounties to buy men wherever they could be found. The agent appointed by a county in one of the middle states learned that some Confederate prisoners at Chicago were about to be released and enlisted in the United States army for service against the Indians in the northwest. He therefore decided to pay them bounties, and get them credited to his district, although they would do only what they were about to do any way. He then obtained from the President an order to have them credited. Stanton refused to have the credit allowed. The agent, who was acquainted with Lincoln, returned to him, and got him to repeat the order, but it was without effect.

The President then went to the Secretary's office, and had General Fry present to state the facts. Fry said that these men, being prisoners of war, could not be used against the Confederates, and that, as they belonged to the government, all that was needed to use them against the Indians was their release. To allow the bounty and the credit, therefore, would merely waste money, and deprive the army of men.

" Now, Mr. President," said Stanton, " those are the facts, and you must see that your order cannot be executed."

" Mr. Stanton," replied Lincoln, " I reckon you'll have to execute the order."

" Mr. President, I can't do it. The order is an improper one, and I cannot execute it."

" Mr. Secretary, it will have to be done."

On a hint Fry withdrew, and a few moments later he received instructions from Stanton to carry out Lincoln's order.

Colonel McClure is the witness to another incident that brings out the President's methods in dealing with the situation which any rigid code might have ruined. McClure, who was chairman of the military committee of the Senate, was to execute the first army draft made in Pennsylvania. Dissatisfaction was intense throughout the state, and in Cass Township, Schuylkill County, the centre of the criminal band of " Molly Maguires," open rebellion was threatened. The draft was made with difficulty, and a day fixed for the conscripts to take the cars and report at Harrisburg. The criminals not only refused to go themselves, but they violently drove the other conscripts from the station.

On being informed of this, Secretary Stanton replied at once that the draft must be enforced, and he put one Philadelphia regiment and one at Harrisburg at the orders of Governor Curtin, with instructions to send them immediately to the scene of the revolt. Suggestions were sent back that the situation was dangerously complicated, but Stanton again ordered the law enforced at the point of the bayonet. The soldiers started toward the scene of the revolt. Curtin gave McClure orders to telegraph the whole situation fully, in cipher, to Lincoln. This was done early in the day. Night came and no reply. When Colonel McClure entered the breakfast room at his hotel, Assistant Attorney-General Townsend of the United States army was seated at the table. He had arrived at three A.M., and was watching for McClure. He said: " I have no orders to give you, but I came solely to deliver a personal message from President Lincoln in these words: 'Say to McClure that I am very desirous to have the laws fully executed, but it might be well in an extreme emergency to be content with the appearance of executing the laws. I think McClure will understand.' I have now fulfilled my mission. I do not know to what it relates."

McClure made no explanation to Townsend, but summoned Benjamin Bannan from Pottsville, and explained that in a number of cases, after the quotas had been adjusted and the draft ordered, evidence had been presented to prove that the quotas had been filled by volunteers who had enlisted in towns or cities outside of their township. In such cases, where the evidence was clear, the draft was revoked. By the next evening evidence was secured and properly endorsed, which made the draft in that district inoperative, and released the conscripts.

Another experience related by the same politician shows Lincoln's habit of accomplishing what he wanted. The conscripts from various parts of Pennsylvania were pouring into the capital by thousands. The demand for reinforcements was pressing. The commanding officer mustered only about two companies a day. McClure telegraphed Stanton that he could forward a regiment every day if the government would furnish the officers to muster and organize them. Stanton replied that it would be done. The next day a new officer appeared, but, as he was subordinate to the commandant who had charge, he was, after mustering an entire regiment the first day, re-

lieved from duty. The secret of the commandant's action was the desire to make money out of army contracts while the men were in his neighborhood. McClure, after telegraphing ahead, went to see Lincoln in Washington. The President immediately sent for a major's commission, and told McClure to show it to the commanding officer, who was a captain. He also gave him an order assigning him to duty at Harrisburg. All McClure had to do was to exhibit these documents, and tell the captain there must be a regiment mustered every day. Then he sent back to the President the commission, which had served its purpose.

On April 13, Lincoln wrote to General Curtin : —

" If, after the expiration of your present term as governor of Pennsylvania, I shall continue in office here, and you shall desire to go abroad, you can do so with one of the first-class missions."

The meaning of this was that it was feared that with Cameron's hostility Curtin could not be elected in Pennsylvania. There was not one of the states in which the President was not in the closest touch with the political situation. On May 15, he wrote to certain Missouri politicians : —

" Your despatch of to-day is just received. It is very painful to me that you in Missouri cannot or will not settle your factional quarrel among yourselves. I have been tormented with it beyond endurance for months by both sides. Neither side pays the least respect to my appeals to your reason. I am now compelled to take hold of the case."

On May 27, he wrote to General John M. Schofield a letter which explained what he did when he "took hold of the case": —

"Having relieved General Curtis and assigned you to the command of the department of the Missouri, I think it may be of some advantage for me to state to you why I did it. I did not relieve General Curtis because of any full conviction that he had done wrong by commission or omission. I did it because of a conviction in my mind that the Union men of Missouri, constituting, when united, a vast majority of the whole people, have entered into a pestilent factional quarrel among themselves — General Curtis, perhaps not of choice, being the head of one faction, and Governor Gamble that of the other. After months of labor to reconcile the difficulty, it seemed to grow worse and worse until I felt it my duty to break it up somehow; and as I could not remove Governor Gamble, I had to remove General Curtis. Now that you are in the position, I wish you to undo nothing merely because General Curtis or Governor Gamble did it, but to exercise your own judgment, and do right for the public interest. Let the military measures be strong enough to repel the invader and keep the peace, and not so strong as to unnecessarily harass and persecute the people.

It is a difficult rôle, and so much greater will be the honor if you perform it well. If both factions, or neither, shall abuse you, you will probably be about right. Beware of being assailed by one and praised by the other."

Once, according to General Fry, in talking over the selection of brigadier generals, the President told Stanton that he concurred in pretty much everything he had been saying, but that something had to be done in the interest of the Dutch, and that he therefore wished Schmell-finnig appointed. Stanton said that possibly he was not as highly recommended as some other German officer.

"No matter," said Lincoln. "His name will make up for any difference there may be, and I will take the risk of his coming out all right."

In dealing with the Copperheads, who sprung up in unexampled rankness in the gloomy spring of '63, the President's most notable feat was accomplished on one Vallandigham, who made such offensive speeches in Ohio that General Burnside, whose headquarters were at Cincinnati, arrested him. A military tribunal convicted him, and the general approved the finding. He was imprisoned, and an effort to get him out on *habeas corpus* failed. Lincoln's correspondence with Burnside shows a doubt about the need of this act, combined with a willingness to stand by it. There was an immense outcry all over the North. Governor Seymour, of New York, denounced the arrest as dishonorable despotism. He said: " The action of the administration will determine in the minds of more than one-half of the people of the loyal states whether this war is waged to put down rebellion in the South, or to destroy free institutions in the North."

The President met the complaints by commuting the sentence in an original and adroit manner. He sent him to the South, and on May 25 he was accepted by a Confederate picket.

Still the noise continued, and June 11 the Ohio Democrats nominated Vallandigham for governor.

To some of the resolutions denouncing the arrest the President thought it best to reply, and his answer to the New York Democrats is among his ablest and most famous arguments. A few sentences may give some idea of its clear and logical power: —

" I understand the meeting whose resolution I am considering to be in favor of suppressing the rebellion by military force by armies. Long experience has shown that armies cannot be maintained unless desertion shall be punished by the severe penalty of death. The case requires, and the law and the Constitution sanction this punishment. Must I shoot a simple-minded soldier boy who deserts, while I must not touch a hair of the wily agitator who induces him to desert? This is none the less injurious when effected by getting a father, or brother, or friend into a public meeting, and there working upon his feelings till he is persuaded to write the soldier boy that he is fighting in a bad cause for a wicked administration of a contemptible government, too weak to arrest and punish him if he shall desert. I think that, in such a case, to silence the agitator and save the boy is not only constitutional, but withal a great mercy. . . . Nor am I able to appreciate the danger apprehended by this meeting, that the American people will by means of military arrests during the rebellion lose the right of public discussion, the liberty of speech and the press, the law of evidence, trial by jury, and *habeas corpus* throughout the indefinite peaceful future which I trust lies before them, any more than I am able to believe that a man could contract so strong an appetite for emetics during temporary illness as to persist in feeding upon them during the remainder of his healthful life."

Now a story of Lincoln's was about to have its vindication in a result brought about by his argument and the people's sense. He told of the boy who was particularly effective in knocking away the last support when a vessel was to be launched, and then lying down while the vessel passed over him. Yet he always screamed violently during the process. He was not afraid, and he liked to do it, but his noise made him more important.

Vallandigham was defeated by the people of Ohio by over 100,000 votes.

A few other miscellaneous features of these six months of stress add variety to a period which did so much to test this most thoroughly tested President. In reference to privateers he had acted with prudence, checking the desire for mere revenge as he always did, but Great Britain was particularly annoying just now by the aid she gave the South in preparing vessels to prey on commerce. The country and Congress were in a mood to quarrel with England, and still more in a mood to indulge in privateers on their own account, so on the 3d of March, the last day of the session, an act was passed declaring, "that in all domestic and foreign wars the President of the United States is authorized to issue to private armed vessels of the United States, commissions or letters-of-marque and general reprisal in such form as he shall think proper, and under the seal of the United States, and make all needful rules and regulations for the government thereof, and for the adjudication and disposal of the prizes and salvages made by each vessel — provided that the authority conferred by this act shall cease and terminate at the end of three years from the passage of this act."

The results of this fiery move, however, were easily escaped by the administration, which found none of the offers of privateers proper for acceptance. The case against England was handled with firmness and dignity by the minister to England, the Secretary of State, and the President, and later ended in full indemnity instead of a fatal war. It was in this situation in 1863 that Mr. Adams wrote to Lord Russell his famous and effective words. " This is war." Offers of mediation were also thick from foreign powers and they were declined with courtesy.

Another aspect of these times is suggested in this effusion by the voluble Secretary of the Treasury.

" Had there been here an administration in the true sense of the word — a President conferring with his cabinet and taking their united judgments, and with their aid enforcing activity, economy, and energy, in all departments of public service — we could have spoken boldly and defied the world. But our condition here has always been very different. I preside over the funnel; everybody else, and especially the Secretaries of War and the Navy, over the spigots — and keep them well open, too. Mr. Seward conducts the foreign relations with very little let or help from anybody. There is no unity and no system, except so far as it is departmental. There is progress, but it is slow and unvoluntary — just what is coerced by the irresistible pressure of the

vast force of the people. How under such circumstances can anybody announce a policy which
can only be made respectable by union, wisdom,
and courage ? "

It was true that Chase was allowed to attend
alone to the finances. Lincoln knew nothing
about them, and it was not his nature to meddle
with the unknown, unless, as in the case of military matters, it was pressed upon him by necessity. That Chase was not allowed to meddle with
the other departments grieved him sorely. As to
his talk about a "policy" it is answered by Lincoln's famous frank confession that he made no
pretence of controlling events, but admitted willingly that they had controlled him. That was
his way, and it worked. Whether an arbitrary
hand could have guided the State as safely must
remain a speculation. Lowell speaks of him as
"avoiding innumerable obstacles with noble bends
of concession," and of his "cautious but sure-footed
understanding." It is the general later opinion
that even if a less tentative, more aggressive nature
had succeeded in rapidly crushing the rebellion,
the disease would have been less effectively eradi-
cated than it was by allowing the people to be
the motive force. At any rate it is no wonder
that the President, in all his trouble, remarked:
"It's a good thing for individuals that there's a
government to shove their acts upon. No man's

shoulders are broad enough to bear what must be."

A glimpse into one corner of the inner life of the man at this time is caught through the following telegram: —

"WASHINGTON, January 9, 1863.

"MRS. LINCOLN, Philadelphia; Pennsylvania.

"Think you had better put Tad's pistol away. I had an ugly dream about him.

"A. LINCOLN."

Now, as always, however, no matter what strange and attractive light on the man's nature may be thrown by other aspects of his activity, the military was the most important if not psychologically the most significant part of his career. In this winter and spring he gave a full trial to one more general, who also was found wanting. On Lincoln himself a flood of blame for the army reverses continually poured. *Harper's Weekly*, on January 3, printed a cartoon in which Columbia confronted the President and demanded an accounting for the thousands slain at Fredericksburg. "This," replied Lincoln, "reminds me of a little joke." "Go," replied the angry nation, "tell your joke at Springfield." For a later generation it is not easy to realize that thousands actually believed that the awful slaughter was a matter for coarse Western jests by the

President. It was perhaps when he felt most terribly that he needed his stories most. Stanton sometimes used abruptly to leave the room when Lincoln began a tale, and other members of the cabinet would bite their lips when he started one of his stories in the presence of strangers. They took him with no sense of humor. He took them with the humorous comprehension of a Sancho Panza. A man who had presented to Stanton a certain order from the President returned and repeated the Secretary's comment. "If," said Lincoln, "Stanton said I was a damned fool, then I must be one; for he is nearly always right and generally says what he means. I must step over and see him."

In February one of the cartoons showed P. T. Barnum presenting Tom Thumb and Commodore Nutt to the President, and under the picture was this dialogue:—

The Great Showman: — "Mr. President, since your military and naval heroes do not seem to get on, try mine."

Lincoln: — "Well, I will do it to oblige you, friend Phineas, but I think mine are the smallest."

He began the experiment with General Hooker with one of his most characteristic messages:—

(Private.)

"EXECUTIVE MANSION,
"WASHINGTON, D.C. Jan. 26, 1863.

"MAJOR-GENERAL HOOKER:

"*General:*—I have placed you at the head of the Army of the Potomac. Of course I have done this upon what appears to me sufficient reasons; and yet I think it best for you to know that there are some things in regard to which I am not quite satisfied with you.

"I believe you to be a brave and skilful soldier, which of course I like. I also believe you do not mix politics with your profession, in which you are right. You have confidence in yourself, which is a valuable, if not indispensable, quality. You are ambitious, which, within reasonable bounds, does good rather than harm. But I think that during General Burnside's command of the army you have taken counsel of your ambition solely, and thwarted him as much as you could; in which you did a great wrong to the country and to a most meritorious and honorable brother officer. I have heard, in such a way as to believe it, of your saying that both the country and the army needed a dictator. Of course it was not for this, but in spite of it, that I have given you the command. Only those generals who gain success can set themselves up as dictators. What I ask of you is military success, and I will risk the dictatorship. The government will support you to the utmost of its ability, which is neither more nor less than it has done and will do for all its commanders.

"I much fear that the spirit which you have aided to infuse into the army, of criticising their commander and withholding confidence from him, will now turn upon you; and I shall assist you as far as I can to put it down. Neither you nor Napoleon, if he were alive again, could get any good out of an army while such a spirit prevails in it.

"And now, beware of rashness, but with energy and sleepless vigilance go forward and give us victories.

"Yours very truly,

"A. LINCOLN."

Secretary Welles tells us that the President once went so far in conversation as to say this: "There has been a design, a purpose, in breaking down Pope, without regard to the consequences to the country, — which is atrocious. It is shocking to see and know this, but there is no remedy at present. McClellan has the army with him." So he recalled McClellan. Now there was a slightly similar situation. He believed Burnside had been injured by jealousies, yet he called to the command one of the guilty generals and told him to do his best. He urged on him especially the importance of an early and energetic movement of the Army of the Potomac, for its political effect at home and abroad. Hooker proved efficient in getting the demoralized army into form, but slow to act. Finally the able Southerners saw their opportunity. Stonewall Jackson, on May 2, won the victory which cost his life, and the next two days General Lee inflicted on

Hooker the heavy defeat of Chancellorsville, won by superior generalship. One of Hooker's errors was failing to use all of his men, a mistake against which Lincoln had emphatically warned him. The President was learning a good deal about the kind of mistakes to expect from his generals.

Lee now made his great error by deciding to invade the North. Hooker wished to attack the Confederate rear at Fredericksburg, but Lincoln, who was afraid of this plan, made a famous comment: —

"If he should leave a rear force at Fredericksburg, tempting you to fall upon it, it would fight in intrenchments and have you at disadvantage, and so, man for man, worst you at that point, while his main force would in some way be getting an advantage of you northward. In one word, I would not take any risk of being entangled upon the river, like an ox jumped half over a fence and liable to be torn by dogs front and rear without a fair chance to gore one way or kick the other."

A few days later he said, in answer to Hooker's scheme of advancing upon Richmond: —

"If left to me, I would not go south of the Rappahannock upon Lee's moving north of it. If you had Richmond invested to-day, you would not be able to take it in twenty days; meanwhile your communications, and with them your army, would be ruined. I think Lee's army, and not Richmond, is your true objective point. If he comes toward the upper Potomac, follow on his flank and on his inside track, shortening your lines while he lengthens his. Fight him, too, when opportunity offers. If he stays where he is, fret him and fret him."

Hooker was slow, and Lincoln telegraphed : —

"So far as we can make out here, the enemy have Milroy surrounded at Winchester, and Tyler at Martinsburg. If they could hold out a few days, could you help them? If the head of Lee's army is at Martinsburg and the tail of it on the plank road between Fredericksburg and Chancellorsville, the animal must be very slim somewhere. Could you not break him?"

The Confederates under Ewell entered Pennsylvania June 22. Now there was more bickering among the Federal generals, and Lincoln told Hooker he would have to submit to Halleck. Halleck was hostile and annoying and Hooker on June 27 asked to be relieved. General Meade was straightway appointed, for which, among other reasons, the following have been given.

1. He was a good soldier, if not a brilliant one.

2. He was a native of Pennsylvania, the present battle-ground.

3. He was a Democrat, and the President wished to check a threatened demand for McClellan's restoration.

A few days later came the turning-point in the war.

CHAPTER XIV

THE TURNING OF THE TIDE

AFTER Chancellorsville one of Lincoln's private secretaries, working at the office over his mail until 3 A.M., heard the President's footfall as he left. Returning at eight o'clock he saw his chief still in the room eating a solitary breakfast, before him the written instructions to Hooker to push forward and fight again.

A few weeks later the President had a dream. A ship passed before his sleeping vision, sailing away rapidly, badly damaged, with victorious Union vessels in close pursuit. Also there appeared the close of a battle on land, the enemy routed, our forces in possession of a position immensely important. The same dream had come to him before Antietam. Coming before Gettysburg it heralded fortune of far greater scope.

For three days the Confederates attacked the Federal army, charging and recharging up the hills with fearful slaughter, and when they were driven back for the last time, July 3, the total in killed and wounded Union soldiers was 23,186, with a total almost as great for the Southern army, which could ill afford the equal loss. Lee slowly retired across the Potomac, and Meade, reënforced, with fresher troops, refused to attack. Lincoln was as sharp as his patient nature would allow. Meade's phrase, "driving the invaders from our soil," particularly displeased him, partly, perhaps, because the whole country was our soil, but more because it showed that he had not yet found a general who could conceive the idea of following up advantage and destroying his adversary. On account of the President's comments Meade asked to be relieved. Lincoln wrote, in a letter which he never sent, this view of the struggle: —

"I am very, very grateful to you for the magnificent success you gave the cause of the country at Gettysburg; and I am sorry now to be the author of the slightest pain to you. But I was in such deep distress myself that I could not restrain some expression of it. I have been oppressed nearly ever since the battles at Gettysburg by what appeared to be evidences that yourself and General Couch and General Smith were not seeking a collision with the enemy, but were trying to get him across the river without another battle. What these evidences were, if you please, I hope to tell you at some time when we shall both feel better. The case, summarily stated, is this: You fought and beat the enemy at Gettysburg, and, of course, to say the least, his loss was as great as yours. He retreated, and you did not, as it seemed to me, pressingly pursue him; but a flood in the river detained him till, by slow degrees, you

Y

were again upon him. You had at least twenty thou
sand veteran troops directly with you, and as many
more raw ones within supporting distance, all in addition to those who fought with you at Gettysburg, while
it was not possible that he had received a single recruit,
and yet you stood and let the flood run down, bridges be
built, and the enemy move away at his leisure without
attacking him. And Couch and Smith! The latter
left Carlisle in time, upon all ordinary calculation, to
have aided you in the last battle at Gettysburg, but he
did not arrive. At the end of more than ten days,
I believe twelve, under constant urging, he reached
Hagerstown from Carlisle, which is not an inch over
fifty-five miles, if so much, and Couch's movement was
very little different.

"Again, my dear general, I do not believe you appreciate the magnitude of the misfortune involved in Lee's
escape. He was within your easy grasp, and to close
upon him would, in connection with our other late suc-
cesses, have ended the war. As it is, the war will be
prolonged indefinitely. If you could not safely attack
Lee last Monday, how can you possibly do so south of
the river, when you can take with you very few more
than two-thirds of the force you then had in hand? It
would be unreasonable to expect, and I do not expect
you can now effect much. Your golden opportunity is
gone, and I am distressed immeasurably because of it.

"I beg you will not consider this a prosecution or per-
secution of yourself. As you had learned that I was dissatisfied, I have thought it best to kindly tell you why."

Things dragged along. Meade thought of attacking Lee later, at a disadvantage, merely to

satisfy the administration, an idea which Lincoln rejected. By October, however, we find the President writing to General Halleck: —

"Doubtless, in making the present movement, Lee gathered in all available scraps, and added them to Hill's and Ewell's corps; but that is all, and he made the movement in the belief that four corps had left General Meade; and General Meade's apparently avoiding a collision with him has confirmed him in that belief. If General Meade can now attack him on a field no worse than equal for us, and will do so with all the skill and courage which he, his officers, and men possess, the honor will be his if he succeeds, and the blame may be mine if he fails."

The same Fourth of July which told the nation of the saving victory of Gettysburg saw another almost equally important and far more brilliant victory in the West, the part of the country where most of the best Federal generals had been working with little knowledge from Washington. The capture of Vicksburg brought for the first time very prominently before the President's notice the general who of all the Union soldiers best combined ability with the offensive spirit necessary for an actual conquest by beating his way into the heart of the enemy's country. Lincoln had commented in a few appreciative words on a kindly and tactful proclamation made by General Grant early in the war, but had paid no special attention to him, as, indeed, nobody had. "Keep still and saw wood" was a maxim which Lincoln appreciated. Grant acted on it. While the other generals quarrelled for promotion he only asked to fight. There were ten pegs where there was one hole to put them in, as Lincoln said. The urgency of Fremont's friends that he should have a command reminded the President of the youth who was advised to take a wife. "Willingly. But whose wife shall I take?" To General Rosecrans, who, troubled by the dawning appreciation that Grant was the fighter, began to pull wires, the President said the country would "never care a fig whether you rank General Grant on paper, or he so ranks you."

In 1862, when the other generals were voluminously telling what they needed, Grant telegraphed to Halleck, "If permitted, I could take and hold Fort Henry on the Tennessee." Five days after he received permission the fort was his. Grant then moved upon Fort Donelson. He had virtuously informed Halleck of his intention, but the superior officer's instructions to confine himself to fortifying Fort Henry came after Grant already had his grip on Donelson. The commander asked for terms, and Grant said none would be considered except "unconditional surrender." Grant in his memoirs explains his haste: "I was very impatient to get at Fort

Donelson because I knew the importance of the place to the enemy, and supposed he would reënforce it rapidly. I felt that 15,000 on the 8th would be more effective than 50,000 a month later." The talking generals did not like this, and Halleck immediately claimed the credit for Grant's achievements. Grant, as usual, said nothing, but "sawed wood," while Stanton and Lincoln conceived a higher opinion of Halleck. Grant fared like the commonest soldier in his command, often sleeping on the ground with no covering, without overcoat or blanket, and at one time having as his entire baggage for several days nothing but his tooth-brush. Just after Donelson he arranged for the capture of Nashville, and a little latter Halleck and McClellan had him arrested on a charge of drunkenness. An inquiry by the War Department cleared Grant of the charge, and gave him another chance to work. He at once moved toward Pittsburg Landing, to wait for Buell, and then attack Johnston's army, which was fortifying itself there. Johnston, however, with superior forces attacked him before Buell came, and after the first day's fighting Grant, now reënforced, attacked in turn the next morning at Shiloh, and won. Halleck promptly gave credit to everybody except Grant, and took command of the army himself, while the stories of Grant's drunkenness were again industriously circulated. Lincoln then and after was frequently asked to remove him. " I can't spare that man; he fights," was one reply, and to another delegation he said he would like to know what brand of whiskey Grant used, that he might feed it to his other generals. Passing over other important work by Grant we come, in July 1863, to the act which practically made it certain that he was to be the main reliance of the President and the nation. Vicksburg, by its tremendously strong fortifications, and its position on the Mississippi, was of immeasurable importance. After having Sherman try an assault, and experimenting with canal schemes to get at the almost impregnable citadel, Grant finally decided to risk destruction by running the batteries with his transports and getting his army below the fortifications, which gave the only opportunity for successful siege. This meant prompt victory or annihilation. The result was surrender on July 4. The total outcome of this campaign, to say nothing of the value of the Vicksburg position, was, according to Grant's official summaries, the occupation of Jackson, the capital of Mississippi, a loss to the Confederates of 37,000 prisoners, 10,000 killed and wounded, many more missing, and arms and munitions for an army of 60,000 men, while the Federals lost in killed, wounded, and missing less than 8000. A series of brilliant victories by Grant, with Sherman, Sheridan, Thomas, and Hooker as lieutenants, very soon completed this work in the West.

Thus Lincoln found his soldier. On July 13 he wrote to him: —

"MY DEAR GENERAL: I do not remember that you and I ever met personally. I write this now as a grateful acknowledgment for the almost inestimable service you have done the country. I wish to say a word further. When you first reached the vicinity of Vicksburg, I thought you would do what you finally did — march the troops across the neck, run the batteries with the transports, and thus go below; and I never had any faith, except a general hope that you knew better than I that the Yazoo Pass expedition and the like could succeed. When you got below and took Fort Gibson, Grand Gulf, and the vicinity, I thought you should go down the river and join General Banks, and when you turned northward, east of the Big Black, I feared it was a mistake. I now wish to make the personal acknowledgment that you were right and I was wrong."

On the 27th of the same month Lincoln, explaining to Burnside why he could not give him certain information, remarked, " General Grant is a copious worker and fighter, but a very meagre writer or telegrapher." The country, however, was beginning to understand him, in spite of all wire-pulling, and there grew rapidly a demand for his command of all the forces. The difference

between him and even so able a general as Rosecrans, a sort of second McClellan, not quite so slow,
is gently hinted in the memoirs. Of this officer
General Grant says: "He came into my car and
we held a brief interview, in which he described
very clearly the situation at Chattanooga, and
made some very excellent suggestions as to what
should be done. My only wonder was that he
had not carried them out." It will hardly be out
of place to insert here Grant's opinion of the
President who, as soon as he once came to know
his general, gave over the whole military conduct of the war to him. Grant says of Lincoln: "A man of great ability, pure patriotism,
unselfish nature, full of forgiveness to his enemies, bearing malice toward none, he proved
to be the man above all others for the struggle through which the nation had to pass to
place itself among the greatest in the family of
nations."

Another soldier who was coming to his proper
place was General Sherman. He had first met
Lincoln in March, 1861, when he was introduced
by his brother John, who said, "Mr. President,
this is my brother, Colonel Sherman, who is just
up from Louisiana; he may give you some information you want."

"Ah," said Lincoln, "how are they getting
along down there?"

"They think they are getting along swimmingly —they are preparing for war."

"Oh, well," replied the President, "I guess we'll manage to keep house."

The young soldier was disgusted enough, and emphatically told his brother what he thought of politicians in general.

After Bull Run Sherman received a pleasanter impression of his chief. He saw him riding one day with Seward in an open hack and asked if they were going to his camps.

"Yes," said Lincoln; "we heard that you had got over the big scare, and we thought we would come over and see the boys."

As always after a defeat, the President wanted to encourage everybody, and wished to address the soldiers. Sherman asked him to discourage cheering, noise, or other confusion, saying they had had enough of that before Bull Run to ruin any lot of fighting men. Lincoln took the suggestion with good nature. He then made from his carriage what Sherman calls "one of the neatest, best, and most feeling addresses I ever listened to." At one or two points the soldiers began to cheer. "Don't cheer, boys," said Lincoln, "I confess I rather like it myself, but Colonel Sherman here says it is not military, and I guess we had better defer to his opinion." In conclusion, he told the men that as he was their commander-in-chief, he was determined the soldiers should have everything the law allowed, and re· quested them to appeal to him personally if they were wronged. " The effect of this speech," says Sherman, " was excellent."

Later an officer forced his way through the crowd, and said, " Mr. President, I have a grievance." He then told that Colonel Sherman had threatened to shoot him. After looking at him, and then at Sherman, Lincoln, stepping toward the officer, said, in a stage whisper, " Well, if I were you, and he· threatened to shoot, I wouldn't trust him, for I believe he would do it."

The officer left, and the men laughed. Sherman explained the facts, and Lincoln said, " Of course, I didn't know anything about it, but I thought you knew your own business best."

Lincoln's relations to Sherman after he came to high command were of the most friendly sort. He told him later in the war that he was always grateful to him and to Grant because they never scolded him.

The discovery of the proper generals made an immense difference in the life of the President. He could confine himself largely to other than military matters, and politics were soon to need his closest attention. At the beginning of the spring Grant was made lieutenant general, and took command of the forces in the East, to begin the final struggle. Lincoln gave few suggestions and no orders. Once he had sat in deep meditation, and finally remarked: " Do you know that I think General —— is a philosopher? He has proved himself a really great man. He has grappled with and mastered that ancient and wise admonition, ' Know thyself '; he has formed an intimate acquaintance with himself; knows as well for what he is fitted and unfitted as any man living. Without doubt he is a remarkable man. This war has not produced another like him. He has resigned. And now I hope some other dress-parade commanders will study the good old admonition, ' Know thyself,' and follow his example." By the end of 1863 the dress-parade commanders were pretty nearly gone. Of a cavalry raid, which filled the papers with enthusiasm, but did not cut the communications at which it was aimed, Lincoln remarked that it "was good circus riding." When the final struggle began in the spring, instead of the current joke, " Who ever saw a dead cavalryman ? " Washington was to have a sample of Philip Sheridan's cavalry methods.

Before finishing the year 1863, however, there remain to be noted a number of details about the President, among them a few half pathetic personal touches. To the actor, James H. Hackett, who had sent him a book, Lincoln said in his reply:—

" For one of my age I have seen very little of the
drama. The first presentation of Falstaff I ever saw
was yours here, last winter or spring. Perhaps the best
compliment I can pay is to say, as I truly can, I am very
anxious to see it again. Some of Shakespeare's plays
I have never read, while others I have gone over perhaps as frequently as any unprofessional reader. Among
the latter are 'Lear,' 'Richard III.,' 'Henry VIII.,'
'Hamlet,' and especially 'Macbeth.' I think nothing
equals 'Macbeth.' It is wonderful. Unlike you gentlemen of the profession, I think the soliloquy in 'Hamlet' commencing, 'Oh, my offence is rank,' surpasses
that commencing, 'To be or not to be.' But pardon
this small attempt at criticism. I should like to hear
you pronounce the opening speech of 'Richard III.'"

Perhaps the President did not appreciate the
usual vanity of actors. Hackett gave the letter
to the press, wrote Lincoln again, and received
in return these words: —

" My note to you I certainly did not expect to see in
print; yet I have not been much shocked by the newspaper comments upon it. Those comments constitute a
fair specimen of what has occurred to me through life.
I have endured a great deal of ridicule without much
malice; and have received a great deal of kindness, not
quite free from ridicule. I am used to it."

In a letter to his wife in August, he says: —

" Tell dear Tad poor 'Nanny Goat' is lost, and Mrs.
Cuthbert and I are in distress about it. The day you

left Nanny was found resting herself and chewing her little cud on the middle of Tad's bed; but now she's gone! The gardener kept complaining that she destroyed the flowers, till it was concluded to bring her down to the White House. This was done, and the second day she had disappeared, and has not been heard of since. This is the last we know of poor Nanny."

There were two goats, and Lincoln used to play with them in the White House yard. The next year a telegram to Mrs. Lincoln referred to them thus, " Tell Tad the goats and father are very well — especially the goats."

The fall elections went well, and one of the President's comments was this: —

" I am very glad the elections this autumn have gone favorably, and that I have not, by native depravity or under evil influences, done anything bad enough to prevent the good result. I hope to ' stand firm ' enough to not go backward, and yet not go forward fast enough to wreck the country's cause."

His attitude toward Stanton and toward certain tests for office are shown in this note to the Secretary of War: —

" I personally wish Jacob Freese, of New Jersey, to be appointed colonel for a colored regiment, and this regardless of whether he can tell the exact shade of Julius Cæsar's hair."

A germ of the doctrine of preference for the veteran, so fully extended since, was planted by the President:—

" Yesterday little indorsements of mine went to you in two cases of postmasterships sought for widows whose husbands have fallen in the battles of this war. These cases occurring on the same day brought me to reflect more attentively than I had before done as to what is fairly due from us here in the dispensing of patronage toward the men who, by fighting our battles, bear the chief burden of saving our country. My conclusion is that, other claims and qualifications being equal, they have the better right ; and this is especially applicable to the disabled soldier and the deceased soldier's family."

That his view of the delinquent soldier did not harden as time made him more familiar with the facts is shown by this : —

" The case of Andrews is really a very bad one, as appears by the record already before me. Yet before receiving this I had ordered his punishment commuted to imprisonment for during the war at hard labor, and had so telegraphed. I did this, not on any merit in the case, but because I am trying to evade the butchering business lately."

The fall of 1863 saw one of the President's most noted literary efforts. About the famous address at the dedication of Gettysburg Cemetery many contrary statements have been made, both about its preparation and about its recep- tion. The most plausible view is that it was rather carefully prepared, that it was received by the assemblage in comparative silence, and that Lincoln and others present thought it a failure, only to learn their mistake when they saw its re- ception by the world. Lamon says that a few days before the dedication Lincoln spoke to him of his short time for preparation and his fear of not coming out of the situation with credit. From his hat he drew a sheet of foolscap, on one side of which was a closely written memorandum of the intended address. After the delivery he said he regretted that it had not been done more care- fully. "Lamon," he said also, "that speech won't *scour!* It is a flat failure. The people are dis- appointed." Edward Everett, the orator of the day, whose long speech is unremembered now, and Secretary Seward also thought, according to Lamon, that Lincoln had failed and that the crowd was disappointed. The story that it was written on the train probably grew out of a final revision. The whole speech was : —

"Fourscore and seven years ago our fathers brought forth on this continent a new nation, conceived in lib- erty, and dedicated to the proposition that all men are created equal.

"Now we are engaged in a great civil war, testing

Address delivered at the dedication of the Cemetery at Gettysburg.

Four score and seven years ago our fathers brought forth on this Continent, a new nation, conceived in Liberty, and dedicated to the proposition that all men are created equal.

Now we are engaged in a great civil war, testing whether that nation, or any nation so conceived and so dedicated, can long endure. We are met on a great battle field of that war. We have come to dedicate a portion of that field, as a final resting place for those who here gave their lives, that that nation might live. It is altogether fitting and proper that we should do this.

But, in a larger sense, we can not dedicate — we can not consecrate — we can not hallow — this ground. The brave men, living and dead, who struggled here, have consecrated it, far above our poor power to add or detract. The world will little note, nor long remember what we say here, but it can never forget what they did here. It is for us the living, rather, to be dedicated here to the unfinished work which they who fought here have thus far so nobly advanced. It is rather for us to be here dedicated to the great task remaining before us — that from these honored dead we take increased devotion to that cause for which they gave the last full measure of devotion — that we here highly resolve that these dead shall not have died in vain — that this nation, under God, shall have a new birth of freedom — and that government of the people, by the people, for the people, shall not perish from the earth.

Abraham Lincoln.

November 19. 1863.

whether that nation, or any nation so conceived and so dedicated, can long endure. We are met on a great battle-field of that war. We have come to dedicate a portion of that field as a final resting-place for those who here gave their lives that that nation might live. It is altogether fitting and proper that we should do this.

"But, in a larger sense, we cannot dedicate — we cannot consecrate — we cannot hallow — this ground. The brave men, living and dead, who struggled here, have consecrated it far above our poor power to add or detract. The world will little note nor long remember what we say here, but it can never forget what they did here. It is for us, the living, rather, to be dedicated here to the unfinished work which they who fought here have thus far so nobly advanced. It is rather for us to be here dedicated to the great task remaining before us — that from these honored dead we take increased devotion to that cause for which they gave the last full measure of devotion; that we here highly resolve that these dead shall not have died in vain; that this nation, under God, shall have a new birth of freedom; and that government of the people, by the people, for the people, shall not perish from the earth."

The classical, lasting qualities of this brief address are no longer subject to doubt. They stand with the few best known pieces of English prose. The last phrase is one that the world had been working at, and Lincoln had marked something very much like it in one of Theodore Parker's lectures; but it was chosen for this final place

with literary skill, and the whole address, which has
no other echo in it, is too nobly right to gain by
praise. Nothing could better prove how thoroughly
the man of the people could be the man of taste;
how the absolute Democrat could perfectly speak
the highest language of literary simplicity. Nothing seems too ripe or cultivated for him, just as
nothing seems too humble or crude to deserve
his fellowship. With the highest he never entirely lost the air of familiarity; when easily
meeting the lowest it was always with an inalien-
able dignity. How different, it might be natural
to exclaim, the Lincoln who penned these lines
from the Lincoln who listened to Lamon's songs;
yet the surprise would be as shallow as it would
be natural. He was a man, and deemed nothing
human foreign to him; yet his soul dwelt alone,
" silent upon a peak in Darien." This solitary
greatness, this elevation and distinction in the
midst of unconventionality and equality, are well
set in the outer habits of his life. A French
marquis has left this singularly vivid impression
of him. " He wittingly laughed either at what
was being said to him, or at what he said himself.
But all of a sudden he would retire within himself; then he would close his eyes and all his features would at once bespeak a kind of sadness as
indescribable as it was deep. After a while, as
though it were by an effort of his will, he would

shake off this mysterious weight under which he seemed bowed; his generous and open disposition would again reappear. In one evening I happened to count over twenty of these alternations and contrasts."

One of the last acts of the year 1863 showed the President's never sleeping wish for leniency. To his annual message to Congress he added, unexpectedly to everybody, a proclamation granting amnesty to all rebels, barring certain classes, who would take a simple oath to support the Constitution, the Union, and the legislation and proclamations concerning slavery. By the same proclamation one-tenth of the voters in a seceded state were given the right, after taking and keeping the oath, to reëstablish a state government. Almost immediately Congress showed displeasure at the President's undertaking reconstruction alone, it being uncertain which branch of the government had the better right to accomplish that duty. Naturally also many people felt sternness where Lincoln felt none. His constant desire for compensation to the slaveholders may be contrasted with the sentiment voiced even by so gentle a soul as Emerson: —

> " Pay ransom to the owner,
>   Ay, fill it up to the brim !
>   Who is the owner? The slave is owner,
>   And ever was. Pay him."

This moral indignation applied equally to reconstruction; but in the one case as in the other indignation was of a quality which to Lincoln's character was entirely foreign. Whatever he believed about the Christian religion, he practised as few others did some of the extreme Christian virtues. He very genuinely believed that the way to establish the new order of things without bitterness was to treat the vanquished rebel as if he were a beloved and trustworthy brother who had just been convinced in an argument. This state of mind, looked upon as impractical, did a good deal to add to the considerable opposition which existed, especially among politicians, to Lincoln's renomination in the following spring. The leader of the House of Representatives said that the President had but one political friend in that body. Lincoln, however, had his convictions fully ripened. Sometimes he felt sure of renomination, sometimes he saw little hope of it, but in either case his way lay clear before him. He could do the right, as it seemed clearly marked out before him, and silently endure whatever he could not remedy; but in the meantime he would " saw some wood." He would trust the great engine of sane public opinion, but he also knew when to put a little oil in it, and how to touch a spring here or tighten a screw there to make it work better. The his-

tory of the next presidential campaign will be
the story of destiny and justice grandly vindi-
cating the work of the servant who, according
to Emerson, had " been permitted to do more for
America than any other American man "; but if
correctly read it will also show that American
statesman astutely and subterraneously guiding
destiny to its just conclusion.

CHAPTER XV

AMONG the obstacles to Lincoln's renomination Secretary Chase reckoned himself a large one. He used his position as Secretary of the Treasury in every way he could to strengthen his own chances against those of the President. General Butler tells us that a friend of Chase offered him the nomination for vice-presidency on condition that Chase should win at the convention. The criticisms of the Secretary of the Treasury on the administration were unceasing and severe. His letters contain frank admissions that if the country shall look upon him as the ablest standard-bearer he will not dispute the choice. Senator Pomeroy brought matters to a head by issuing a circular calling for efforts by the friends of the Union who disapproved of the administration, to counteract the work being done for Lincoln's renomination. The President's re-election was stated to be practically impossible as well as undesirable, among other reasons on account of Lincoln's "tendency toward compromises and temporary expedients of policy." The document also stated that the friends of Chase had already established conventions in all the states. The circular soon got into the press, and Chase saw that his only course was to resign, which he did. Lincoln replied that he would not allow himself to consider the question from any standpoint other than his judgment of the public service, and in that view he saw no occasion for a change. To his friend Raymond, whose omission of Chase's name hardly creates a doubt, he gave a rather more racy estimate of the situation : —

" Raymond, you were brought up on a farm, were you not? Then you know what a chin-fly is. My brother and I were once ploughing corn on a farm, I driving the horse, and he holding plough. The horse was lazy, but on one occasion rushed across the fields so that I, with my long legs, could scarcely keep pace with him. On reaching the end of the furrow, I found an enormous chin-fly fastened upon him, and knocked him off. My brother asked me what I did that for. I told him I didn't want the old horse bitten in that way. 'Why,' said my brother, 'that's all that made him go.' Now, if Mr. —— has a presidential chin-fly biting him I am not going to knock him off, if it will only make his department go."

Chase's hopes came to an end in February, when his own state, Ohio, renominated Lincoln. That statesman's view of the result he has stated himself : —

"Your views of policy coincide with my own, and had it seemed to be the will of the people that I should take the responsibilities of government I should not have refused, though I could not seek such a place. But, through the natural partialities of the people for the President, and the systematic operation of the Postmaster-General, and those holding office under him, a preference for the reëlection of Mr. Lincoln was created, to which I thought it my duty to bow cheerfully and unhesitatingly. It did not cost me a regret to do so. That, since then, I have been so maliciously pursued by the Blair family, is what was wholly unexpected. That their slanders have the apparent, though I am sure not the real, indorsement of the President, is a new source of pain to me. No good can, I think, come of the probable identification of the next administration with the family. The political future, in consequence of it, has already become clouded and doubtful."

The reference to the Blair family meant merely that Lincoln would not join in a feud between General Blair and Chase. The bad blood continued, especially as each wished to control the patronage connected with the Treasury Department. Finally, in June, Chase resigned, for the fourth time, it is said, and Lincoln accepted, frankly on the ground that their relations had become too strained for further work together. The President made a bad nomination, David Todd of Ohio, who declined, and then Senator Fessenden of Maine, chairman of the Committee on Finance, an excellent choice, was with difficulty induced to accept. Chase, within a week after his retirement, said that he was then inclined to agree with Pomeroy, who would not support Lincoln, but he added that he was " not willing now to decide what duty may demand next fall." In September he visited Washington, saw Lincoln, and declared in his favor. Just after this Chief Justice Taney died. Sumner, Stanton, and others were in favor of giving Chase the place. Opponents of the move said he did not know enough law, as his life had been almost entirely political. Lincoln waited several weeks before acting, although his mind was probably made up. Chase says in his diary that Lincoln told a friend of his June 30 that he intended to appoint Chase if a vacancy occurred in the chief justiceship, Taney then being ill. Warden, Chase's biographer, quotes Sumner as telling him that Lincoln proposed to Sumner the plan of sending for Chase, and frankly telling him that he would make the best chief justice we ever had if he could only get rid of his presidential ambition. Sumner thought that this course would lead to misinterpretation of Lincoln's motives, and also displease Chase, so the President made the appointment without exacting any pledge. As Chase was already removed from Lincoln's own way, the President's motive in wishing him out of politics was doubtless mainly the genuine belief that dabbling in them would injure his work on the bench.   To George S. Boutwell, however, Lincoln said, after Chase's nomination: " There are three reasons why he should be nominated, and one why he should not be.   In the first place, he occupies a larger place in the public mind, with reference to the office, than any other person.   Then we want a man who will sustain the Legal Tender Act and the Proclamation of Emancipation.   We cannot ask a candidate what he would do, and if we did and he should answer, we should only despise him for it.   But he wants to be President, and if he does not give that up it will be a great injury to him and a great injury to me.   He can never be President."

Another seeker of the same prize was Fremont. Among his supporters the best known was Wendell Phillips, who said he should look upon Lincoln's reëlection as meaning the end of the Union, or reconstruction on terms worse than disunion. Other Fremont men described the President's "imbecile and vacillating policy."   They got together in small numbers for a mass convention in May, and nominated their man.   Lincoln, when told that the convention was so small, took up the Bible, and read from Samuel these lines, " And every one that was in distress, and every one that was discontented, gathered themselves unto him;

and he became a captain over them; and there were in all about four hundred men."

In reference to the opposition of Wendell Phillips, Wade, Davis, and others, he recalled an Illinois farmer who, at his repast, was interrupted by the exclamation of his son: —

" Hold on, dad! there's skippers in that cheese you're eating."

" Never mind, Tom, if they can stand it, I can."

Fremont's letter of acceptance attacked the President, and hinted that if the Republicans in their approaching convention at Baltimore, would choose another candidate, he would withdraw. The Fremont people attacked the administration not only for its vacillation but for its use of patronage. It was undoubtedly true that all the resources of the administration, including the War Department, in spite of Stanton's opposition to some of the methods, were used to secure the President's renomination and reëlection. But these things did not bother the people. The only thing that counted much with them was military success, and Lincoln's chances, in spite of his real popularity, seemed to hang largely on the army. Fremont soon saw that he was in for little more than ridicule, but he would only retire on condition that the arch-enemy of the radicals, Blair, should leave the cabinet. Lincoln did not feel strong enough to take needless chances, and he secured Blair's resignation without losing his support. Fremont withdrew. In commenting on his difficulty in satisfying the politicians when he was choosing successors to Blair and to Bates, who also resigned in this year, Lincoln said, " I suppose that if the twelve apostles were to be chosen nowadays, the shrieks of locality would have to be heeded." Some idea of the constant pressure for office is given by a little tale about a delegation that called on the President to request the appointment of a certain man as commissioner to the Sandwich Islands. They urged among other things that he was in bad health and residence in the Islands would benefit him. " Gentlemen," said Lincoln, " I am sorry to say that there are eight other applicants for the place, and they are all sicker than your man."

Lincoln was certainly a politician among the politicians, as a number of illustrations will show. George W. Julian, one of the malcontent members of Congress, whom Lincoln had every reason to wish to please, was renominated, but not recognized as the regular nominee by one of the Republican newspapers, the editor of which happened to be commissioner of patents. Lincoln assured Julian that the editor should support him or lose his head, and the paper shortly after changed its mind. His letters show him trying for an opportunity to conciliate Governor Seymour, which was in vain, and also Thurlow Weed, which succeeded better. R. E. Fenton tells of being called to Washington by a telegram from one of the President's private secretaries, and addressed by Lincoln, as nearly as he could remember, as follows: "You are to be nominated by our folks for governor of your state. Seymour of course will be the Democratic nominee. You will have a hard fight. . . . There is some trouble among our folks over there, which we must try and manage. Or, rather, there is one man who may give us trouble, because of his indifference, if in no other way. He has great influence and his feelings may be reflected in many of his friends. We must have his counsel and coöperation if possible." Thurlow Weed, in short, was not pleased with the disposition of the Federal patronage in New York, being particularly hostile to the collector and surveyor. Nicolay, the secretary, and Fenton returned to New York that evening. The next day Fenton had a consultation with Weed, Nicolay returned to Washington with the resignation of the surveyor, and a friend of Weed was the successor. The state went Republican in the fall.

It has been frequently said that Lincoln as far back as 1862 offered to get out of the way in 1864 if Seymour would take the right ground in his annual message; but Seymour remained as violent as ever. Lamon also says that the President then made an offer to McClellan looking to his nomination by the Democrats with Republican support; but these stories have little to rest upon. As far as can now be seen, Lincoln, in spite of certain strong moods and consequently strong expressions, was in the field for renomination from the beginning. His correspondence indicates some of the directions of his political activity during the first part of 1864. He was once heard to say that honest statesmanship was the employment of individual meanness for the public good. He played on most of the keys of human nature and he never failed to aim at the public good. He held a sharp rein on the politicians in his party, and yet he treated them leniently. "I am in favor of short statutes of limitations in politics," he said, which was only another side of his love for forgiveness and his lack of rancor. He worked hard for his renomination and his reëlection, and he faced much malice but bore none. Speaking of resentment he said: "Perhaps I have too little of it; but I never thought it paid. A man has no time to spend half his life in quarrels." Again, to Mr. Hay, "It is singular that I, who am not a vindictive man, should always, except once, have been before the people for election in canvasses marked for their bitterness." In the present contest he saw that those who opposed him were working against the public good and he knew that every point he could make for himself was a point for his country. After his nomination he said to a delegation: " But I do not allow myself to suppose that either the convention or the league have concluded to decide that I am either the greatest or best man in America, but rather they have concluded that it is not best to swap horses while crossing the river, and have further concluded that I am not so poor a horse that they might not make a botch of it in trying to swap."

Nothing could better show his combination of frankness and modesty.

Three days before the Republican convention a mass meeting was held in New York to thank Grant, and there was thought to be a design to present him as a candidate. The general, however, firmly refused the use of his name. It is said that the President, warned about him, had sounded him through friends earlier in the season. When the convention was actually held, June 7, Lincoln received 484 votes on the first ballot, the 32 from Missouri going to Grant, but being immediately transferred to Lincoln.

About the vice-presidency there has been some controversy in print, but the facts are in no reasonable doubt. General Butler tells us that he was offered the second place, but said he would not take it unless the President would agree to die during the term. Colonel McClure confirms this, and gives a full and apparently exact account of the movement against Hamlin's renomination. The Vice-President had apparently given at least passive support to the Republican opposition to Lincoln led by Wade of Ohio and Davis of Maryland, although he is reported to have refused to be nominated against the President. Lincoln felt an underlying despondency in the North, after the effect of Gettysburg and Vicksburg had passed and the heavy drafts in 1864 were being felt. He therefore decided early in the year that it would strengthen him to have on the ticket with him a conspicuous war Democrat who had opposed him in 1860, but was now in the military service. Hamlin did not belong in this class. After Butler declined, Lincoln expressed his preference for Andrew Johnson, war-governor of Tennessee. He summoned General Sickles to Washington, and sent him to Tennessee to make a confidential report on Johnson's record as military governor. The report was favorable, and relieved the President's mind of the fear that charges of violence and despotism might be successfully brought against Johnson during the campaign. The Wade–Davis faction charged that Lincoln's determination not to have

2 A

the question of reconstruction settled in the summer of 1864 by Congress was caused by his desire to guard against defeat at the polls, by
putting himself in a position to have the votes
of certain partly reconstructed Southern states
counted if it became necessary. Wade and Davis
published an attack on Lincoln in the *Tribune*
of August 5 in which they said, " The President, by preventing this bill from becoming a
law, holds the electoral votes of the Southern
states at the dictates of his personal ambition."
The most promising situation was in Tennessee,
but McClure believes that if the contest was
close Lincoln intended to have Louisiana, Arkansas, and West Virginia also organized into some
sort of state-hood. He had delegates elected
from these states to the national convention, and
the battle for their admission was led by Lincoln's
confidants. Tennessee's position being the strongest it was chosen for the test fight. The opposition came from the anti-Johnson men. After a
struggle, that delegation was admitted, and Louisiana and Arkansas were then given the right to
representation almost as a matter of course. Their
votes in the end were not counted, but the result
might have been different had they been needed.

One of the ways in which Lincoln's political
shrewdness was shown was in the care he took
to consult Cameron early on this matter of the

vice-presidency.   Seward and Weed were both taken early into the movement for Johnson's nomination.   McClure says that Lincoln's friends Swett and Lamon knew nothing of the selection until within a day or two of the convention.   Then Swett said to the President that if it were known in New England that he was in favor of leaving Hamlin off the ticket, "it would raise the devil among the Yankees."   He urged that New England politicians were rankling over what they deemed Lincoln's tardiness about slavery and haste about reconstruction, and that it would be dangerous to offend them further.   Swett was persuaded by Lincoln, however, to go to the convention, prepared to support Johnson if necessary, though he was to avoid suspicion by having another candidate as his first choice, and he was not to reveal the President's preference for Johnson.   According to Lamon, Lincoln said: "I will address a letter to Lamon here, embodying my views, which you, McClure, and other friends may use if it be found absolutely necessary.   Otherwise it may be better that I should not appear on the stage of this theatre."   Lamon took the letter to Baltimore, but found no need of it, and it was then returned at the President's request. Another point in Johnson's favor, in Lincoln's mind, according to McClure, was that he believed the election of a Southern man to the vice-presidency would have a good effect in England and France. Johnson had 200 on the first ballot, to 150 for Hamlin and 108 for D. S. Dickinson, and his nomination was promptly made unanimous.

The Democrats did not meet until the end of August, when they nominated General McClellan on a platform calling the war policy a failure and demanding peace. Before that they devoted themselves to attacking the Republicans, who were badly divided among themselves. The attitude of Senator Wade was described by Lincoln himself to Lamon, at the same time that he showed his way of treating him. Wade had come in to demand the dismissal of Grant. In reply to one of his remarks Lincoln said, " Senator, that reminds me of a story." " Yes, yes," Wade replied, " it is with you, sir, all story, story! You are the father of every military blunder that has been made during the war. You are on your road to hell, sir, with this government, by your obstinacy; and you are not a mile off this minute." Lincoln answered, " Senator, that is just about the distance from here to the Capitol, is it not?" Wade, as Lincoln put it, "grabbed up his hat and cane and went away."

The President's moods about the outcome probably varied greatly. According to one report he said early in the campaign:—

"I am glad you have come in.   Lamon, do you know that 'we have met the enemy, and they are *ourn?*'   I think the cabal of obstructionists 'am busted!'   I feel certain that if I live, I am going to be reëlected.   Whether I deserve to be or not, it is not for me to say; but on the score even of remunerative chances for speculative service, I now am inspired with the hope that our disturbed country further requires the valuable services of your humble servant.   'Jordan has been a hard road to travel,' but I feel now that, notwithstanding the enemies I have made and the faults I have committed, I'll be *dumped* on the right side of that stream.   I hope, however, that I may never have another four years of such anxiety, tribulation, and abuse.   My only ambition is and has been to put down the rebellion and restore peace; after which I want to resign my office, go abroad, take some rest, study foreign governments, see something of foreign life, and in my old age, die in peace with all of the good of God's creatures."

On the other hand, on August 23 he prepared this memorandum: —

"This morning, as for some days past, it seems exceedingly probable that this administration will not be reëlected.   Then it will be my duty to so coöperate with the President-elect as to save the Union between the election and the inauguration, as he will have secured his election on such ground that he cannot possibly save it afterward."

Nicolay and Hay, who publish the memorandum, also report the following later remarks on this subject at a cabinet meeting : —

"The President said : 'You will remember that this was written at the time, six days before the Chicago nominating convention, when as yet we had no adversary, and seemed to have no friends. I then solemnly resolved on the course of action indicated in this paper. I resolved, in case of the election of General McClellan, being certain that he would be the candidate, that I would see him, and talk matters over with him. I would say : "General, the election has demonstrated that you are stronger, have more influence with the American people, than I. Now let us together, you with your influence and I with all the executive power of the government, try to save the country. You raise as many troops as you possibly can for this final trial, and I will devote all my energies to assist and finish the war." '

"Seward said, 'And the general would have answered you, "Yes, yes," and the next day when you saw him again and pressed these views upon him he would have said, "Yes, yes;" and so on forever, and would have done nothing at all.'

"'At least,' said Lincoln, 'I should have done my duty, and have stood clear before my own conscience.'"

Before McClellan's nomination and after, Lincoln pushed constantly the argument that a vote for union was in all reasonableness a vote for him, and he tried constantly to bring the meaning of union home to his hearers. To one regiment he said: —

" I happen, temporarily, to occupy this White House. I am a living witness that any one of your children may look to come here as my father's child has. It is in order that each one of you may have, through this free government which we have enjoyed, an open field and a fair chance for your industry, enterprise, and intelligence; that you may all have equal privileges in the race of life, with all its desirable human aspirations."

To another regiment: —

" But this government must be preserved in spite of the acts of any man or set of men. It is worthy of your every effort. Nowhere in the world is presented a government of so much liberty and equality. To the humblest and poorest amongst us are held out the highest privileges and positions. The present moment finds me at the White House, yet there is as good a chance for your children as there was for my father's."

The soldiers' vote was an element on which Lincoln put a good deal of his effort. To General Sherman he wrote, September 19: —

" The state election of Indiana occurs on the 11th of October, and the loss of it, to the friends of the government, would go far toward losing the whole Union cause.

The bad effect upon the November election, and especially the giving the state government to those who will
oppose the war in every possible way, are too much to
risk, if it can possibly be avoided. The draft proceeds,
notwithstanding its strong tendency to lose us the state.
Indiana is the only important state, voting in October,
whose soldiers cannot vote in the field. Anything you
can safely do to let her soldiers, or any part of them, go
home and vote at the state election will be greatly in
point. They need not remain for the presidential election, but may return to you at once. This is in no sense
an order, but is merely intended to impress you with the
importance, to the army itself, of your doing all you
safely can, yourself being the judge of what you can
safely do."

In Pennsylvania the Republican state committee
advised the President to guard against bad results
from McClellan's popularity there by asking Grant
to furlough some thousands of Pennsylvania soldiers, not for their votes, since they could vote in
the field, but for the influence of their presence
during the campaign, and for the prestige of carrying the home election without the "bayonet
vote," as the vote in the army was called. Lincoln said he was doubtful about Grant's attitude
in such a matter. The delegate from the committee then suggested that it be done through
Meade, the direct commander of the Army of the
Potomac, and Sheridan; and one of the assistant
secretaries of war was sent with an unofficial mes-

sage to Meade, and another agent to Sheridan, with the desired result. McClure says it was at Lincoln's special request that General Logan left his command and the march to the sea in order to stump Illinois and Indiana in this campaign. General Carl Schurz wished to perform a similar service, but he was a horse of a somewhat different color, and he was at first told on high grounds to remain with his command. Years later Grant said to McClure that he supposed no one would have doubted his desire for Lincoln's reëlection. " It would," he added, " have been obviously unbecoming on my part to have given a public expression against a general whom I had succeeded as commander-in-chief of the army." When Washburne of Illinois asked Grant to publish a letter in favor of Lincoln's election, the general replied that he thought that "for the President to answer all the charges the opposition would bring against him would be like setting a maiden to work to prove her chastity." Several acquaintances say that Lincoln felt hurt by Grant's aloofness, but this interpretation of whatever the President may have said is improbable, and in contradiction to his intellectual magnanimity. Grant at this period had a great distrust of politicians in general. Letters exchanged between him and Sherman show that both generals looked upon Washington as a hotbed of danger and corruption. When Grant was appointed lieutenant general, Lincoln asked him to make a short speech in answer to his few words at the formal presentation, and in it to say something to prevent jealousy from any other generals, and to put the new commander on good terms with the Army of the Potomac. Grant made his little reply, and entirely ignored the President's suggestions, but on the contrary rather emphasized the fact that he felt the responsibility centred directly on himself and all the armies. There was nothing about other generals, and nothing about the Army of the Potomac. His reason for staying East was that he believed "no one else could probably resist the pressure that would be brought to bear upon him to desist from his own plans and pursue others." It has been said that he made a special stipulation against interference, particularly by Stanton, and that he was warned not to talk over his plans with Lincoln; but the way he treats both men in his own written words shows his sympathy with the President and his hostility to the Secretary. Lincoln's own position toward his new general is honestly set forth in this letter of April 30: —

"Not expecting to see you again before the spring campaign opens, I wish to express in this way my entire satisfaction with what you have done up to this time, so far as I understand it. The particulars of your plans I neither know nor seek to know. You are vigilant and self-reliant; and, pleased with this, I wish not to obtrude any constraints or restraints upon you. While I am very anxious that any great disaster or capture of our men in great numbers shall be avoided, I know these points are less likely to escape your attention than they would be mine. If there is anything wanting which is within my power to give, do not fail to let me know it. And now, with a brave army and a just cause, may God sustain you."

It is not likely that the man who, accustomed to exercise authority on generals who needed it, could treat in this manner the first commander who had an equally firm character of his own, would feel any real resentment if that general's distrust of political machinery made him give less assistance in the election than the President thought due to the cause. Lincoln knew how to treat each man. He let Grant alone but he put the screws on to many others. The Secretary of State of New York during this campaign gives this account of what befell him in one of his functions: —

"A law was passed by the legislature, which was Republican, to take the soldier's vote. Well, ordinarily this duty would have devolved upon the governor. Because the legislature in this instance imposed it upon me, I spent much time in Washington endeavoring to get the data to send out the necessary papers enabling the New

York soldiers to vote. Under the act each soldier was to make out his ballot, and it was to be certified by the commanding officer of his company or regiment, and then sent to some friend at his last voting place to be deposited on election day. It was therefore necessary for me to ascertain the location of every New York company and regiment. They were scattered all over the South, and in all the armies. Secretary Stanton refused to give me any information whatever, and, finally, with a great deal of temper, informed me one day that information of that character given to politicians would reach the newspapers, and through them the enemy, and in that way the Confederates would know by the location of the New York troops precisely the condition and situation of every army, corps, brigade, and battery. As I was leaving the War Department I met Mr. Washburne and the marshal of the district coming in. Mr. Washburne said, 'Depew, you seem to be in a state of considerable excitement.' I told him of my interview with Mr. Stanton, and that I was going home to New York, and would publish in the morning papers a card that the soldiers' votes could not be taken, owing to the action of Secretary Stanton. And I added, 'I can inform you that a failure to get them will lose Mr. Lincoln the electoral vote of New York.' Mr. Washburne said: 'You don't

know Lincoln; he is as good a politician as he is
a President, and if there was no other way to get
those votes he would go round with a carpet-bag
and collect them himself.'   He then asked me to
wait until the President could be informed as to
the facts.   I stood in the corridor leading to Mr.
Stanton's room, and in about fifteen minutes an
orderly came out and said the Secretary wanted
to see Mr. Depew.   I went in, and Secretary
Stanton met me with the most cordial politeness;
inquired when I arrived in Washington, if I had
any business with his department, and whether
he could do anything for me.   I restated to him
what I had already stated at least half a dozen
times before.   He sent me with an order so per-
emptory to the head of one of the bureaus, that I
left Washington that night with a list and location of every organization of New York troops."

Another example of Lincoln's political dexterity in this fight for reëlection is shown by his
offer of the French mission to James Gordon
Bennett.   The *Herald* had favored McClellan's
nomination by the Democrats.   After McClellan
was nominated, Lincoln wrote in his own hand
to Bennett making this offer, just the kind of
attention to flatter the well-known nature of the
powerful editor.   Bennett responded in a round-
about, but obvious manner.   First he suggested
an entirely new nomination.   " Lincoln has proved

a failure," he said in one editorial. " Fremont has proved a failure. Let us have a new candidate." The *Herald*, not obtaining its new man, as it had not expected to, came out squarely for Lincoln. Bennett declined the office, but there is little doubt that this famous offer, which is here told in the form given by Colonel McClure, was made by the President for the direct purpose of securing the *Herald's* support. There is also little doubt that when Charles A. Dana says that the whole power of the War Department was used to secure Lincoln's reëlection he calmly states the facts exactly as they were. Purists may turn pale at these things and try to pull the blankets over any exhibition of them, but the world loves and admires the great War President as he was and desires no prettified portrait of him. That his jesuitical ability to use the fox's skin when the lion's proved too short was one part of his enormous value to the land, no competent thinker can doubt.

Opposite this brilliant ability in political manipulation stands another picture, not the contradiction of it but the complement. During those same long and dubious months in which Lincoln pulled every wire pointing to success, we see him giving some of his most unmistakable proofs of moral independence, trust in the right, and political courage. He let the draft go on in spite of

all the howls.   What use to him, he asked, was a
second term if he had no country?   When General Grant asked for 300,000 soldiers Lincoln
was able to reply that he had already called for
500,000.   How he treated some protests against
this call is well shown in an account which Joseph
Medill, the editor of the *Chicago Tribune*, gave
to Miss Tarbell shortly before his death : —

"In 1864, when the call for extra troops came, Chicago revolted.   She had already sent 22,000 men up to
that time, and was drained.   When the new call came,
there were no young men to go, no aliens except what
were bought.   The citizens held a mass-meeting, and
appointed three persons, of whom I was one, to go to
Washington and ask Stanton to give Cook County a
new enrolment.   I begged off, but the committee insisted, so I went.   On reaching Washington, we went
to Stanton with our statement.   He refused entirely to
give us the desired aid.   Then we went to Lincoln.   'I
cannot do it,' he said, 'but I will go with you to Stanton and hear the arguments of both sides.'   So we all
went over to the War Department together.   Stanton
and General Fry were there, and they, of course, contended that the quota should not be changed.   The
argument went on for some time, and finally was referred to Lincoln, who had been sitting silently listen-
ing.   I shall never forget how he suddenly lifted his
head and turned on us a black and frowning face.

"'Gentlemen,' he said, in a voice full of bitterness,
'after Boston, Chicago has been the chief instrument in
bringing this war on the country.   The Northwest has

opposed the South as New England has opposed the
South. It is you who are largely responsible for making blood flow as it has. You called for war until we
had it. You called for emancipation, and I have given
it to you. Whatever you have asked you have had.
Now you come here begging to be let off from the call
for men which I have made to carry out the war you
have demanded. You ought to be ashamed of yourselves. I have a right to expect better things of you.
Go home, and raise your 6000 extra men. And you,
Medill, you are acting like a coward. You and your
Tribune have had more influence than any paper in the
Northwest in making this war. You can influence great
masses, and yet you cry to be spared at a moment when
your cause is suffering. Go home and send us those
men.'

"I couldn't say anything. It was the first time I
ever was whipped, and I didn't have an answer. We
all got up and went out, and when the door closed, one
of my colleagues said: 'Well, gentlemen, the old man is
right. We ought to be ashamed of ourselves. Let us
never say anything about this, but go home and raise
the men.' And we did — 6000 men — making 28,000
in the war from a city of 156,000. But there might
have been crape on every door almost in Chicago, for
every family had lost a son or a husband. I lost two
brothers. It was hard for the mothers."

Politicians from all over the country begged Lincoln to suspend the draft until after the election.
Sherman, on the contrary, telegraphed from the
field that if the President modified it to the ex-

tent of one man the army would vote against him. This was one of the cases where the right was clear, and Lincoln did not know a moment's hesitation.

Perfect dexterity was shown by him in his manipulation of the peace cranks. The schemes for reconciliation were as numerous as they were futile. Several came to a head during the most uncertain part of the campaign. One was initiated by a man named Jaques, who thought that if he could only see Davis everything would be all right. Lincoln refused to let him speak for the administration, but gave his ideas privately and allowed him to go as a citizen accompanied by a journalist friend named Gilmore, who has left in his memoirs a full account of what happened. Davis was perfectly firm that any peace proposals must proceed on the basis of recognizing the independence of the Confederacy. When Gilmore talked with Lincoln the President at once took control of the publication of the facts about Davis's attitude, which was just what he expected and desired. It was to be written up by Gilmore for the *Atlantic*, but as that periodical could not print the article for some time, and as immediate publication would have a good effect, it was proposed to put a card into a Boston paper giving the central demand of the Southern President. " That is it," said Lincoln, "put Davis's ' we are

2 B

not fighting for slavery, we are fighting for independence,' into the card, that is enough; and
send me the proof of what goes into the *Atlantic*. Don't let it appear till I return the proof.
Some day all this will come out, but just now
we must use discretion." The President retained
the *Atlantic* proofs seven days, and struck out a
full page and a half, including a statement of the
terms which he was willing to give the rebels and
all references to compensation for slaves.

When Henry J. Raymond, chairman of the
National Executive Committee of the Republican
party, made similar proposals, Lincoln took the
same method, offering to let him execute his own
schemes, which treatment stopped Raymond.
Horace Greeley had a few weeks before been
impressed by the statements of some pretended
Confederate emissaries, who said they were authorized to treat for peace, and the editor made
a great noise about it. Lincoln easily saw through
the sham, but Greeley was so busily proving to
the public that the administration had no wish
for peace that the President sent him to confer
with these creatures, and, although the resulting
fiasco did not enlighten his obstinate soul, it had
its effect on the public. In the following year,
when all considerations of reëlection had passed,
and the end of the war was in sight, General
Blair hatched another peace scheme. Lincoln

would not listen to it, but let him go South to talk with Davis, and his visit only showed that the Confederate president was determined to insist on recognition as an independent nation, one of the points on which Lincoln, of course, would not yield an inch. He decided finally to meet some Southern commissioners nominated by Davis, and to them he insisted that he could make no agreement with "parties in arms against the government." R. M. T. Hunter, one of the commissioners, mentioned as precedents certain doings between Charles I. and his rebellious subjects. Lincoln replied that on historical matters he must refer to Seward. "All I distinctly recollect about the case of Charles I. is that he lost his head," he remarked. During the conference he found occasion to say that the rebel leaders had forfeited all right to immunity from punishment for the highest crime known to the law. There was a pause. At length Hunter said: "Then, Mr. President, if we understand you correctly, you think that we of the Confederacy have committed treason; that we are traitors to your government; that we have forfeited our rights, and are proper subjects for the hangman. Is not that about what your words imply?"

"Yes," said Lincoln, "you have stated the proposition better than I did. That is about the size of it."

There was another pause, after which Hunter, with a pleasant smile, replied: " Well, Mr. Lincoln, we have about concluded that we shall not be hanged as long as you are President, if we behave ourselves."

One of the hardest attacks for Lincoln to parry, during the campaign of 1864, related to the negro question.   The Democrats kept strenuously announcing that the war was now being conducted not for union but for emancipation.   Lincoln had so often said the opposite that it was difficult to admit now, in the midst of a campaign, that negro freedom was a necessary condition of peace, although he knew it was.   In April he had written : " To this day, I have done no official act in mere deference to my abstract judgment and feeling on slavery."   He then told how events had finally forced him to emancipation and arming the negroes, in spite of all his efforts for compensation and all his interference with military emancipation by generals early in the war.

" In telling this tale I attempt no compliment to my own sagacity.   I claim not to have controlled events, but confess plainly that events have controlled me. Now, at the end of three years' struggle, the nation's condition is not what either party, or any man, devised or expected.   God alone can claim it.   Whither it is tending seems plain.   If God now wills the removal of a great wrong, and wills also that we of the North, as well as you of the South, shall pay fairly for our complicity in that wrong, impartial history will find therein new cause to attest and revere the justice and goodness of God."

Yet he found this no easy position to maintain. It is never a soft task to explain to the public that learning by experience and changing with the facts is not inconsistency. He spoke as little as he conveniently could of the direct fact that negro freedom must now be included in any arrangement for peace, but he did argue often in favor of his wisdom in arming the blacks and of the justice of emancipating them.

"The world," he said in April, "has never had a good definition of the word 'liberty,' and the American people, just now, are much in want of one. We all declare for liberty; but in using the same word we do not all mean the same thing. With some the word 'liberty' may mean for each man to do as he pleases with himself, and the product of his labor; while with others the same word may mean for some men to do as they please with other men, and the product of other men's labor."

In the same address he went so far as to promise revenge if the rumors of Fort Pillow massacres turned out to be true. An unfinished draft of a letter, dated August 6, says: —

"The President has received yours of yesterday and is kindly paying attention to it. As it is my business to assist him whenever I can, I will thank you to inform me, for his use, whether you are either a white man or black man, because in either case you cannot be regarded as an entirely impartial judge. It may be that you belong to a third or fourth class of yellow or red men, in which case the impartiality of your judgment would be more apparent."

His sharpest repartees were usually left unsaid. The next month he made this vigorous statement of the military impossibility of escaping emancipation : —

" An armistice — a cessation of hostilities — is the end of the struggle, and the insurgents would be in peaceable possession of all that has been struggled for. Any different policy in regard to the colored man deprives us of his help, and this is more than we can bear. We cannot spare the hundred and forty or fifty thousand now serving us as soldiers, seamen, and laborers. This is not a question of sentiment or taste, but one of physical force, which may be measured and estimated as horse-power and steam-power are measured and estimated. Keep it and you can save the Union. Throw it away, and the Union goes with it. Nor is it possible for any administration to retain the service of these people with the express or implied understanding that, upon the first convenient occasion, they are to be reënslaved. It cannot be, and it ought not to be."

More than once he said he was willing to stake his election on these principles.

First, however, among all political dangers lay, as usual, military reverses. Sherman fought hard through the spring without notable victories. Grant had Lee in a position which meant death, but the cost was awful, and the North could not even see how inevitable it was that her armies should now win. In this situation Lincoln behaved perfectly. He knew that Grant's military ideas might prevent his reëlection, but he knew also that the only right step was to let the bloody fight go on under the conduct of the commander. After the fearful struggle in the Wilderness, Schuyler Colfax heard Lincoln exclaim: "Why do we suffer reverses after reverses? Could we have avoided this terrible, bloody war? Was it not forced upon us? Is it ever to end?" A little after, however, he referred with hope to Grant's famous words, "I shall fight it out on this line if it takes all summer," and in June he even went so far as to say in a speech at a fair:—

"We accepted this war for an object, a worthy object, and the war will end when that object is attained. Under God, I hope it never will end until that time. Speaking of the present campaign, General Grant is reported to have said, 'I am going through on this line if it takes all summer.' This war has taken three years; it was begun or accepted upon the line of restoring the national authority over the whole national domain, and for the American people, as far as my knowledge enables me to speak, I say we are going through on this line if it takes three years more."

It will be seen that these two firm and clear minds understood each other. When Grant failed in his assaults on the desperate Confederate army in those jungles of the South, instead of marching toward Washington he marched by flank movements still nearer Richmond and the Northern soldiers cheered. Asked by Justin McCarthy in after years what he deemed the first requisite of a general, Grant replied "patience." With that he mixed freely the other virtue of energetic aggressiveness. Even the frightful defeat at Cold Harbor did not dazzle him. From beginning to end of the series of unexampled battles he sent Lincoln telegrams of encouragement, assuring him that final victory became more certain every day; that his army had the feeling of conquerors and the Southerners the feeling of defeat; and that much of the credit was due to the prompt reënforcements and supplies from Washington. After McClellan and the rest, it is, perhaps, safe to infer that Lincoln enjoyed this tone. June 15 he telegraphed:—

"I have just received your despatch of 1 P.M. yesterday. I begin to see it; you will succeed. God bless you all."

The next month he again became anxious about the capital. It was not personal fear, but a knowledge of the political effect the capture of Washington would have. At first Grant thought Early's designs on the Northern capital were not serious, but he soon changed his mind, and Lincoln was relieved, although he left everything to the general. He was also glad to hear Grant say that he should try to get along without such heavy losses, although in that matter, too, he made no interference. Grant finally sent Sheridan to take care of the situation in the Shenandoah. Lincoln was a little disappointed, as he hoped for the commander himself, but he soon learned more about Grant's young favorite. His cipher despatch of August 3 to Grant was not needed, but it shows his state of mind: —

"I have seen your despatch in which you say: 'I want Sheridan put in command of all the troops in the field, with instructions to put himself south of the enemy, and follow him to the death. Wherever the enemy goes, let our troops go also.' This, I think, is exactly right as to how our forces should move; but please look over the despatches you may have received from here, ever since you made that order, and discover, if you can, that there is any idea in the head of any one here of 'putting our army south of the enemy,' or of following him to the 'death,' in any direction. I repeat to you, it will never be done nor attempted, unless you watch it every day and hour, and force it."

He soon came to agree more actively with Grant's view of the situation. On August 17 he telegraphed : —

"I have seen your despatch expressing your unwillingness to break your hold where you are. Neither am I willing. Hold on with a bulldog grip, and chew and choke as much as possible."

He ventured to suggest that Sheridan might be reënforced and an attack made on Early. Eight days later he had occasion to telegraph Sheridan thus : —

"Have just heard of your great victory. God bless you all, officers and men. Strongly inclined to come up and see you."

Everybody knows the final outcome, but probably only students of history realize how much Sheridan had to do with Lincoln's reëlection. His brilliant series of victories over Early changed the whole moral atmosphere at the North. The picturesqueness of the young leader, quietly riding back from Washington, finding his own demoralized troops flying along the road, rallying them, making them decide on reflection, as he puts it, that they had not done themselves justice, riding up and down the lines, assuring his men that the captured guns and camps must be recaptured, and wrecking Early's army so completely that it never counted in the history of the war again, was the kind of an apparition the President needed. Sheridan's despatch to Grant, "We have just sent them whirling through Winchester, and we after them to-morrow" put one of the finishing strokes on the political campaign. It went to every home in the North and brought the flush of pride to every cheek. When Lincoln had read the telegrams relating the last fight with Early, he told his companions about the man who filled a piece of punk with powder, set it on fire, clapped it under a biscuit, and gave it to a dog. "As for the dog, *as a dog*, I was never able to find him," said the man.

Farragut had already taken Mobile Bay and Sherman had just captured Atlanta. "We are coming, father Abraham, 300,000 strong" went through the land after Atlanta. "Sherman and Farragut," said Seward in a speech at Chicago, "have knocked the planks out of the Chicago platform,"—that platform which declared the war a failure. Sheridan demolished whatever was left of it. When Lincoln, on November 8, went to read the telegrams, it was without a reasonable doubt of the result.

He stayed in Stanton's office, following the returns. When there was a lull in the news he read aloud the writings of Petroleum V. Nasby.

The result of the election was the most complete victory ever won in a presidential contest in America.

Two days after he told some serenaders what his election meant: —

"It has long been a grave question whether any government, not too strong for the liberties of its people, can be strong enough to maintain its existence in great emergencies. On this point the present rebellion brought our republic to a severe test, and a presidential election occurring in regular course during the rebellion, added not a little to the strain.

"If the loyal people united were put to the utmost of their strength by the rebellion, must they not fail when divided and partially paralyzed by a political war among themselves? But the election was a necessity. We cannot have free government without elections; and if the rebellion could force us to forego or postpone a national election, it might fairly claim to have already conquered and ruined us. The strife of the election is but human nature practically applied to the facts of the case. What has occurred in this case must ever recur in similar cases. Human nature will not change. In any future great national trial, compared with the men of this, we shall have as weak and as strong, as silly and as wise, as bad and as good. Let us, therefore, study the incidents of this as philosophy to learn wisdom from, and none of them as wrongs to be revenged. But the election, along with its incidental and undesirable strife, has done good too. It has demonstrated that a people's government can sustain a national election in the midst of a great civil war. Until now, it has not been known to the world that this was a possibility.   It shows also, how sound and how strong we still are.   It shows that, even among the candidates of the same party, he who is most devoted to the Union and most opposed to treason can receive most of the people's votes."

Of this address he said to the secretary who stood beside him lighting the page with a candle: "Not very graceful, but I am growing old enough not to care much for the manner of doing things."

CHAPTER XVI

VICTORY AND DEATH

WHEN the President sent his annual message to Congress, December 6, 1864, he included among other things this short paragraph, " Civil war continues in the Spanish port of San Domingo, apparently without prospect of an early close." On this conflict hang an act of prudence by the President and one of his most characteristic stories. Seward one day came to a cabinet meeting with clouded brow. Spain, he said, was already sick of the European alliance, and was beginning to view the United States with a more friendly eye. Her government had never gone as far as Palmerston and Louis Napoleon in the effort for intervention, yet she had been led a certain distance by her hope of recovering her possessions in San Domingo. The negroes, however, had put up a good fight, and they had the sympathy of American abolitionists. It was important to separate Spain from the alliance, and yet not to offend those who sympathized with San Domingo. To the President, however, there seemed to be no difficulty. He was merely reminded of an interview between two negroes in Tennessee. One was a preacher and the other an erring brother. " Dar are," said Josh the preacher, "two roads befo' you, Joe; be careful which ob dem you take. Narrow am de way dat leads straight to destruction; but broad am de way dat leads right to damnation." Joe opened his eyes, and exclaimed, " Josh, take which road you please; I shall go troo de woods." " I am not willing," concluded the President, " to assume any new trouble or responsibilities at this time, and shall therefore avoid going to the one place with Spain or with the negro to the other, but shall take to the woods. We will maintain an honest and strict neutrality."

The references to the war in the annual message were few, confident, and positive. He gave figures to show that the national resources, both in wealth and in men, were " unexhausted and, as we believe, inexhaustible "; and he told why the war should be fought to the bitter end.

"The public purpose to reëstablish and maintain the national authority is unchanged, and, as we believe, unchangeable. The manner of continuing the effort remains to choose. On careful consideration of all the evidence accessible, it seems to me that no attempt at negotiation with the insurgent leader could result in any good. He would accept nothing short of severance of the Union — precisely what we will not and cannot give.

His declarations to this effect are explicit and oft repeated. He does not attempt to deceive us. He affords
us no excuse to deceive ourselves. He cannot voluntarily reaccept the Union; we cannot voluntarily yield
it. Between him and us the issue is distinct, simple, and
inflexible. It is an issue which can only be tried by war,
and decided by victory."

What was true of Davis, however, was not
necessarily true of his followers. Some of them
already desired peace and reunion, and the number might increase. They could have peace at
any moment by mere submission.

"If questions should remain, we would adjust them
by the peaceful means of legislation, conference, courts,
and votes, operating only in constitutional and lawful
channels. Some certain, and other possible, questions
are, and would be, beyond the executive power to adjust;
as, for instance, the admission of members into Congress, and whatever might require the appropriation of
money. The executive power itself would be greatly
diminished by the cessation of actual war. Pardons and
remissions of forfeitures, however, would still be within
executive control. In what spirit and temper this control would be exercised, can be fairly judged of by the
past."

About the negroes he was more than usually
strict in tone.

"In presenting the abandonment of armed resistance
to the national authority on the part of the insurgents as

the only indispensable condition to ending the war on
the part of the government, I retract nothing heretofore
said as to slavery. I repeat the declaration made a year
ago that, ' while I remain in my present position I shall
not attempt to retract or modify the Emancipation Proclamation, nor shall I return to slavery any person who
is free by the terms of that proclamation, or by any of
the acts of Congress.'

"If the people should, by whatever mode or means,
make it an executive duty to reënslave such persons,
another, and not I, must be their instrument to perform
it."

The increasing severity of his manner on this
subject may be indicated by his remark to a
woman from Tennessee, who had called, a few
days before this message, to request the release of
her husband, partly on the ground that he was a
religious man : —

"You say your husband is a religious man; tell him
when you meet him that I say I am not much of a judge
of religion, but that, in my opinion, the religion that sets
men to rebel and fight against their government, because,
as they think, that government does not sufficiently help
some men to eat their bread in the sweat of other men's
faces, is not the sort of religion upon which people can
get to heaven."

Some months later he said, referring to the
Confederate plan to enlist negroes : —

2 C

" **I** may incidentally remark that having **in my life** heard many arguments — or strings of words meant to pass for arguments — intended to show that the negro ought to be a slave — if he shall now really fight to keep himself a slave, it will be a far better argument why he should remain a slave than I have ever before heard. He perhaps ought to be a slave, if he desires it ardently enough to fight for it. Or, if one out of four will, for his own freedom, fight to keep the other three in slavery, he ought to be a slave for his selfish meanness. I have always thought that all men should be free; but if any should be slaves, it should be first those who desire it for themselves, and secondly those who desire it for others. Whenever I hear any one arguing for slavery, I feel a strong impulse to see it tried on him personally."

Convinced as he was that freedom was now no longer an open question, his desire to have it brought about by constitutional methods was intense. Of emancipation he had once said: " We are like whalers, who have been on a long chase; we have at last got the harpoon into the monster, but we must now look how we steer, or with one flop of his tail he will send us all into eternity." He had steered with care, and the rest of the course was clear. It was an amendment to the Constitution. Motions to this end had been offered in the House in December, 1863, and in the Senate in 1864. How the President worked for the success of the effort is vividly shown in one of his conversations, recorded by Charles A. Dana:—

"Dana, I am very anxious about this vote. It has got to be taken next week. The time is very short. It is going to be a great deal closer than I wish it was. . . . There are three that you can deal with better than anybody else, perhaps, as you know them all. I wish you would send for them."

"What will they be likely to want?" asked Dana.

"I don't know. It makes no difference, though, what they want. Here is the alternative: that we carry this vote, or be compelled to raise another million, and I don't know how many more men, and fight no one knows how long. It is a question of three votes or new armies."

"Well, sir," said Dana, "what shall I say to these gentlemen?"

"I don't know, but whatever promise you make to them I will perform."

With all his efforts, however, he was beaten in the House when on June 15 it came to a vote. At his special request a demand for such an amendment was then inserted in the Republican platform on which he was to be so overwhelmingly elected. After that election, with the immense Republican gain in Congress, the measure seemed sure, but the President wished to hurry it through and he urged in his message of December 6 that the legislature should obey the unmistakable voice of the majority. The vote came in January, and when it was over Lincoln was able to congratulate the people who crowded the White House that "the great job is ended." The thirteenth amendment, making slavery forever impossible in the United States, was then substantially a fact. On February 25 *Leslie's* published a cartoon showing Lincoln holding an envelope inscribed, "Thirteenth Amendment to the Constitution," and observing, with a smile, "This is like a dream I once had in Illinois." It was, indeed, and like the dream which had occupied the better part of his life.

The fears which had always gone with this dream, however, were not unabated; but before taking up this last problem of his life, reconstruction and its dangers, we may pause to see him as he appeared in this last year of his life. Happily the picture has been drawn for us by a vigorous hand—the hand of America's prophet poet, the apostle of Democracy, to whom Lincoln meant the ideal of his country's manhood.

" From my note-book in 1864, at Washington City," says Walt Whitman, "I find this memorandum, under date of August 12 : —

" I see the President almost every day, as I happen to live where he passes to or from his lodgings out of town. He never sleeps at the White House during the hot season, but has quarters at a healthy location, some three miles north of the city, the Soldiers' Home, a United States military establishment. I saw him this morning about 8.30 coming in to business, riding on Vermont Avenue, near L Street. He always has a company of twenty-five or thirty cavalry, with sabres drawn, and held upright over their shoulders. The party makes no great show in uniforms or horses. Mr. Lincoln, on the saddle, generally rides a good-sized, easy-going gray horse, is dressed in plain black, somewhat rusty and dusty, wears a black stiff hat, and looks as ordinary in attire, etc., as the commonest man. A lieutenant, with yellow straps, rides at his left, and following behind, two by two, come the cavalrymen in their yellow-striped jackets. They are generally going at a slow trot, as that is the pace set them by the one they wait upon. The sabres and accoutrements clank, and the entirely unornamental *cortege*, as it trots toward Lafayette Square, arouses no sensation, only some curious stranger stops and gazes. I see very plainly *Abraham Lincoln's* dark brown face, with the deep cut lines, the eyes, etc., always to me with a latent sadness in the expression. We have got so that we always exchange bows, and very cordial ones.

" Sometimes the President goes and comes in an open barouche. The cavalry always accompany him, with drawn sabres. Often I notice as he goes out evenings — and sometimes in the morning, when he returns early — he turns off and halts at the large and handsome residence of the

Secretary of War on K Street, and holds conference there. If in his barouche, I can see from
my window he does not alight, but sits in his
vehicle, and Mr. Stanton comes out to attend him.
Sometimes one of his sons, a boy of ten or twelve,
accompanies him, riding at his right on a pony.

"Earlier in the summer I occasionally saw the
President and his wife, toward the latter part of
the afternoon, out in a barouche, on a pleasure
ride through the city. Mrs. Lincoln was dressed
in complete black, with a long crape veil. The
equipage of the plainest kind, only two horses,
and they nothing extra. They passed me once
very close, and I saw the President in the face
fully, as they were moving slow, and his look,
though abstracted, happened to be directed steadily in my eye. He bowed and smiled, but far
beneath his smile I noticed well the expression I
have alluded to. None of the artists or pictures
have caught the subtle and indirect expression of
this man's face. One of the great portrait paint-
ers of two or three centuries ago is needed."

As late as February 5, 1865, the President
drafted a message to Congress, which he never
sent, recommending that he be empowered to pay
$400,000,000 (in compensation for their negroes)
to such of the slave states as should have ceased
resistance by April 1. The same day Lincoln
made on the memorandum this indorsement, —

"To-day these papers, which explain themselves, were drawn up and submitted to the cabinet and unanimously disapproved by them."

A day later Secretary Welles wrote in his diary: "There was a cabinet meeting last evening. The President had matured a scheme which he hoped would be successful in promoting peace. It was a proposition for paying the expenses of the war for two hundred days, or four hundred millions, to the rebel states, to be for the extinguishment of slavery or for such purpose as the states were disposed. This, in few words, was the scheme. It did not meet with favor, but was dropped. The earnest desire of the President to conciliate and effect peace was manifest, but there may be such a thing as so overdoing as to cause a distinct or adverse feeling. In the present temper of Congress the proposed measure, if a wise one, could not be carried through successfully; I do not think the scheme would accomplish any good results. The rebels would misconstrue it if the offer were made. If attempted and defeated, it would do harm." So the President sadly folded it up and laid it away. How unpopular his views were among the politicians even after his death, may be judged by this passage from the "Political Recollections" of George W. Julian: "I spent most of the afternoon in a political caucus, held for the purpose of considering the necessity for a new cabinet and a line of policy less conciliatory than that of Mr. Lincoln; and while everybody was shocked at his murder, the feeling was nearly universal that the accession of Johnson to the Presidency would prove a godsend to the country." Lincoln read the Bible more in the last years of his life than he ever had before, and gave signs of taking many of the Christian principles as intense realities. All his plans of reconstruction were in harmony not with the Mosaic law but with the Sermon on the Mount.

The latest expressions by the President on the subject of reconstruction were given shortly before his death. Some of them were made to his generals when their work was about ending. Grant told him that surrender might be expected at any time, so Lincoln went down March 22 and established himself at City Point, probably to make negotiations easier. Sheridan in his memoirs hints that the President was a little uneasy about a possible rebel capture of that point, but Grant says: "Mr. Lincoln was not timid, and he was willing to trust his generals in making and executing their plans. The Secretary was very timid and it was impossible for him to avoid interfering with the armies covering the capital when it was sought to defend it by an offensive movement against the army guarding the Confederate capital. He could see our weakness, but he could not see that the enemy was in danger. The enemy would not have been in danger if Mr. Stanton had been in the field." This judgment makes an amusing comparison to Stanton's remark about McClellan, " If he had a million men he would swear the enemy had two millions, and then he would sit down in the road and yell for three." It is, perhaps, significant also that Sherman had the friendliest feelings for Lincoln and the most thorough hostility to Stanton.

When, toward the end of March, Grant, Sherman, and Admiral Porter visited Lincoln on the *River Queen* and told him that one more bloody battle was probably necessary, he showed the greatest disappointment. Sherman asked if he was ready for the end of the war, and what would be done with Jeff Davis and the rebel armies. " He said," Sherman records, " he was all ready. All he wanted of us was to defeat the opposing armies, and to get the men comprising the Confederate army back to their homes, at work on farms and in the shops. As to Jeff Davis, he was hardly at liberty to speak his mind fully; but intimated that he ought to 'clear the country,' only it would not do for him to say so openly. As usual he illustrated his meaning by a story." This story has been told by various hearers in various ways, of which the following is the best:

"When I was a boy in Indiana, I went to a neigh-bor's house one morning and found a boy of my own size holding a coon by a string. I asked him what he had and what he was doing. He says, 'It's a coon. Dad cotched six last night, and killed all but this poor little cuss. Dad told me to hold him until he came back, and I'm afraid he's going to kill this one too; and oh, Abe, I do wish he would get away!' 'Well, why don't you let him loose?' 'That wouldn't be right; and if I let him go, Dad would give me hell. But if he would get away himself, it would be all right.' Now, if Jeff Davis and those other fellows will only get away, it will be all right. But if we should catch them, and I should let them go, 'Dad would give me hell.'"

On March 3, when Grant first sent word that Lee was likely to surrender and asked about a conference, Lincoln had written immediately, with his own hand, this despatch: —

"WASHINGTON, March 3, 1865. 12 P.M.

"LIEUTENANT-GENERAL GRANT:

"The President directs me to say that he wishes you to have no conference with General Lee unless it be for capitulation of General Lee's army, or on some minor or purely military matter. He instructs me to say that you are not to decide, discuss, or confer upon any politi-cal questions. Such questions the President holds in his own hands, and will submit them to no military con-

ferences or conventions.   Meanwhile, you are to press
to the utmost your military advantages.

"EDWIN M. STANTON, *Secretary of War.*"

Grant was now soon to use as much authority
as was his in regard to peace.   March 29 he
wrote to Sheridan that he felt like ending the
matter then.   After victories on April 1 and 2,
Grant sent a note to City Point, saying, " I think
the President might come and pay us a visit
to-morrow," and about the same time Lee sent
word to Davis that Petersburg and Richmond
must be abandoned.   April 3 Grant and Meade
entered the deserted Petersburg, Lincoln joined
them, and they three walked alone through the
streets.

On the same morning General Weitzel, with a
few attendants, entered Richmond, which was in
confusion, with buildings afire, men·drunk, and
negroes crazy with excitement.   The next day
Lincoln entered the Confederate capital with so
little care for his safety that he walked without
protection through streets full of drunken rebels.
When he reached Weitzel's headquarters, a house
from which Jeff Davis had just made a sudden
flight, Lincoln, weary and without exultation,
sank, it is said, into the very chair which the Confederate President used at his writing-table.   One
account of Lincoln's trip through the city says : —

" Mr. Lincoln was evidently perplexed and suf‹
fering — he had his hat in his hand trying to fan
his furrowed face, which was streaming with per-
spiration ; he had mopped his face till his hand-
kerchief was too wet to absorb more. But the
negroes were happy in their frenzy, and they took
no further note of events or the sober world. One
old 'Aunty' had a sick white child in her arms,
who was alarmed at the surrounding riot, and
was crying to go home ; but the good negress kept
trying to get the child to gaze at the President,
which she was afraid to do, and she would try to
turn the child's head in that direction, and would
turn around herself, in order to accomplish the
same object. 'See yeah, honey, look at de Saviour,
an' you'll git well.' 'Touch the hem of his gar-
ment, honey, an' yur pain will be done gone,'
she would urge. 'Glory! Hallelujah!' 'God
bress Massa Linkum!' 'Open de pearly gates.'
' I'se on the mount ob rejoicin'.' 'He's de Mes-
siah shuah.' 'Heah am de promise land.' 'Rally
round de flag, boys.' 'Jerusalem, my happy home.'
'I'se on Mount Pisgah's stormy top.' 'I'se bound
for de lan' of Canaan.' 'De Lord save us!' 'Dis
am de judgment day.' 'Come, Lord, I'se ready
to go.' 'Chariot ob fire.' 'De mount ob trans-
figurashun.' 'My tribulations all done gone.' 'No
more sighin' an' a-weepin'.' These were some of
the expressions used. They would shout in each

other's ears; negroes and negresses alike would suddenly spring in the air; and young negresses would spin themselves on the edge of the crowd like a teetotum."

On April 6 Sheridan reported, " If the thing is pressed, I think that Lee will surrender." Grant sent the despatch to Lincoln, who replied, " Let the thing be pressed." After various negotiations, Grant, on April 9, appearing "with no sword, travel-stained, and severely plain both in dress and manner," had a conference with Lee, in which he agreed to parole the Confederates, and allow the officers their side arms, private horses, and baggage. " Each officer and man will be allowed to return to their homes, not to be disturbed by United States authorities so long as they observe their parole and the laws in force where they may reside." Although this sentence exceeded the general's authority, the President made no objection, and Admiral Porter, who took notes at the time, says that when Lincoln heard Grant's terms, he exclaimed a dozen times, " Good!" " All right!" " Exactly the thing!" and similar expressions. General Sherman says that he then argued that he could get his own terms for the surrender of Johnston's army, but that Lincoln insisted that he must obtain a surrender on any terms. One who was present when Lincoln heard the news of Lee's surrender, said that Jeff

Davis ought to be hung.   The President quoted from his inaugural, " Let us judge not, that we be not judged."   It was then said that the sight of Libby Prison forbade mercy.   " Let us judge not," Lincoln repeated, " that we be not judged."

Steaming up the Potomac on this day, April 9, the President read aloud to his companions, for several hours, passages from Shakespeare, mainly from " Macbeth," including the lines which follow Duncan's murder.

Whatever was said at these various steamboat conversations about the treatment of the South merely confirms what is implied in the President's whole course.   " We should," he had said a year before, " avoid planting and cultivating too many thorns in the bosom of society."   Two days after he reached Washington, April 11, 1865, in his last public address, he said : —

" Let us all join in doing the acts necessary to restoring the proper practical relations between these states and the Union, and each forever after innocently indulge his own opinion whether in doing the acts he brought the states from without into the Union, or only gave them proper assistance, they never having been out of it.   The amount of constituency, so to speak, on which the new Louisiana government rests, would be more satisfactory to all if it contained 50,000 or 30,000, or even 20,000, instead of only about 12,000, as it does.   It is also unsatisfactory to some that the elective franchise is not given to the colored man. I would myself prefer that it were now conferred on the very intelligent, and on those who serve our cause as soldiers.

" Still, the question is not whether the Louisiana government, as it stands, is quite all that is desirable. The question is, will it be wiser to take it as it is and help to improve it, or to reject and disperse it ? Can Louisiana be brought into proper practical relation with the Union sooner by sustaining or by discarding her new state government ? Some twelve thousand voters in the heretofore slave state of Louisiana have sworn allegiance to the Union, assumed to be the rightful political power of the state, held elections, organized a state government, adopted a free-state constitution, giving the benefit of public schools equally to black and white, and empowering the legislature to confer the elective franchise upon the colored man. Their legislature has already voted to ratify the constitutional amendment recently passed by Congress, abolishing slavery throughout the nation. These twelve thousand persons are thus fully committed to the Union and to perpetual freedom in the state — committed to the very things, and nearly all the things, the nation wants — and they ask the nation's recognition and its assistance to make good their committal.

" Now, if we reject and spurn them, we do our utmost to disorganize and disperse them. We, in effect, say to the white man, 'You are worthless or worse; we will neither help you nor be helped by you.' To the blacks we say, 'This cup of liberty which these, your old masters, hold to your lips we will dash from you, and leave you to the chances of gathering the spilled and scattered contents in some vague and undefined when, where, and how.' If this course, discouraging and paralyzing both white and black, has any tendency to bring Louisiana into proper practical relations with the Union, I have so far been unable to perceive it. If, on the contrary, we recognize and sustain the new government of Louisiana, the converse of all this is made true. We encourage the hearts and nerve the arms of the twelve thousand to adhere to their work and argue for it and proselyte for it and fight for it and feed it and grow it and ripen it to a complete success. The colored man, too, in seeing all united for him, is inspired with vigilance and energy and daring, to the same end. Grant that he desires the elective franchise, will he not attain it sooner by saving the already advanced steps toward it than by running backward over them? Concede that the new government of Louisiana is only to what it should be as the egg is to the fowl, we shall sooner have the fowl by hatching the egg than by smashing it."

April 14, the last day of Lincoln's life, the cabinet discussed reconstruction. As members differed as to whether trade between the states should be carried on under military supervision or more liberally, the President appointed Stanton, Welles, and McCulloch, the three Secretaries who had expressed divergent views, a commission with power to examine the whole subject, and he said that he should be satisfied with their conclusions.

About the reëstablishment of civil government, Lincoln, trusting himself and his cabinet and distrusting Congress, was anxious to get the Southern state governments in operation before the December session, and that with as little discussion as possible.

"No one need expect he would take any part in hanging or killing these men," runs Secretary Welles's abstract of the President's words, "even the worst of them. Frighten them out of the country, open the gates, let down the bars, scare them off," said he, throwing up his hands as if scaring sheep. "Enough lives have been sacrificed; we must extinguish our resentments if we expect harmony and union."

As Lincoln did not live to enforce and modify his own ideas of reconstruction, he cannot be judged by the results. Those results were bad enough. They are still bad enough. Whether they could have been better, no man knows. Lincoln always looked with horror on the race problems that would come with freedom, and he fought desperately to have the negroes removed and colonized. Told by the almost universal voice of the people that it was impracticable, he made the best of necessity and henceforth tried everything — compensation, kind words, amnesty — to remove bitterness in the South. Had he lived four years longer, it is probable that his skilful hand would have done much to make his Christian charity effective in the rebel states; and, as always, he would have learned with every step

2D

how best to take the next. We may drop this subject with one incident. When the negro Frederick Douglass attended the reception on the evening of the second inauguration, a policeman tried to stop him at the door. Lincoln ordered the negro admitted, and he always took pains to speak of him as " my friend Douglass." [1]

The last high literary effort of the doomed President was his second inaugural — a paper which stands, on a plane with the Gettysburg address, at the height of his more solemn utterances. It is : —

" FELLOW-COUNTRYMEN : At this second appearing to take the oath of the presidential office, there is less occasion for an extended address than there was at the first. Then a statement, somewhat in detail of a course to be pursued, seemed fitting and proper. Now, at the expiration of four years, during which public declarations have been constantly called forth on every point and phase of the great contest which still absorbs the attention and engrosses the energies of the nation, little that is new could be presented. The progress of our arms, upon which all else chiefly depends, is as well known to the public as to myself ; and it is, I trust, reasonably satisfactory and encouraging to all. With high hope for the future, no prediction in regard to it is ventured.

[1] This is one of the many significant stories in the volume of reminiscences edited bv Mr. Rice.

"On the occasion corresponding to this four years ago, all thoughts were anxiously directed to an impending civil war. All dreaded it; all sought to avert it. While the inaugural address was being delivered from this place, devoted altogether to saving the Union without war, insurgent agents were in the city seeking to destroy it without war — seeking to dissolve the Union, and divide effects, by negotiation. Both parties deprecated war; but one of them would make war rather than let the nation survive; and the other would accept war rather than let it perish. And the war came.

"One-eighth of the whole population were colored slaves, not distributed generally over the Union, but localized in the Southern part of it. These slaves constituted a peculiar and powerful interest. All knew that this interest was, somehow, the cause of the war. To strengthen, perpetuate, and extend this interest was the object for which the insurgents would rend the Union, even by war; while the government claimed no right to do more than to restrict the territorial enlargement of it.

"Neither party expected for the war the magnitude or the duration which it has already attained. Neither anticipated that the cause of the conflict might cease with, or even before, the conflict itself should cease. Each looked for an easier triumph, and a result less fundamental and astounding. Both read the same Bible, and pray to the same God; and each invokes his aid against the other. It may seem strange that any men should dare to ask a just God's assistance in wringing their bread from the sweat of other men's faces; but let us judge not, that we be not judged. The prayers of both could not be answered — that of neither has been answered fully.

"The Almighty has his own purposes. 'Woe unto the world because of offences! for it must needs be that offences come; but woe to that man by whom the offence cometh.' If we shall suppose that American slavery is one of those offences which, in the providence of God, must needs come, but which, having continued through his appointed time, he now wills to remove, and that he gives to both North and South this terrible war, as the woe due to those by whom the offence came, shall we discern therein any departure from those divine attributes which the believers in a living God always ascribe to him? Fondly do we hope — fervently do we pray — that this mighty scourge of war may speedily pass away. Yet, if God wills that it continue until all the wealth piled by the bondman's two hundred and fifty years of unrequited toil shall be sunk, and until every drop of blood drawn with the lash shall be paid by another drawn with the sword, as was said three thousand years ago, so still it must be said, 'The judgments of the Lord are true and righteous altogether.'

"With malice toward none; with charity for all; with firmness in the right, as God gives us to see the right, let us strive on to finish the work we are in; to bind up the nation's wounds; to care for him who shall have borne the battle, and for his widow, and his orphan — to do all which may achieve and cherish a just and lasting peace among ourselves, and with all nations."

Some of his frequent warnings about plans to kill him, Lincoln kept in his desk marked "Assassination Letters." He deemed it impossible to avoid this risk, and he took few steps for protection, even when his dreams were of evil omen.

On the last day of the President's life Grant arrived in Washington, and attended the cabinet meeting, where he showed some anxiety about Sherman. Lincoln assured him that there would soon be good news, as he had had his dream about the vessel, the same which had presaged Antietam, Murfreesboro, Gettysburg, and Vicksburg. Members of the cabinet looked impressed, but Grant replied simply that " Murfreesboro was no victory, and had no important results." He was not a poet, and the President, in his way, was.

He referred, a few days before the end, to the number of warnings by dream in the Bible, the book which had of late taken such a hold upon him. Finally he said: —

" About ten days ago, I retired very late. I had been up waiting for important despatches from the front. I could not have been long in bed when I fell into a slumber, for I was weary. I soon began to dream. There seemed to be a deathlike stillness about me. Then I heard subdued sobs, as if a number of people were weeping. I thought I left my bed and wandered downstairs. There the silence was broken by the same pitiful sobbing, but the mourners were invisible. I went from room to room; no living person was in sight, but the same mournful sounds of distress met me as I passed along. It was light in all the rooms, every object was familiar to me; but where were all the people who were grieving as if their hearts would break? I was puzzled and alarmed. What could be the meaning of all this? Determined to find the cause of a state of things so mysterious and so shocking, I kept on until I arrived at the east room, which I entered. There I met with a sickening surprise. Before me was a catafalque, on which rested a corpse wrapped in funeral vestments. Around it were stationed soldiers who were acting as guards; and there was a throng of people, some gazing mournfully upon the corpse, whose face was covered, others weeping pitifully. 'Who is dead in the White House?' I demanded of one of the soldiers. 'The President,' was his answer; 'he was killed by an assassin!' Then came a loud burst of grief from the crowd, which awoke me from my dream. I slept no more that night; and although it was only a dream, I have been strangely annoyed by it ever since."

This dream continued to disturb him. A few days after, he said to Lamon: "To sleep, perchance to dream. Ay, there's the rub."

On the evening of April 14, Good Friday, he went to the theatre. In the door of his box a hole had been cut by a body of conspirators, so that the occupants could be watched. Just after ten o'clock, John Wilkes Booth, an actor, entered the box, shot the President with a pistol in the back of the head, stabbed one of the theatre party who tried to stop him, and leaped upon the stage. In the folds of the American flag he caught his spur, and broke his leg. Limping across the stage, swinging his dagger, he cried, " *Sic semper tyrannis*," the motto of Virginia, and escaped, soon to be killed. The bullet, passing through the brain, left its victim unconscious, and at twenty-two minutes past seven on the following morning Abraham Lincoln was dead.

CHAPTER XVII

A LAST WORD

VICTORY and death were needed to give Lincoln immediately his place at home and abroad. Criticism subsided and appreciation began. From that day to this the tide has flowed without an ebb.

Immediately after the assassination the extreme radicals — the men of more heat than judgment, of more self-appreciation than patience — were pleased, and they alone. When the President had been one day dead the committee on the conduct of the war called upon the new President, and Senator Wade said : " Johnson, we have faith in you. By the gods, there will be no trouble now in running the government!"

There was trouble, however, and the country is not proud of the men who undertook to do what Lincoln was prevented from doing.

The funeral was on the 19th, and behind the coffin, at the head of the line, marched a detachment of negro troops. Two days the body lay in state, while the people came to the capital to look their last on Lincoln's face. The body rests in Springfield, the town in which the President had made the beginnings of his fame.

Later a monument was built there, and when it was dedicated Sherman spoke, and Grant said: " With all his disappointments from failures on the part of those to whom he had intrusted commands, and treachery on the part of those who had gained his confidence but to betray it, I never heard him utter a complaint, nor cast a censure, for bad conduct or bad faith. It was his nature to find excuses for his adversaries. In his death the nation lost its greatest hero; in his death the South lost its most just friend."

Among the expressions of grief that passed over the land none was more elevated than the mourning cry of our Democracy's first poet, WALT WHITMAN : —

O CAPTAIN! MY CAPTAIN

"O Captain ! my Captain ! our fearful trip is done,
The ship has weathered every rack, the prize we sought is won,
The port is near, the bells I hear, the people all exulting,
While follow eyes the steady keel, the vessel grim and daring ;
But O heart ! heart ! heart !
Oh, the bleeding drops of red,
Where on the deck my Captain lies,
Fallen cold and dead.

"O Captain ! my Captain ! rise up and hear the bells,
Rise up — for you the flag is flung — for you the bugle trills,
For you bouquets and ribboned wreaths — for you the shores
a-crowding,
For you they call, the swaying mass, their eager faces turning ;
Here Captain ! dear father !
This arm beneath your head !

> **It** is some dream that on the deck
> You've fallen cold and dead.

> " My Captain does not answer, his lips are pale and still,
> My father does not feel my arm, he has no pulse nor will,
> The ship is anchored safe and sound, its voyage closed and
> done,
> From fearful trip the victor ship comes in with object won ;
> Exult, O shores, and ring, O bells !
> But I with mournful tread,
> Walk the deck my Captain lies,
> Fallen, cold and dead."

To the instinctive Democracy of Whitman in the same year of Lincoln's death, was added the aristocratic Democracy of Lowell : —

> " For him her Old World moulds aside she threw,
> And, choosing sweet clay from the breast
> Of the unexhausted West,
> With stuff untainted shaped a hero new,
> Wise, steadfast in the strength of God, and true.
> How beautiful to see
> Once more a shepherd of mankind indeed,
> Who loved his charge, but never loved to lead ;
> One whose meek flock the people joyed to be,
> Not lured by any cheat of birth,
> But by his clear-grained human worth,
> And brave old wisdom of sincerity !
> They knew that outward grace is dust ;
> They could not choose but trust
> In that sure-footed mind's unfaltering skill,
> And supple-tempered will
> That bent like perfect steel to spring again and thrust.
> His was no lonely mountain peak of mind,

Thrusting to thin air o'er our cloudy bars,
A sea-mark now, now lost in vapors blind ;
Broad prairie rather, genial, level-lined,
Fruitful and friendly for all human kind,
Yet also nigh to heaven and loved of loftiest stars.
Nothing of Europe here,
Or, then, of Europe fronting mornward still,
Ere any names of Serf and Peer
Could Nature's equal scheme deface
And thwart her genial will ;
Here was a type of the true elder race,
And one of Plutarch's men talked with us face to face.
I praise him not ; it were too late ;
And some innative weakness there must be
In him who condescends to victory
Such as the Present gives, and cannot wait,
Safe in himself as in a fate.
So always firmly he :
He knew to bide his time,
And can his fame abide,
Still patient in his simple faith sublime,
Till the wise years decide.
Great captains, with their guns and drums,
Disturb our judgment for the hour,
But at last silence comes ;
These all are gone, and, standing like a tower,
Our children shall behold his fame.
The kindly-earnest, brave, foreseeing man,
Sagacious, patient, dreading praise, not blame,
New birth of our new soil, the first American."

With these two tributes but one other in poetry deserves to stand, and it came as a noble retraction from the nation whose leading men had been unable to see clearly across the sea until Lee's surrender and Booth's pistol taught them how. John Bright had spoken boldly for the Union from the first, and John Stuart Mill, to plead our cause, had left the closet for the platform; but these were single figures, society and the politicians sympathizing with the haughty slave-owners, and despising the Northern tradesmen. It was late in the war that the organ of prosperous British thought, the *London Times*, described those who believed in the possibility of restoring the Union as a "small knot of fanatics and sciolists." When we remember that even Gladstone believed that Davis and his supporters had created a nation, we understand something of the difficulties met by Lincoln, Adams, and Seward in their foreign relations. No nobler confession could have been made than the one Tom Taylor, a few weeks after the murder, printed in the *London Punch*: —

> " *You* lay a wreath on murdered Lincoln's bier !
>   *You*, who with mocking pencil wont to trace,
>   Broad for the self-complacent sneer,
>   His length of shambling limb, his furrowed face,

> " His gaunt, gnarled hands, his unkempt, bristling hair,
>   His garb uncouth, his bearing ill at ease,
>   His lack of all we prize as debonair,
>   Of power or will to shine, of art to please ;

> " *You*, whose smart pen backed up the pencil's laugh,
>   Judging each step, as though the way were plain ;

Reckless, so it could point its paragraph,
  Of chief's perplexity, or people's pain !

" Beside this corpse, that bears for winding sheet
  The stars and stripes he lived to rear anew,
Between the mourners at his head and feet,
  Say, scurrile jester, is there room for *you* ? "

Surely there is room for all. As Lincoln felt for mankind, so now every kind of men can feel for him.

" He was the Southern mother, leaning forth
  At dead of night to hear the cannon roar,
Beseeching God to turn the cruel North
  And break it that her son might come once more;
He was New England's maiden, pale and pure,
  Whose gallant lover fell on Shiloh's plain." [1]

From France, immediately after his death, came one of the most just recognitions of what formed the President's political significance. Some French liberals sent Mrs. Lincoln a medal on which part of the inscription was, " Saved the Republic, without veiling the Statue of Liberty." That he used great power without in any degree injuring the Republican system will always be a corner-stone of his fame. In his very last public address he pointed out that the ability of the nation to preserve itself without checking its freedom was the most hopeful lesson of the war. If Democracy is the best government, it is be-

[1] Maurice Thompson.

cause it is well that the people should rule themselves, make their own errors, and find their own
remedies. Lincoln helped them to do this. He
was sure that the great body of his fellow-citizens
needed only time and the facts to sail safely
through the roughest sea. His object was to
persuade and not to coerce. He knew that such
was the meaning of Democracy. "Come, let
us reason together about this matter," Lowell
imagines him always saying. His life he measured out alone, without intimate friends, with the
universal heart of the people for his friend. Like
them he was careless of many little things, and
profoundly just on big ones. Like them he was
not quick, but sure. He took his wisdom and
his morals from the range of his country, east
and west, north and south, hearing the distant
voices with a keener ear than most, and not caring
to theorize until he had weighed the messages
from every corner.

In natural harmony with his breadth in great
things went his easy tact in small ones. The
course of the story has taken us through many
proofs of this, has given pictures of anxious steer-
ing around obstacles, where a straight course
would have meant shipwreck; but a tale of his
mild superiority, told by Lowell in his powerful
essay on Democracy, adds another to a list which
can hardly be too long. The Marquis of Harting-

ton, although he wore a secession badge at a public ball at New York, yet was led by curiosity and
bad taste to seek an introduction to the President.
Lincoln, with the dignity of ease, kept his gentleness, without quite hiding his contempt, by innocently and persistently addressing the foreign
nobleman as Mr. Partington. The critic who
tells this story, referring to Lincoln's writing, says
that the tone of familiar dignity is perhaps the
most difficult attainment of mere style, as well as
an indication of personal character. Certainly,
the power to speak, act, and write with humility
and elevation, with familiarity and dignity, with
common equality and personal distinction, sprang
from the roots of Lincoln's character. It was no
feat of literary or intellectual skill. It was altogether the man. It was what was left after the
storms and wastes of a gloomy life had given
their large and solitary schooling to a noble soul.
In one of his dreams he was in a great assembly, where the people made a lane to let him
pass. "He is a common-looking fellow," said one
of them. "Friend," replied Lincoln, even in his
dream, "the Lord prefers common-looking people;
that is why he made so many of them." Even
Disraeli, hypocritically no doubt, said that in Lincoln's character there was "something so homely
and innocent that it takes the question, as it
were, out of all the pomp of history and the cere-

monial of diplomacy," and "touches the heart of nations."

" I never," says his assistant Secretary of War, "heard him say anything that was not so." He could refrain from speaking at all, but when the time came he told the truth. In his later years experience had so mellowed him that he saw the truth almost without moral indignation; but in his early days, before the burden of the world had chastened him, he could, as we have seen, "skin defendant." One law case he refused with these words, "I could set a neighborhood at logger-heads, distress a widowed mother and six father-less children, and get you the $600, which, for all I know, she has as good a right to as you have; but I will not do it."

" There are," said Phillips Brooks, "men as good as he, but they do bad things. There are men as intelligent as he, but they do foolish things. In him goodness and intelligence com-bined and made their best result of wisdom." Strangely mingled wisdom of Æsop and of the apostle, it was sought most willingly in the lowli-est haunts and applied with fitness in the high-est. When Sherman came to the *River Queen* from his march to the sea, what Lincoln asked him about with particular zest was the "bum-mers" on the routes, and the devices to collect food and forage. He cared little for great men,

not overmuch for great books; but from Shakespeare, the Bible, sentimental ballads, American
humorists, and above all from the ebb and flow
of daily life, he learned the essential lessons.
Pomp and ceremony were tiresome, ludicrous,
or unnoticed. He wrote messages of moment
to generals and secretaries on cards and slips of
paper. A long letter about a law case, containing a desire to retain him, he returned with the indorsement: "Count me in. A. Lincoln." His first
spectacles, which he bought in 1856 in a tiny jewel-
lery shop in Bloomington, with the remark that he
"had got to be forty-seven years old and kinder
needed them," cost him 37½ cents. At one o'clock,
on a night after Lincoln had been away for a week,
his Springfield neighbor heard the sound of an
axe. Leaving his bed he saw Lincoln in the moon-
light chopping the wood for his solitary supper.

Thus, from whatever angle we approach this
nature, we glide inevitably from the serious to
the amusing, and back again from the homely
to the sublime. The world no longer sees the
leisure and manners of a few as a compensation
for the suppression of the many. The law of
universal sympathy is upon us. Some imagine
that in this levelling lies the loss of poetry, of
great natures, of distinction, the impressive and
stirring being laid upon the altar of a gloomy
right. To them the life of Lincoln need have

2 E

little meaning.   Others rejoice in the new truth, and trust the world, and smile at prophecies. For them Lincoln represents soundness.   For them his rule is as full of pictures and inspiration as anything in the past, as full of charm as it is of justice, and his character is as reassuring as it is varied.   He had no artificial aids.   He merely proved the weapon of finest temper in the fire in which he was tested.   In the struggle for survival in a social upheaval he not only proved the living power of integrity and elasticity, but he easily combined with his feats of strength and shrewdness some of the highest flights of taste. As we look back across the changes of his life, — see him passing over the high places and the low, and across the long stretches of the prairie; spending years in the Socratic arguments of the tavern, and anon holding the rudder of state in grim silence; choosing jests which have the freshness of earth, and principles of eternal right; judging potentates and laborers in the clear light of nature and at equal ease with both; alone by virtue of a large and melancholy soul, at home with every man by virtue of love and faith, — this figure takes its place high in our minds and hearts, not solely through the natural right of strength and success, but also because his strength is ours, and the success won by him rested on the fundamental purity and health of the popular will of which he was the leader and the servant. Abraham Lincoln was in a deep and lasting sense the first American. All the world can see his worth, but perhaps only we who know the taste of the climate, the smell of the prairie, the tone of fresh and Democratic life, can quite appreciate his flavor. General and President Washington, who, standing firm, with wisdom and power, gave the opportunity to build a nation, has left a name that grows with the onward march of his country. Abraham Lincoln, nearly a century later, found the nation grown, about to test the sufficiency of its creed, and with the comprehension of lifelong intimacy helped it to understand itself. His fame also has risen, and will rise, with the fortunes of his country. His deeds stand first, but his story becomes higher through the pure and manifold character which accomplished them and the lastingly fair and vital words in which he defended them.

INDEX